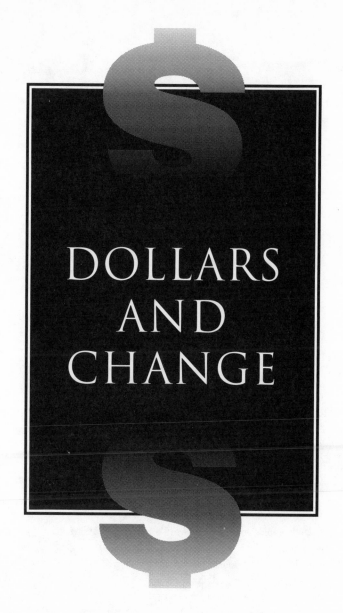

DOLLARS
AND
CHANGE

ECONOMICS IN CONTEXT

LOUIS PUTTERMAN

YALE UNIVERSITY PRESS   NEW HAVEN & LONDON

Set in Janson and Meta types by Keystone Typesetting, Inc.,
Orwigsburg, PA.
Printed in the United States of America by R. R. Donnelley.
Library of Congress Cataloging-in-Publication Data
Putterman, Louis G.
Dollars and change : economics in context / Louis Putterman.
    p.   cm.
Includes bibliographical references and index.
ISBN 0-300-08709-8 (cloth : alk. paper) —
ISBN 0-300-08710-1 (paper : alk. paper)
    1. Economics.   2. Economic history.   3. Social history.   I. Title.
HB171.5 .P974 2001
330—dc21   00-044919

A catalog record for this book is available from the British Library.

The paper in this book meets the guidelines for permanence and
durability of the Committee on Production Guidelines for Book
Longevity of the Council on Library Resources.

10 9 8 7 6 5 4 3 2 1

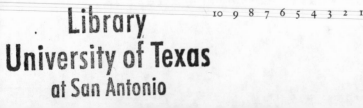

For my friends and family

CONTENTS

PREFACE

Economics is about the way people earn their livelihoods. Although there are other interesting and important subjects of study, this one certainly ranks high among the things that interest us as human beings. How we acquire the means to live and how our economies are organized help to determine what opportunities we have to fulfill our aspirations — not only the aspiration for financial security but also that for satisfying work and stable and fulfilling family and social relationships. The economy affects our well-being in the broadest sense because economic opportunities influence how our families form and are dissolved, where we live and for how long, the relations we have with our parents and children, our inter-actions at the workplace, and much more. Whether our societies know tranquility or tension, whether we can judge them to be just or not, whether we are at war or at peace, whether we are satisfied or dissatisfied with our political institutions, and whether our physical environment is healthful or noxious are all critically affected by economic arrangements and the outcomes associated with them. The pursuit of scientific knowl-edge, the arts, and religion are also all influenced by the economic ar-rangements of society and by the outcomes of those arrangements.

Every year, about a million students in the United States and perhaps more still in a great many other countries take an introductory course in college or university economics. Increasingly, students are exposed to economics in high school as well, and a considerable fraction of college students go beyond the introductory course to take a variety of advanced courses in economics. Aside from economics majors, students of political science, history, and sociology are encouraged to take courses in eco-nomics, and the subject is a mainstay for students preparing for business or law school.

As students, young or old, embark on the study of economics as it is known these days in countries throughout the world, they encounter an impressive if sometimes dismayingly abstract edifice of ideas. The economy is depicted, in mathematical or graphical models, as a system of interactions between consumers and producers, each of whom attempts to attain his or her objectives to the maximum degree possible subject to the constraints imposed by limited resources, wealth, and knowledge. After generations of efforts to refine the theoretical models that are used in their field of study, economists of the mid–twentieth century demonstrated that a competitive economy should have some very nice abstract properties indeed. In the equilibrium of the ideal economy, each participant was shown to be as well off as he or she can possibly be given the levels of well-being achieved by all other participants, and assuming that individuals know what makes them well off and act accordingly. To this extent, the models support the normative claims of those who have asserted the virtues of free markets for the past two centuries and more. The models also allow economists to study the effects of taxes and tariffs, the impact of monopoly power, the influence of changes in consumers' tastes, the alternative ways of curbing environmental pollution and their costs, and a host of other issues. And they provide foundations for studies of such problems as the relations between interest rates, money supply, and inflation, and the connections between these and the levels of employment, investment, and output in a nation's economy.

But standard textbook approaches to economics often seem unsatisfying to students hoping that their understanding of the subject will help them sort out larger social issues or make better sense of world affairs, politics, or history. In most economics books, the institutions of a modern industrial economy — business firms, banks, and regulatory agencies — are assumed to exist from the get-go. Economics is treated as a more or less complete corpus of scientific knowledge, rather than as an evolving body of ideas that can be challenged and that appear in many varieties. This is not necessarily to be regretted; after all, it is the business of economists to teach about the economy as they know it, using the approaches that they have been taught and that they use in their own research. Unfortunately, though, the typical student comes to the subject ill equipped to put what he or she is learning into a larger context. Moreover, her professors may lack the time or knowledge to provide the links she is seeking, and teachers in neighboring fields may also fail to establish these links or may prefer to criticize rather than to engage in a constructive interaction with what economics offers.

Because business firms and wage-earning households are found everywhere in our modern industrial society, it is easy to forget that firms and markets, money and taxes, have been around for only a few centuries, or at most a few millennia, out of humanity's thousands of centuries of existence. Because of the dramatic successes of capitalism and the main variety of economic thought associated with it in the late twentieth century, it is easy to forget that capitalist principles have been challenged on moral and ideological battlefronts since the system made its first appearance, and that economic science has known and still knows a variety of contending schools. Because many college students can look forward to life "in the fast lane" of an economy pouring out a seemingly endless stream of consumer goods and services, conflicts over economic policies, wealth distribution, and the philosophical basis of the economy may also be easily forgotten.

A standard economics textbook will introduce you to the ways in which economists understand the economy, from the factors underlying the behavior of consumers to the sources of producer choice and the interaction of supply and demand. But the broader context of these tools and concepts may be left a bit unclear. Why is the economy organized in the way that it is? Is it possible to marry economic efficiency with economic justice? Is the economy optimally arranged from the standpoint of maximizing human well-being and fulfillment? From that of maintaining the life-sustaining capacity of our planet? Will the two-billion-plus people who still live in poor countries be able to join the already well off? Where did the prevailing paradigm of economic thought come from, how adequate is it to the issues that it studies, and is it the only plausible way of understanding the economy?

No one field can be expected to answer all of the big questions facing the individual and society, and economics is like all others in having its own particular place in our modern intellectual division of labor. However, for the student — whether matriculating or a life-long learner — who is looking for integrative answers, it is frustrating to find important questions falling between the stools of the different disciplines. Being neither fish nor fowl, they are addressed by no one, or are addressed unsatisfactorily by specialists (in, say, history or philosophy) who are not sufficiently acquainted with some of their important dimensions. This short book is intended to make up for some of these gaps by helping you to begin thinking about important questions surrounding the models that constitute the core of modern economics. It provides basic background on where both economics and the economy come from, what we know about the potentials of differing economic arrangements, and how economics relates to questions of social justice and of life quality.

The book is organized into six chapters. Chapter 1 discusses the origins of the modern economy, putting the staggering changes of the past century or two into the perspective of mankind's thousands of generations of life. In Chapter 2, economics itself—that is, our accumulating set of understandings about economic life—is put in its own developmental perspective. The chapter looks at how modern economics evolved along with the economy, and it gives a sense of the varieties of economic thought. Chapter 3 discusses our economic arrangements as a system of interrelated institutions, putting those institutions into comparative perspective. The chapter considers differences in the nature and extent of governments' roles in economic life, the varying conceptions of property, the lessons learned from experiments with alternative economic arrangements, including planned socialism, and the variety of economic systems in the contemporary world.

Chapter 4 looks at those countries where the benefits of modern technology are still limited, in which vast populations live under conditions dramatically different from the economic arrangements of the industrial world. It asks why so much of the world remains poor, and what the prospects are for a more universal prosperity. Chapter 5 discusses problems of economic justice. It considers how justice has been defined by different approaches, and it discusses what economics teaches us about the possibility of achieving justice, however defined. Chapter 6 considers the broader effects of the way in which economic life is organized upon the types of people we become and the quality of the lives that we lead. Does a market economy encourage competitiveness, selfishness, and materialism to the detriment of higher human aspirations, or is it, on the contrary, the ideal way for getting the job done given an inherently self-interested and acquisitive human nature? Do advertising and career pressures lead us to wrongly associate our happiness with consumption, and to have too high a willingness to sacrifice job satisfaction for pay? Are we sufficiently alert to the danger that we are turning our planet into an unlivable wasteland for the sake of short-term economic growth? This chapter shows how some economists have grappled with these issues, and it explains why the study of economics can contribute to their understanding and resolution.

As a beginning student of economics years ago, I felt a need for answers to the types of questions this book considers, and found them hard to come by in any of the assigned or listed texts. I was impressed by economic analysis, but at the same time distrustful of it, given its seeming separation from, or even indifference to, the complexities and trials of real life. The struggle to make the connections among disparate fields of knowledge on one's own, and the excitement that comes from discovering the occasional nugget of wisdom in existing writings, can be an invigorating process. But over the years, as more and more students come to me looking for guidance on how to fill in the pieces that are missing in their courses in both economics and its neighboring fields, I have often wished there were something I could recommend to help them along the way. Curiosity about the big picture clearly varies from one person to another. My hope is that the pages that follow will help those who are intent on surveying the landscape before them to better understand the possibilities for a lifetime of continuing inquiry and engagement.

ACKNOWLEDGMENTS

This book was written over the course of several years, its contents influenced by teachers, colleagues, authors, and friends too numerous to mention. What can be mentioned is the direct assistance of a series of able and enthusiastic research assistants, each of whom, at the time, was an undergraduate at Brown University. In particular, David Jefferson helped research Chapter 1 and commented on parts of Chapter 6; Shu-yi Oei did research for chapters 1 and 2; and Peter Cabral and Kyuhey Lee did portions of the research for Chapter 4. Jefferson, Oei, and Lee worked with the financial support of the Undergraduate Teaching and Research Assistantship (UTRA) program at Brown University.

Mention also must be made of Areendam Chanda, a Ph.D. candidate in economics and a collaborator on other projects, who helped to write the vignette on India that appears in Chapter 4 and to answer some data queries. Carol Heim read a draft of Chapter 1 and provided helpful criticism. Toby Page shared his collection of books on environmental economics along with his collegiality and good cheer. Rick Shor read portions of a related manuscript and added encouragement. Eleven other readers, who remain anonymous to me, read drafts of most of the book at different stages in its preparation, and their comments and encouragement were invaluable. Indeed, after members of my family saw their reports, they suffered supportively the remaining months to the book's completion. Finally, it was John Harney, a book consultant and a gentleman, whose interest led me to undertake the project, and the people at Yale University Press, including my editor, John Covell, who provided much useful criticism and encouragement. To all of them, my sincere thanks and good wishes.

1

THE
INDUSTRIAL
ECONOMIES
IN
PERSPECTIVE

Observe the accommodation of the most common artificer or day laborer in a civilized and thriving country, and you will perceive that the number of people of whose industry a part, though but a small part, has been employed in procuring him this accommodation, exceeds all computation. The woolen coat, for example, which covers the day laborer . . . is the produce of the joint labor of a great multitude of workmen. The shepherd, the sorter of wool, the wool comber or carder, the dyer, the scribbler, the spinner, the weaver, the fuller, the dresser, with many others, must all join their different arts in order to complete even this homely production. How many merchants and carriers, besides, must have been employed in transporting the materials from some of those workers to others who often live in a very distant part of the country! How much commerce and navigation in particular, how many shipbuilders, sailors, sail makers, rope makers must have been employed in order to bring together the different drugs made use of by the dyer, which often come from the remotest corners of the world! What a variety of labor too is necessary in order to produce the tools of the meanest of those workmen! To say nothing of such complicated machines as the ship of the sailor, the mill of the fuller, or even the loom of the weaver, let us consider only what a variety of labor is requisite in order to form that very simple machine, the shears with which the shepherd clips the wool. The miner, the builder of the furnace for smelting the ore, the feller of the timber, the burner of the charcoal to be made use of in the smelting house, the brick maker, the bricklayer, the workmen who attend the furnace, the millwright, the forger, the smith must all of them join their different arts in order to produce them.
— *Adam Smith,*
     The Wealth of Nations, *1776*

The millennial record seems simple enough. From a world of great and little empires and kingdoms, more or less equal in wealth and power, we have become a world of nation-states, some far richer and stronger than others. From hundreds of millions of people, we have become 6 billion and counting. From working with modest if ingenious tools and techniques, we have become masters of great machines and invisible forces. Putting aside magic and superstition, we have passed from tinkering and intelligent observation to a huge and growing corpus of scientific knowledge that generates a continuing flow of useful applications. Most of this is to the good . . .
— *David Landes,*
     The Wealth and Poverty of Nations, *1998*

It is 1200 B.C., and you are an artisan in the town of Ur in Mesopotamia. Most of your income comes from carving statues of the local gods and selling them to rich officials and merchants. This occupation was inherited from your father, who inherited it from his; you hope to pass it on to your son. However, you have distant cousins who herd sheep in the wilderness west of the Euphrates, and the boy has taken to daydreaming about their way of life. How can he even think of giving up the security of civilization to go off to lands where there is no king, where a dozen tribes speaking strange tongues lead unknown ways of life? The workers you and the neighboring craftsmen employ would happily pledge to serve you for twenty years for the right to replace your son in the business. But there would be no pleasure for you in that. How are you going to talk sense into the boy?

The year is 1646. You are the grandson of English peasants evicted from their land by a baronet who chose to convert his estate to raise sheep for the growing wool market. Your father found work for a while in a shipbuilding establishment and had hoped to become an apprentice in one of the skilled trades, but he lost a hand in an accident, leaving him unable to work. Your mother supported the family as a seamstress until her death last month from smallpox. Your only hope may be to sign up for an expedition to the New World. You'll receive a payment upon signing that you can turn over to your father. If your ship reaches America, you'll have to work for a gentleman farmer for seven years; then you will be free to start your own farm or look for another occupation. But the trip is treacherous and conditions in the New World are harsh. An older brother who went there several years ago lasted only a year before succumbing to dysentery.

In today's industrialized world, people earn their livings by working at specialized jobs — assembling automobile parts or working in a medical lab, say — that pay them money, which they then exchange for the products of thousands of other producers, some working half a world away. A typical individual spends twelve or more years being educated for a life as worker and citizen, then works for three or four decades before what is sometimes a lengthy retirement.

Things were very different during most of human existence. For hundreds of thousands of years, people survived by hunting and gathering animal and vegetable foodstuffs from places they could reach on foot, using tools fashioned from stone, wood, and bone. There was no formal education, and both children and the elderly played active roles in the band's economy. Even after the agricultural revolutions of seven to ten thousand years ago, and until very recently, most people continued to grow their own food, build their own dwellings, and with the help of family and neighbors produce for themselves the bulk of what they consumed. Unlike today's industrial nations, which exhibit the complex hierarchies of large corporations and governments responding to the needs of millions of people, and in which only 3 percent of the population is engaged in food production, the largest organizations known in most of the past were bands of no more than a few dozen people, which were essentially self-sufficient in providing for their own needs and had relatively simple internal divisions of labor. One need go back no more than a few hundred years to find a time when the vast majority even in today's most developed nations were more or less self-sufficient farmers living in small villages.

Why do we need to know anything about the world prior to the one we know today? To be sure, it is of intrinsic interest to the curious to know something about how the world worked over the greater part of human history. But there are good practical reasons why the origins of today's economy need to be recalled. Understanding how the modern economy evolved may be important for addressing problems of continuing underdevelopment in parts of today's world, for appreciating the dynamics of population growth, and for moving toward the achievement of an environmentally sustainable economy.

Furthermore, the very concept of a "modern industrial economy" does not correspond to something static. Change has occurred not only in the past. It continues and has accelerated since the core ideas of modern economics were first laid down. It is useful to know how and why institutions like firms, markets, and governments came into being. By understanding past changes, we may gain insight into what changes to expect in the future — or, more important perhaps, which changes we ought to resist and which we should facilitate or attempt to bring about. Finally, the economics of our textbooks is a product of the era in which economics as a science came into being, so some understanding of economic history is useful to comprehending economics itself.

To illustrate the relevance of past changes, consider that corporations, taken as given in most discussions of the economy today, were thought to be inherently inefficient forms of organization as recently as the late eighteenth century. How did the corporate form overcome the problems that the founding figure of economics, Adam Smith, saw in it then?

As to the rootedness of today's economics in the economy of the past, this can be illustrated by many examples. Modern textbooks, for instance, still discuss "labor, land, and capital" as basic inputs to production. It is worth appreciating the fact that this practice follows the tradition established in the days of Smith and his immediate successors, when workers, landlords, and capitalists were viewed by most social observers as the fundamental classes of the society then emerging from a still-recent feudal past. Perhaps it is more important today than it was in their time to separate "labor" into distinct skill types and market structures, and to distinguish between the number of workers a firm hires and the amount of effective work that each performs. The distinction between capitalist and working classes may also have to be reexamined in our own time, since workers jointly provide nearly half of the capital used by firms via their savings and pension funds. In many applications, by contrast, it may be less important for us today than in the eighteenth century to distinguish real estate from other investments, since landowners and capitalists are no longer distinct social groups. Although each of these points is debatable, it is nevertheless clearly useful to know where the vocabulary of modern economics has locked in terminology from a world since transformed.

The transition from subsistence-oriented societies to modern commercial economies has been fairly gradual, from the standpoint of any one generation. That transition was quite abrupt, however, if we take the long view of human history. Much as the human species as a whole is a very late addition to the history of life's evolution on earth (less than a million years for *Homo sapiens* but about three and a half *billion* for life!), so living in complex industrial societies also appears only at the most recent moments on the clock counting down our history as a species (only about two centuries out of at least sixty thousand years).[1] Moreover, just as organic evolution accelerated, taking about 2.7 *billion* years to become multicellular but producing a panoply of mammalian species in spans of just tens of millions of years, so human social evolution at first progressed slowly, but then began cumulating at increasingly explosive rates. Thousands of generations passed from the time that humans emerged from the African savanna until the appearance of societies relying mainly on settled agricultural production. Following the appearance of such agricultural societies, however, only another three or four hundred generations were required to bring about the development of written languages and complex large-scale empires with specialized administrators, soldiers, and priests. Radical change continued to accelerate. It took only another hundred-some generations until the appearance of the commercial city-states of the third century B.C., and a hundred more until the start of the industrial revolution. From the start of the industrial revolution to the computer age, only ten generations passed.

A major reason for the accelerating trend illustrated by these numbers is that technological advances have been central to the changes in question. Technological progress tends to be cumulative in character. Scientists in the twentieth century were not smarter than those who lived two hundred years earlier, nor were the latter likely to have had larger brains than did the first foragers to experiment with plant cultivation over ten thousand years ago. Each later generation simply had the benefit of the knowledge that had accumulated in the interim. And with each step from the advent of writing to its dissemination to the invention of the print-

1. Collapse terrestrial history into a week and suppose that the earth came into being at midnight at the start of a Monday. The first organisms appear early Tuesday morning, but the first large animals (fish) do not arise until 1:30 A.M. the following Saturday. The first mammals appear on Sunday evening, primates on Sunday at 10:00 P.M., *Homo erectus* three and a half minutes before midnight, *Homo sapiens* in the last thirty seconds of this busy week. Written human history would occupy two-thirds of the final second of the week only (see Brower, 1995). Rescaling and setting the beginning of the minimum of sixty thousand years of existence of anatomically modern humans at midnight as a Monday begins puts the emergence of agriculture at 8:00 P.M. on Saturday, the first coins at 4:30 P.M. on Sunday and the first writings on economics by Aristotle at 5:30, the industrial revolution at a half hour before midnight, and the information age in the last three minutes of the human week.

ing press and finally electronic information storage and communication, the likelihood that knowledge would be retained and transmitted has increased.

Changes in technology do not represent an isolated chamber of knowledge — "science." Rather, they are aspects of broader patterns of change in culture and in social and economic arrangements quite generally. A major reason why the development of sedentary agriculture stimulated further social change is that agriculturally based societies were able to support much larger, denser populations than could those based on hunting and gathering. And with storable food surpluses evolved stratified societies containing specialized classes, including rulers, priests, soldiers, and philosophers. The transfer of surpluses to specialized classes encouraged the development of writing and mathematics for purposes of record keeping. The need to protect surpluses, trade routes, and the position of the rulers also contributed to the emergence of the specialized occupation of soldier. Culture, changing in accordance with changes in technology and social organization, ultimately facilitated further the development of still more technical knowledge.

In the remainder of this chapter, we take a bird's-eye view of the main stages on the way to the modern economy, beginning with the hunting and gathering bands that were the starting point of human society. From there, we will visit ancient empires, feudal economies, and the world of the early industrial revolution. We'll end with an overview of the varieties of modern industrial economy, leaving discussion of economies that are still relatively non-industrialized for consideration in Chapter 4.

A theme running throughout the chapter will be the idea that economic development has been inseparable from economic complexity — that is, from specialization and the division of labor. Increases in productivity and living standards have gone hand in hand with changes in modes of organization, production, transportation, and communications that have made it possible for more and more people to engage in more and more specialized activities and to exchange the results of those activities (directly or indirectly) with ever greater numbers of others located on ever more diverse and widely separated nodes of ever larger networks of trade and interaction. In the two and a quarter centuries since Adam Smith wrote that the division of labor and the lowering of trading costs is key to the increasing wealth of nations, an abundance of further evidence has accumulated in support of that insight.

A second, and cautionary, theme is that increasing specialization did not immediately improve the well-being of the ordinary person in the complex societies of history's initial millennia. It is only in modern times that productivity has risen sufficiently, and that the fruits of productivity have been distributed widely enough, so that increases in prosperity have become widespread in a significant number of societies. The economy of prosperity is young, its generalization to the world as a whole still in doubt, its internal stability still fragile, and its ecological sustainability still difficult to determine. Recognizing that our moment of prosperity in less than one-half of the globe could be a short-lived phenomenon if we do not make adequate efforts to understand it is another reason why a long-term perspective may be critical. A proper respect for the recentness and uniqueness of today's prosperity is central to such a perspective.

THE FIRST HUMAN ECONOMIES

Based on orally transmitted history, the authors of the early biblical narratives and many other texts of antiquity supposed the world to be a few thousand years old. This may have been a reasonably good guess about the age of the world as *they* knew it, for agricultural societies in their transitions to early civilizations would have dated to roughly the time the writers of the period associated with "Creation." Until at least the sixteenth century, the idea that the world was a few thousand years old continued to be given credence by European scholars and lay persons alike. It came as a shock when geological and archeological discoveries of the nineteenth century revealed the planet to be hundreds of thousands of times older than had been thought, with a record of human occupation dating back sixty thousand to a million years or longer.

For hundreds of thousands of years, humans and their proto-human ancestors were hunters and gatherers who fashioned their most sophisticated tools from stone, wood, bark, and animal hides.[2] This period before

2. Anthropologists differ over the date at which human beings reached their fully modern form, with the benchmarks of sixty thousand to one hundred thousand years being common suggestions in recent years. However, no obvious sharp break in technology has been discovered between *Homo sapiens sapiens* and its immediate precursors, so members of the broader *Homo* family may have lived similarly for a million years or longer.

money and formal institutions might seem largely irrelevant to us. However, it has left us with important legacies, not least of which are the genes that define our human nature: for to the extent that there is such a nature, biologists agree that it had essentially evolved by the end of the Paleolithic period, before the development of agriculture. Hunter-gatherers, though not perhaps the particular ones pictured in your *National Geographic*, were our direct ancestors. We carry their genes, and we are genetically adapted to *their* world of hunting and gathering, not to *our* world of jet airplanes and fax machines.

It is difficult to know much about the way of life of early hunter-gatherers because the physical record they left us is sparse and hard to interpret. Although there still exist hunter-gatherers today in such places as the upper Amazon River and the Kalahari Desert, their numbers are small, and the fact that they have survived mainly in environments too inhospitable to have invited earlier encroachment may make them unrepresentative of our most typical ancestors. Nevertheless, by combining careful analysis of the artifacts left by prehistoric people with contemporary anthropological studies and with study of the records of earlier contacts with the hunting-gathering peoples who were far more widely dispersed a few centuries ago, scholars have pieced together a plausible picture of their ways of life.

Students of prehistory believe that hunter-gatherers generally lived in small groups or bands, averaging thirty or forty members. They lived lives of relative self-sufficiency, with the band or families within it alternating in the roles of production and consumption unit, depending on the scale of the activity in question. The daily life of hunter-gatherer bands revolved around the search for food. In a hunter-gatherer band, you would not have spent much time wondering what you would be when you grew up. After a year or so being carried around on your mother's back or playing at an older relative's feet, you would soon have taken on some responsibilities of your own, and your "career path" would depend mainly on your gender and physical strength. If a man, you would specialize in hunting for animals, if a woman, you would gather edible plants, water, and firewood, and would give birth to, nurse, and care for children. Within the band, you might have become known for your tool making or storytelling or hunting skills, but complete specialization among tasks was probably rare.

Initially, interaction with other bands may have been minimal and leaving one's band to join another almost impossible, so in a hostile environment of changing food availabilities and dangerous animals, adherence to the norms of one's group was critical. Within the band, men, women, and offspring formed family groupings that shared gathered vegetable foods, while strong norms of sharing determined that any large game brought in from a hunt would be shared with other band members, with the successful hunter himself often receiving the smallest part so as to underscore the principle of reciprocity.[3] As human evolution progressed, bands may have increasingly interacted with neighboring bands and practiced marriage outside the immediate group. In this connection, ongoing relationships and alliances developed between bands who supported one another in the event of intertribal warfare and who also provided one another with insurance against local calamities.

The extent of trading between groups was limited by the slow movement of goods, restricted storage capabilities, and the broad similarity of production conditions across many neighboring habitats. It was beneficial to share meat within the band because this pooled the risks from the uncertainty of any one hunter's success across a larger number of hunters. But with each neighboring band gathering similar types of vegetables, hunting similar game, and making similar tools, there was little benefit from trade in the modern sense. Still, residents of neighboring but different habitats (those living along the banks of a stream, for instance, and the inhabitants of a nearby forest) might have traded with each other the abundant goods of their territory. Also, the practices of hunter-gatherer cultures recorded by literate observers suggest that the exchange of gifts even between groups sharing a common ecological adaptation was a common practice helping to cement alliances. Moreover, it is reported, "By 200,000 years ago stone tools were traveling long distances from their quarries. By about 60,000 years ago . . . other goods began to appear regularly more than a day's walk from where they were manufactured. By 30,000 years ago in Europe, pierced sea shells, to be used as beads, were traveling 400 miles inland or more to turn up in grave goods and in other places."[4]

Forms of money, such as the cowry shells used by indigenous peoples in parts of the western Pacific, may date back many thousands of

3. For an account of food sharing in a contemporary hunter-gatherer culture, see Kaplan and Hill, 1985.

4. Ridley, 1996, p. 209.

years.[5] But most primitive trade probably took the form of barter. The potential for trade and hence for specialization in economic activity would eventually be expanded when the need for "a double coincidence of wants," which barter entails, was superseded by the existence of a currency that could be accepted by anyone regardless of specific needs.[6] Widespread use of such currencies awaited not only the development of metallurgy but also the evolution of large integrative polities marked by state-level political entities. And even the Roman Empire would collect most of its taxes in the form of grain.

Did our hunter-gatherer ancestors have economies? Did they act in ways permitting meaningful economic analysis? If "economy" refers to what people do in societies to provision themselves with their material needs and wants, then certainly we can talk of hunter-gatherer economies. What anthropologists and others have debated is whether the calculus of rational choice that dominates economics texts has anything to do with the behaviors of premodern peoples. The American economist Thorstein Veblen ridiculed the economic theorists of his day for supposing that utility maximization is a human universal.[7] Some social scientists have argued that behavior in primal bands was governed by customs and magical beliefs, or that it was determined by a social process rather than by individual goal-seeking. Some go so far as to suggest that the concept of the individual was lacking.[8]

5. The cowry shell "was used as a means of payment in India, the Middle East, and China, probably for several thousand years before Christ, and it continued to circulate in historical times over large parts of Asia, Africa, and the Pacific islands, from Nigeria to Siam, and from the Sudan to the New Hebrides. Even now its use is not quite extinct, and when the Japanese invaded New Guinea in 1942 they distributed cowries so freely as to cause a sharp fall in their value and, in the words of an aggrieved district officer, 'endanger the economic and financial stability of the district.'" Morgan, 1965, p. 12.

6. "Double coincidence of wants" refers to the fact that barter between herders and farmers makes sense only when the farmers happen to want skins or other herding products and the herders also happen to want grain or other farming products. More complex webs of barter trade are possible: the herders might trade skins with fishermen who give them fish even though the herders themselves don't eat fish, if the herders know that they can trade the fish with the farmers for grain, which they do eat. But a currency that everyone will accept cuts through the need for any of these particular coincidences.

7. See Veblen, 1908.

8. While statements of this sort might hold relative truth when applied to a

Owing to the restricted social world of a hunter-gatherer, the member of a primitive band faced different constraints from those facing contemporary people. Because few individuals had the choice to leave the band in which they were born, except through marital exchange, good social relationships would have had a large weight in the individual's decision making: being a team player and obeying social norms would have to have figured prominently in a Paleolithic human's decision making. Yet the physical record suggests that human biology was the same sixty thousand years ago as today, so major changes in either cognitive abilities or behavioral predispositions are unlikely.[9] That being the case, Paleolithic men and women are likely to have shared with us such characteristics as a keen interest in the welfare of themselves and their close kin, the ability to reason about what would advance that welfare, and the inclination to act accordingly. The difference in the extent to which behavior was constrained by beliefs and social norms in their day and in ours is a matter of degree, not of kind.

Suppose the question we want to pose, however, is: "Did our ancestors pursue their own interests in as thoroughgoing a manner as do human beings today?" In that case, it may be worth pointing out that the "natural interest" of individuals has *never* been a perfectly selfish one. Biology teaches that natural selection works by favoring those variations of the genes that increase the reproductive success rates of an animal's genetic material. This holds for humans as much as for other species. Strict selfishness is inconceivable in a species in which the young are born immature and are for a long time dependent on adult care. In such animals (most notably ourselves), a genetic propensity to neglect one's young would die out quickly. So a biologically founded concern for the well-

---

culture and to the type of psychology that it fostered, it can hardly be sensible to assert that the individual had no cognizance of his or her personal existence. Even nonhuman primates show plenty of concern for their own interests and an acute awareness of their position in the dominance hierarchy of their "society" (see de Waal, 1996).

9. Here, "behavioral predispositions" refers to the genetic underpinnings of behavior. Of course, these genetic predispositions may very well play out in different ways under different environmental influences, such as cultures. The chronology of human evolution and the common background of all contemporary peoples is discussed by Cavalli-Sforza and Cavalli-Sforza, 1995, Ridley, 1996, and Diamond, 1998, among others.

being of offspring, at least, probably lies behind the parental altruism that is commonly assumed in economic theories of saving, educational choice, and bequests.

Evolutionary theorists go further, however, and conjecture that human beings may be endowed with inclinations toward *reciprocity* and toward keeping accounts of *fairness* in their interactions, even when dealing with others who are not close blood relatives. The argument is that such propensities may have served the interests of the genes of our ancestors, because in primitive band societies it favored survival for members to be cooperative enough to share the unpredictable proceeds of a hunt, and to be sufficiently concerned about fairness that a cheater on such sharing norms could anticipate retribution.[10] Some of our present-day notions of fairness, and such other traits as our desire to be well regarded and our concern with status, may well survive from this era in which most interactions occurred in the small group. The handing down of behavioral traits—whether by way of genes or culture or both—from our preindustrial past provides another reason why understanding the economic environment facing our ancestors may hold important clues to understanding our own behavior when confronting problems of cooperation and competition today.

SPECIALIZATION, AGRICULTURE, AND ANCIENT EMPIRES

Around ten thousand years ago, groups of people began to shift from mainly gathering and hunting their means of sustenance to producing them by growing crops and domesticating animals. It is quite possible that the knowledge that edible plant growth could be enhanced by human

10. The inclinations toward reciprocity and retaliation are not necessarily consistent with the rational self-interest of individuals, but they may be consistent with the long-term interests of our genes. The selection of such inclinations by evolution may help explain why cooperation is far more prevalent in human society than is predicted by the branch of economics called game theory under the assumption of a narrower form of rationality and self-interest. For a fascinating discussion of the evolution of cooperation, kin altruism, and marriage, see Wright, 1994. The implications of this viewpoint for the economics of the family are discussed by Bergstrom, 1996, while the implications for economics of reciprocity among unrelated individuals are discussed by Fehr and Gächter, 1998.

intervention was around for thousands of years before the agricultural way of life took root. Contemporary foragers show such knowledge, and there is archeological evidence of some horticultural practices predating farming villages. It may simply have been that earlier human bands had not found it worth their while to cultivate crops in an intensive fashion, since it was relatively easy for them to locate stands of edible foods, fishable streams, and animals that could be hunted during the tens of thousands of years in which human populations remained small and natural food sources comparatively abundant. Some scientists believe that rather than being a technological leap forward after eons of uneventful backwardness, the shift to agriculture was actually a reluctant adjustment made necessary by the dying out of large animals that are numerous in the fossil record for millions of years before the appearance of human hunters, then suspiciously disappear.[11] The human population on all continents combined at about 10,000 B.C. is thought to have been no more than twenty million and perhaps as little as four or five million people, smaller than the populations of a number of today's cities.

Somewhere along the line, short-run surges in population or declines in the availability of wild food sources may have encouraged the more systematic investigation of ways to cultivate food. As agriculture was refined, cultivation methods improved and the populations of regions where farming was practiced rose dramatically. Eventually there was no turning back, as the resulting populations were now dependent on farming as a way of life.[12]

By 6000 B.C., agriculture is believed to have been well established from western Iran to the Mediterranean and across the Anatolian highlands to both sides of the Aegean Sea. From there, it appears to have spread gradually to Egypt, India, China, western Europe, and other parts of the Old World. It also developed and spread independently more than a thousand years before Europeans arrived in the New World.[13] Different

11. The account by economist Vernon Smith, 1975, of the extinctions of numerous large mammals following the proliferation of hunting populations agrees with those of Ridley, 1996, and Diamond, 1998.

12. The theory that population growth necessitated intensification of agriculture, which in turn led to further population growth, was most notably propounded by Ester Boserup, 1965.

13. Not only is the development of agriculture by native Americans believed to be completely independent of that in the Old World, but agriculture may have

crops were domesticated in different regions: wheat and barley in the Near East, rice in China, corn in the New World. Non-staples were quickly added: olives in the Mediterranean world, apples, peaches, and grapes in central Asia, peanuts and beans in the New World. More important still was the domestication of animals: chickens, ducks, pigs, and sheep, for instance, providing additional protein sources without the effort of hunting; oxen and water buffaloes becoming beasts of burden; and all of these domesticated animals providing valuable manure to increase the yields of field crops. Between 10,000 and 3000 B.C., world population may have risen by three or more times; in the next thousand years it doubled again, although there would still have been fewer than thirty million persons on all the continents combined, according to some estimates.[14]

With agricultural intensification, people began living in larger numbers in proximity to one another, making the band form of organization unworkable. Already by 7000 B.C., a huge stone wall had been erected at Jericho, and there were traces of other "proto-cities" in the Aegean area and in the Near East, which may have served as "primitive manufacturing centers and commercial entrepōts for the surrounding agricultural communities."[15] By 3000 B.C., the first large state had arisen in Mesopotamia. The process was repeated in Egypt, where agriculture was well established by 3600 B.C., with political life centered on small villages ruled by chieftains. After further population growth and agricultural intensification, the chiefdoms were consolidated into kingdoms, and eventually a vast stretch of the Nile River valley was unified under a pharaoh, its estimated population being 1.2 million in the Old Kingdom (around 2700 to 2100 B.C.) and 2 million in the New Kingdom (around 1600 to 1100 B.C.).[16]

---

arisen independently in at least three separate New World regions (the current southeastern United States, Central America, and Peru). Agriculture may also have arisen independently in West Africa, New Guinea, and elsewhere, and its development in China and other parts of the Old World could also be at least partly independent of Fertile Crescent influences. See Diamond, 1998.

14. McEvedy and Jones, 1978, estimates world population in 10,000, 3000, and 2000 B.C. at four million, fourteen million, and twenty-seven million, respectively. Because the evidence available is limited, such estimates have large margins of error.

15. Cameron, 1993, p. 27.

16. See Butzer, 1976, and Trigger, 1993.

Virtually the same progression has been documented by archeologists working in Mesopotamia, Mexico, and elsewhere.[17] The social arrangements that arose were increasingly hierarchical, and they entailed increasing specialization. In Egypt, for instance, while 90 percent of the population may have engaged in food production under a form of serfdom, specialized crafts included baking, brewing, wine making, spinning, weaving, potting, carpentry, and metalworking, and there was a middle class consisting of bureaucrats, scribes, and priests. Mesopotamia, the Indus and Yellow River valleys, and the later kingdoms and empires of sub-Saharan Africa and the New World displayed similar ranges of specialties.

Rapid population increases and growth in the scale and complexity of political structures were especially notable in societies that achieved unprecedented population densities based in part on the use of man-made irrigation systems. The channels and earthworks these entailed were often relatively large in scale and required the administration of a class of officials functioning under the supervision of an overarching political authority usually associated with a priesthood.[18] Members of the economic and priestly hierarchies of early Mesopotamian cities "directed the labor of irrigation, drainage, and agriculture generally, and supervised the collection of the produce as tribute or taxation," according to Rondo Cameron. "The need to keep records of the sources and uses of this tribute led to the use of simple pictographs on clay tablets, sometime before 3000 B.C." Thus, he argues, "Sumer's greatest contribution to subsequent civilizations, the invention of writing, . . . grew out of economic necessity."[19] Defense against competing political entities was provided by another professional class, the soldiers, whose needs were also met by taxing or extracting tribute from the farmers.

Specialization has played a central role in all historical economic development. In a society in which each family or small band produces its own necessities, all must divide their efforts between building and maintaining their dwellings, procuring food, and making the clothing and tools that they require. In a modern society with a complex division of labor, by contrast, most people produce only a small portion of their

17. See Sanders and Marino, 1970.

18. A well-known study of this phenomenon focusing on China is that by Wittfogel, 1957.

19. Cameron, 1993, p. 28.

requirements, concentrating their efforts on one or two goods. Indeed, the typical individual might be engaged in but one particular facet of the production of a good: attaching windshields to automobiles, operating a machine that helps make bailing twine, doing paperwork (or its electronic equivalent) for the twine company's billing department, illustrating the manual for a computer program, and so on.

Such specialization contributes to overall productivity in a number of ways. First, different localities and different individuals have different advantages in skill, resources, and location. If village A, in the mountains, can produce either twenty goats or five bushels of wheat using one acre and one person-year of labor, while village B, in the valley, can produce either ten goats or twenty bushels of wheat using one acre and one person-year of labor, then both villages can enjoy more of both products if each specializes in producing the one in which it has a comparative advantage and, in turn, trades with the other. Residents of A might settle for four bushels of wheat and four goats, and residents of B might live on eight bushels of wheat and six goats, when each village is self-sufficient. But with specialization and trade, enough could be produced to provide each resident of both villages with both ten goats and ten bushels of wheat![20] The same applies to specialization among individuals in doing jobs requiring, say, more dexterity versus more brute strength, computational skill, or speed. Specialization also permits individuals to improve their productivity in particular jobs by intensive repetition and practice. Even more important, it fosters the refinement of techniques and the development of improved methods of production.

But how much a particular village or a particular individual gains from specialization depends not only on such physical factors as how many acres and man-years are required for production, but also on who has control over which resources and what their relative bargaining strengths are. Assuming uncoerced trade between the villages in the example above,

20. The economic theory of trade shows that this principle extends over a considerable range of preferred patterns of goat and wheat consumption, and even to cases in which one village can produce more of both products than the other, so long as their relative or comparative advantages differ. (Thus, if the data for the example were changed so that village B can still produce twenty bushels but can alternatively produce twenty-five goats per acre and person-year, it would still be beneficial for B to specialize in wheat at least to some degree, since its cost of wheat in terms of forgone goats remains higher than that of village A.)

the equal consumption levels used for illustration are by no means an assured outcome. Conceivably, the higher pre-trade incomes of the inhabitants of village B will allow them to extract a more favorable bargain from their counterparts in A. Or perhaps A's mountainous position will give its villagers a military advantage over B, which they will use to extract a better deal for themselves. Indeed, the villagers of A might decide not to trade at all but simply to invade B, take over its land, and enslave its villagers. Likewise, benefits might be distributed quite unequally if land rights or control over labor are unequally distributed within one or both villages. It is probable that specialization of early empires into such classes as rulers, warriors, priests, and artisans helped increase the total amount produced, and thus the productivity of the "average" worker. However, the social stratification that emerged in places like Egypt may well have prevented the ordinary people from enjoying a higher living standard than those in less specialized societies. Life on the periphery of the great civilizations was the preferred option of some — witness the Israelites of the well-known biblical narrative.

Once the Paleolithic world of hunting and gathering had given way to the Neolithic world of improved tool making, husbandry, and agriculture, however, trade was by no means restricted to the great empires. Sophisticated and specialized tools were already evident in the areas where agriculture first spread even before the rise of civilization, and tool making encouraged trading in specialized materials and in the products of special skills. Portions of southern and southeastern Europe were supplying metals to the Near Eastern civilizations thousands of years before their own incorporation into large-scale states. As Matt Ridley reports,

When the 5,000-year-old mummified corpse of a fully equipped Neolithic man turned up in a melting glacier high in the Tyrolean Alps in 1991, the variety and sophistication of his equipment was astonishing. Europe was in his day a tribal, thinly populated place of Stone Age culture. Copper was smelted but not yet bronze. Corn and cattle had long replaced hunting as the main livelihoods, but writing, law and government were unknown. Dressed in furs under a woven grass cloak, equipped with a stone dagger with an ash-wood handle, a copper ax, a yew-wood bow, a quiver and fourteen cornus-wood arrows, he also carried a tinder fungus for lighting fires, two birch-bark containers, one of which contained some embers of his most recent fire, insulated by maple leaves, a hazel-wood pannier, a bone awl, stone drills and scrapers, a lime-wood-and-antler *retoucheur* for fine stone sharpening, an antibiotic birch fungus as a medicine kit and various spare parts. His copper ax was cast and hammered sharp in a way that is extremely difficult to achieve even with modern metallurgical knowledge. It was fixed with millimeter precision into a yew haft that was shaped to obtain mechanically ideal ratios of leverage. . . . Archeologists believe he probably relied upon specialists for the manufacture of much of his equipment.[21]

Yet in the larger empires that left us large-scale architectural legacies and historical records, the main form of interaction between specialized groups was as often that of taxation and redistribution as it was that of trade. The Egyptian pharaoh taxed his subjects, employed slave labor, and dispatched ships to vassal states in the region of present-day Lebanon to procure "gifts" of timber and other goods. Such rulers extracted produce from their farming populations to support their bureaucracies, armies, and priests, providing "in return" some protection against threats of invasion, supervision of irrigation and other infrastructures, and religious services. Markets for some goods, such as spices and cloth for the higher classes, began to emerge in some instances. The contrast between the trading classes of Mesopotamia and the centralized trading of Egypt, indeed, has been compared to that between twentieth-century capitalism and state socialism.[22] Archeological evidence from the Americas shows long-distance trading between the Olmec culture, located along the coast of the Gulf of Mexico, and the central highlands of Mexico, in such things as jade art objects, statuettes, and obsidian, as well as cocoa beans, as early as the eighth century B.C. But even in those premodern societies in which commerce achieved substantial development, it remained far less important than self-sufficiency and taxation as the basic principles of economic life for the ordinary person.

A "bewildering profusion of empires and their rulers" marked the ancient world, in the words of Cameron. This is probably not surprising, in view of the spans of time involved. In Mesopotamia alone, Sumer was succeeded by Akkad, Babylon, Assyria, the Hittite empire, and Persia. Some changes arose with invasions of peoples from beyond the zones of civilization. While establishing themselves as rulers, the invaders often absorbed much of the host culture. In addition to the marauding "barbarians" who

21. Ridley, 1996, pp. 48–49.
22. Trigger, 1993.

menaced the Mediterranean world and China from such regions as central Asia and the Caucasus, the peripheries of larger states saw the emergence of sophisticated, commercially oriented cultures. By 3000 B.C., Phoenician traders, famed for their coins and their alphabet, were established in the eastern Mediterranean, serving as intermediaries between Mesopotamia and Egypt. Greek merchants could be found throughout the Aegean and as far west as Sicily during the Mycenaean period (from the fourteenth to the twelfth centuries B.C.).[23] Carthage, founded originally by the Phoenicians, evolved in a similar direction in later centuries.

By contrast with such commercial city-states, most empires were more adept at projecting military might and extracting taxes than at encouraging trade. This is true even of the Roman Empire, which eventually dominated North Africa, Europe, and the Middle East, with a population in its heyday of fifty to sixty million people. The historian M. I. Finley argues that this empire, while permissive of trade within its borders, showed a lack of sophistication in economic affairs, forgoing the use of taxes as economic levers, for instance. Thus, imports to Rome were taxed at the same rate as exports, without exemptions even for the capital's all-important grain supply. Moreover, taxes were increasingly levied in kind, rather than in cash, with poor farmers being required to pay in grain and the landless in corvée, or unpaid labor, even as large landed estate holders were exempted from taxation. A number of historians, including Cameron, see this taxation as a major factor that eventually drove many peasants to seek refuge on the estates of the large landholders, ushering in an era of feudalism.

The management of currency was also problematic in the ancient world. Cameron states that the earliest surviving coins, dating from the seventh century B.C., came from Asia Minor. These coins "were probably struck by some enterprising merchant or banker of one of the Greek cities on the coast as a form of advertising."[24] A few centuries later, according to Finley, the rulers of the Hellenistic states and thereafter of the Roman Empire were all engaged in coining money, but they did so with their private aims rather than those of their subjects in mind. Thus, they saw no obligation to maintain a sufficient supply of coins except when needed for state payments, as a result of which coins were often in short supply. Also,

23. Cameron, 1993, p. 33.
24. Ibid., p. 36.

emperors frequently debased their currencies for their personal enrich-
ment, it being difficult for the users to ascertain a coin's true composition.
Agreements between states about exchange ratios were the exception,
their absence the rule.

Imperial policies were by no means the only constraint on the growth
of specialization. Exchange of goods across long distances is advantageous only when the cost of transporting the goods is less than the benefits of lower relative production costs. In the wind- and oar-powered ships
that were the fastest means of transportation well into medieval times, it
was difficult for a ship to cover more than ninety miles a day under the
best of circumstances. But costly as this was, transport by sea was far less
expensive than was that overland, given the available means. In the Rome
of the third century A.D., it is said to have been less expensive to ship grain
from Alexandria to Rome at a distance of 1,250 miles than to transport it
50 miles by land from the city's hinterland.[25] Until more than a thousand
years later, most goods other than luxuries for the small elite classes were
considered too costly to transport over long distances.

Although many civilizations encountered and clashed with one another
in the Mediterranean and Near East, with more limited contacts extending to India and China, the ancient world still contained vast expanses in
which simple agriculturalists and even hunter-gatherers existed in relative
isolation, unaware of the advent of writing, improving metallurgy, or
states. At the height of the Mesopotamian and Egyptian empires, for
instance, the southern half of Africa, including today's Congo, East Africa,
Angola, and Mozambique, was probably occupied by hunter-gatherers
speaking languages of the Khoisan family. Not until about 500 B.C. were
these peoples largely displaced by Bantu-speaking Africans who brought
crops and cultivation practices from West Africa. Even when newly settled by Bantu agriculturalists, large areas continued to be sparsely populated, with hundreds of distinct tribal groups having no overarching political structure and practicing shifting, subsistence-oriented agricultural
traditions in small groups. Pockets of hunter-gatherers and traditional
pastoralists like the Masaii survive in eastern and southern Africa to the
present day. In the waning days of the Roman Empire, central and northern Eurasia was also filled with groups like the Goths, Franks, and the
Turkic-speaking peoples and Mongols who later overwhelmed Rome in

25. Crone, 1989, p. 14.

the west and preyed upon the eastern empires of Byzantium, India, and China over the next thousand years.

In the Americas, where human settlement may have begun about thirteen thousand years ago, plant domestication began independently some five thousand years later than it had in the Fertile Crescent. Three civilizations marked by large-scale states were to arise indigenously in Central and South America before the arrival of the Europeans in 1492, but this did not happen much before the Common Era, by which time the earliest civilizations of the Near East had already expired. Parts of North and South America continued to be sparsely populated by hunters and gatherers, a few of whom survive to the present day. Most was peopled by tribes practicing a mix of farming and hunting or fishing.

Australia and New Guinea are believed to have been populated much earlier than the Americas, but the peoples living there still used stone tools when Europeans reached their respective interiors in the nineteenth century. Only the New Guineans had developed an indigenous agriculture. The waves of migrants who would populate the islands of the Pacific and Indian oceans did not leave South China until the time that large states were arising in the Near East. These peoples spread from island to island, reaching Hawaii and Madagascar only around A.D. 500 and New Zealand around 1000. The differences among the paths that economic, social, and political development took on different islands provide for fascinating insights into the relations between environment, economy, and culture.[26]

THE MIDDLE AGES AND THE
TRANSITION TO MODERNITY

On the whole, the largest imperial states with unproductive elites, large armies, and all-powerful emperors proved unstable and ultimately lacking in dynamism. Limited in their ability to generate new wealth and technology, they burdened their common people with the taxation to

26. Overviews of the settlement histories of sub-Saharan Africa, the Americas, Polynesia, and Australia and New Guinea are found in Diamond, 1998. That author also provides a convincing argument that differences in rates of economic and technological development should be attributed to differences in environmental conditions, not genes.

support bureaucracies and the armies needed to defend against competing empires and neighboring tribes. In 476, the western half of the Mediterranean world's last great classical empire, that of Rome, dissolved into
a large number of disunited territories, and a new form of economy,
dubbed feudalism, began to emerge there. The empire's eastern half survived for nearly a thousand years more, but its territory was gradually
eaten away by challenges from without, eventually succumbing to en-
circlement by the Ottoman Turks. Asia's largest empire, China, remained
unified for most of the next fifteen hundred years, reaching what many
consider its cultural apex in the tenth century, with much of what further
technical and organizational change was to occur before modern times
being offset by population growth.

Islam, a new religious culture that became a predominant force from
Morocco through the Near East, southward into Africa and eastward to
Indonesia, maintained the intellectual legacies of ancient Greece and
absorbed the fruits of other civilizations, including India's numerals and
China's paper. But it, too, did not foster major new technological or
organizational breakthroughs. A series of Indian civilizations, which had
begun with the Indus Valley civilization of about 2500–1500 B.C., was
followed by the development under Aryan dominance of various Hindu
dynasties, ending in the rule of most of India by Muslim conquerors, the
Moguls, in A.D. 1526. The empires that sprang up in the New World,
including the Aztecs of Mexico (c. 1325–1519) and the Incas of Peru (c.
1200–1532), retraced many of the steps of ancient Mesopotamia and
Egypt before their further evolution was halted by the horses, ships, and
gunpowder of Spanish invaders in the sixteenth century.

Although the feudalism of Europe was by no means a universal stage
through which all of the world's societies have passed, and although its
characteristics varied from region to region and over time, it was in feudal
economies, rather than the classical empires, that the commercial and
technological changes leading to the industrial revolution — a development that would leave no part of the world untouched — were to occur.
The economic arrangements of the period in Japan and in some other
non-European countries are also viewed by some historians as "feudal."
Thus, it is worth pausing briefly to discuss the economic nature of feudalism, as well as the process of change that led up to the beginning of
capitalism.

As already mentioned, political and economic power in this era was dispersed to a class of hereditary elites who often owed no more than limited obligations to an overlord or king of a smaller or larger territory. As in the great empires, the vast majority of the people remained impoverished tillers of land, and as in the empires these farming people were required to turn over a substantial part of their produce or their labor or both, in this case to the lord of their manor, without compensation. The typical peasant endured a diet poor in vitamins, protein, and variety, was poorly clothed, and lived in quarters that were poorly ventilated, inadequately heated, and crudely furnished. Poor nutrition and low sanitation standards contributed to high death rates, as did frequent violence among the people.

As in the village-based economies that had preceded the great empires, initially the manors were relatively self-sufficient in the production of food, shelter, and clothing, with men specializing in construction work and leather tanning and women in the weaving of rough linen and woolen cloth. Peasants bartered their crops, handicrafts, or labor for such provisions as salt, ale, fuel, and articles of clothing that they could not produce themselves. Light industries including small-scale mining, fishing, and production of wool, iron, cloth, and wooden products were spread across the countryside. Specialized crafts were gradually concentrated in small and medium-sized towns. Enjoying some autonomy from the feudal lords, the craftsmen organized themselves into guilds and recruited new laborers as apprentices who might advance to the status of journeymen and then master craftsmen. The peasant producers also generated enough surplus to support a class of religious specialists and the construction of impressive cathedrals as well as numerous castles and manors, monasteries, and abbeys.

During the early centuries following the collapse of Rome, Europeans with some historical sensibility felt that the best days of mankind had passed. Not only were the great empires defunct, but for a long time there was little advancement in scientific knowledge, and the best that church scholars seemed able to do was to keep alive fragments of Egyptian, Greek, and Roman learning. For a time, both local and long-distance trade contracted, as goods transported overland could be taxed or held up by robbers over and again along their routes, and there was no strong power to police the seas—although, after 700, Arab traders successfully plied the Mediterranean. In the early centuries following Rome's demise, the money economy was negligible, and land and produce were the main forms of wealth. Populations at first declined from A.D. 200 to 600 due to invasions and disease, then grew back to their previous high point of thirty-six million by 1000 and doubled over the next three centuries. Long-distance trading continued in such essentials as salt and iron, and merchants regularly imported luxury goods including spices, silk, porcelain, and precious stones from the East, sending back wool and linen cloth, furs, metalwares, and glass. A similar mix of trading in luxuries and more basic goods was reflected when an eleventh-century Chinese author wrote: "Merchants who trade across the seas value pearls and jade or else rhinoceros horn or tortoise shell. Merchants who trade overland either value salt and iron or else tea."[27]

Increased contact between Europe and the Muslim world and Asia following the Crusades (eleventh to thirteenth centuries) and the short-lived Mongol unification of much of Asia and Europe (late thirteenth century) seemed to spur increased interest in foreign goods and trade. The Italian city-state of Venice initially led the way. By the fifteenth century, Europe had seen notable improvements in its techniques of shipbuilding and navigation, and there was a growing quest for new sources of goods. For the first time, states with Atlantic coastlines began rivaling those of the Mediterranean, seeking new routes to the East by way of the ocean. "Three-, four-, and five-masted ships, with combinations of square and lateen sails capable of sailing across the wind, replaced the oared galleys with auxiliary sails of medieval commerce. The hinged sternpost rudder replaced the steering oar."[28] These advances provided greater maneuverability and dispensed with oarsmen. The compass was invented to aid navigation, and improved methods for projecting cannonballs and bullets using gunpowder, a Chinese invention, enabled Europeans to enter territories where they were not welcomed. By 1492, Europeans reached the New World, and in 1497–99, their ships reached India by sailing around Africa, returning with plentiful spices. In 1513, a Portuguese ship reached Canton, and by the middle of the century trading and diplomatic relations were established with Japan.

In the thirteenth century, Europe was still so poor and fragmented that when the Italian Marco Polo returned to tell his compatriots of the cultural sophistication and political unity of Mongol-ruled China, he was

27. Crone, 1989, p. 22.
28. Cameron, 1993, p. 98.

greeted with disbelief. In the early sixteenth century, the vast territories of the Aztec and Inca emperors likewise caught by surprise the conquistadors of a Spain only recently united. With the revival of trade and the ensuing overseas expansion, however, Europe began a process of economic revival that would lead to a period of world dominance. Its population, which had fallen to as little as twenty million in the eleventh century, began to grow thereafter. Despite the widespread devastation of the Black Death a century earlier, it reached as much as fifty million by the middle of the fifteenth century and around one hundred million by the mid–seventeenth century. More productive and intensive farming techniques appeared, and the higher value of wool led England's landlords to drive peasants from former manorial commons, which they "enclosed" for private grazing.

Meanwhile, non-agricultural pursuits grew in importance. While typically not more than 10 percent of the population had engaged in occupations other than farming in the ancient empires, Patricia Crone estimates that in western Europe around 1300 the non-farm share had reached 15 percent, and by 1500, 20 percent, a sign of important changes in the making. By the late seventeenth century, international trade was booming. Previously unknown foods became European staples: potatoes, tomatoes, squash, pumpkins, and corn spread from the New World to the Old. Imported tobacco, coffee, tea, cocoa, and sugar began to take on the quality of staples rather than luxuries.

Even at the end of the seventeenth century, however, agriculture still employed two-thirds of Europe's population. Manual labor was the most important factor of production, and most non-farm production remained small in scale, the virtues of mass production still not being fully appreciated. Inland trade remained expensive and had to rely heavily on river transport, still much cheaper than that overland. That a new stage of economic development would begin in Europe would hardly have been clear to an observer at the time. China, in particular, despite nostalgia for past cultural heights and few further advances in science, enjoyed a medieval economic revolution that saw increasing agricultural intensification and a peasantry heavily involved in commercial activities. The building of the Grand Canal linking the Yellow and Yangtze rivers, and the movement of the capital to Beijing during the Ming Dynasty, stimulated north-south trade in cotton, the manufacturing of cotton cloth, and increasing regional specialization. Chinese ships traded with Japan, which would

itself later emerge as a modernizing feudal society, and with the Philippines, Southeast Asia, the Malay Peninsula, and Indonesia. In the early
fifteenth century, a Chinese admiral led large naval expeditions into the
Indian Ocean, leaving colonies of Chinese settlers at ports in Ceylon,
India, the Persian Gulf, the Red Sea, and the east coast of Africa.

Unlike Europe, however, China still had an emperor, and the one who
followed Admiral Cheng-Ho's voyages frowned upon foreign adventures.
The empire thus turned increasingly inward.[29] As its improvements in
farming methods and internal commerce were swallowed up by population growth, the country's declining economy would soon become easy
prey for European, Russian, and Japanese encroachment. With a few
other exceptions, most of what remained of the non-European world,
beginning with the Americas and followed by Asia and then Africa, soon
succumbed to a still more blatant European colonization.

THE INDUSTRIAL REVOLUTION AND THE
EMERGENCE OF THE MODERN ECONOMY

As we have seen, the agricultural revolutions of ten to twelve thousand
years ago led to denser populations, larger political entities, more stratified societies, armies, and the flowering of written culture and new techniques in metalworking and other fields. But these early developments
traversed only a portion of the distance separating primitive from modern
economies. Only a small minority of the populations of the ancient and
medieval worlds experienced improvements in their standards of living,
and the gradual improvements in farming techniques and navigation

29. Diamond, 1998, Landes, 1998, and others place emphasis on this government-
dictated ban of overseas trade, arguing that it was Europe's fragmentation, and the
consequent competition among states, that were decisive in determining that it
would be first to industrialize. Others stress the practical mindset of Europeans of
the Enlightenment, or the impractical focus of China's exam system on purely
literary classical learning. A recent argument by Pomeranz (2000) stresses the luck
of early European manufacturing centers in being able to relieve fuel constraints by
having coal deposits at their doorsteps, whereas long distances separated the coal
deposits deep in China's interior from the country's economic heartland. The important point for our purposes is that Europe and China were on an ostensibly equal
footing up to the eve of the industrial revolution. The same might be said for other
centers, including Constantinople, Persia, and India, just a few centuries earlier.

were largely offset by population growth. It was left for the industrial revolution that began in eighteenth-century England to bring about a quantum leap in the complexity of economic life, the scale of production and trade, and the productivity of labor. New gains from specialization, new technologies, and the expansion of the rights of the common person that accompanied the emerging economic order would eventually engender a large jump in the standard of living of more than a small elite.

In medieval Europe and China, as in the ancient empires of the Near East and those that followed in the New World and elsewhere, the specialized positions of soldier, artisan, or merchant were the exceptions, while the common role of peasant or serf was the rule. Modern society was to turn this around. Farmers would occupy a smaller and smaller fraction of the population, and there would be no single modal occupation, but rather a multitude of occupations in industries ranging from mining and manufacturing to transportation and communications, marketing and sales, health care and education, administration and entertainment. Occupation would be less tightly linked to social status, and hereditary classes and castes would gradually vanish. The main element uniting the diverse new occupations was that in them, people would produce little of their own consumption needs. Instead they would work for a wage or to sell their specialized goods or services, and they would meet their own needs by purchasing goods and services from others. Increasingly, too, people did not control their own enterprises, but rather served as employees of companies owned by providers of financial inputs.

The first movements in this direction have already been discussed above. By the early eighteenth century, only about two-thirds of the population of northwestern Europe was still engaged in farming. Although colonization and foreign plunder brought mountains of precious metals to the monarchs of Spain and Portugal, they did not in themselves bring a new form of economic life. Southern Europe remained largely agrarian, and the countries it colonized began recreating a feudal-style system of large haciendas in which serflike hacienda workers lived off the produce of the surrounding minifundia (microplots). In northern Europe, however, a new economy of increased specialization and commercial interaction was beginning to emerge. Although fueled partly by the abundance of foreign markets and resources and of overseas opportunities for the venting of excess population, the evolution of the new economic system was also driven by a number of other forces.

First, internal specialization and commerce were facilitated by improving means and hence lowered costs of transportation. Although England already enjoyed a head start in this respect due to its abundance of coastline, natural harbors, and navigable streams, demand for transportation increased, and from 1660–89 "fifteen private acts of Parliament were passed for river and harbor improvements; from 1690 to 1719, 59 acts (including some for turnpike construction) were passed; and from 1720 to 1749, 130 acts," according to Cameron. Between 1750 and 1820, 3,000 miles of navigable waterways, mainly canals, were added to the 1,000 already in existence; and the 3,400 miles of turnpike network existing in 1750 grew to 15,000 miles in 1770 and 22,000 in 1836, "by which time the railways had begun to render them and the canals obsolete."[30] Not only did each wave of transportation improvements provide a cheaper and more reliable means of moving goods over long distances; their construction also directly stimulated the industries that provided them (for the railroads, for example, iron, coal, bricks, engine and carriage building, and so on). Still more industries were stimulated indirectly by way of the jobs all of these created.

Second, specialization was facilitated by improvements in agriculture, including more scientific animal husbandry methods and nitrogen-restoring crop rotations. These changes, along with enclosures for private sheep raising and later for grain crops, helped cause the proportion of English workers primarily engaged in farming to fall to 60 percent at the end of the seventeenth century, 36 percent at the end of the eighteenth century, and 22 percent by the middle of the nineteenth century. Although food imports from continental Europe eventually played a role, in the century beginning in 1660 England still had surplus food to export. "The relatively prosperous rural population, more specialized and commercially oriented than most continental peasants, also provided a ready market for manufactured goods, ranging from agricultural implements to such consumer products as clothing, pewter ware, and porcelain," Cameron observes. Farms grew in size and showed a new pattern of organization. Where before peasants had aided one another in farming small strips and had grazed their animals on a village commons, now operators of large farms hired both land and farm workers, with the absolute size of the population of farm laborers at first rising even though agriculture's

30. Cameron, 1993, pp. 172, 173.

share in the occupational structure was falling. Meanwhile, the importance of commerce and other non-agricultural sectors rose: "Between
1688 and 1801, while the relative share of agriculture in national income
declined from 40 to 32.5 percent and that of mining, manufacturing, and
building rose from 21 to only 23.6 percent, the relative share of trade and
transport rose from 12 to 17.5 percent."[31]

A third factor opening the way to a new economy was the emergence
of modern ways of *financing* both public and private investments. Early
states had taken a large part of their revenue in kind, or even in labor, and
had applied the bulk of it to defensive and other military expenditures and
to the support of elites and the building of monuments. With control
over the public finances of England in the hands of a Parliament responsive to landowners and merchants, tax collections were increasingly applied to infrastructure investments that contributed importantly to the
process of industrialization. Tax collection was professionalized, taxes
were paid in cash, and the supply of money was better regulated to meet
the needs of an increasingly commercialized economy. And where earlier
private investment had depended mainly on the private accumulation of
wealth, such institutions as deposit banking, joint stock companies, and
the issuing of private bonds began to diversify sources of funding and to
make possible the organization of private commercial and manufacturing
ventures on significantly larger scales — although internal financing was
to remain prominent.

Most important, although in no sense independent of these other
changes, were developments in the techniques of manufacturing, mining,
transportation, and other sectors, which manifested the new empirical
spirit of the times. The eighteenth century saw a series of improvements
in the techniques for producing iron, which became the basis for railroad
building and a major English export. The development of the steam
engine provided a powerful alternative to wind and water power. With
important early applications in mining and textiles, it drove down the
costs of transportation over water and land, as well as powering construction and other equipment before itself being replaced by internal
combustion engines and then, partially, by electricity. Production in the
textile industry was mechanized and organized on a larger scale, and by
the beginning of the nineteenth century, English cotton exports sur-

31. Ibid., pp. 169–70.

passed those of wool, with more than half of the country's cotton goods being marketed overseas. Progress in the production and use of chemicals gave rise to another major industry, producing dyes and bleaches for the textile and paper industries, among others. Many of the industries just mentioned exhibited powerful linkages and synergies: for instance, coal powered the steam-driven equipment that facilitated deeper and less expensive coal mining, and it was also an input in iron production, while iron and coal were used by the railroads, which in turn transported their raw materials to the smelters. The textile industry bought cotton, dyes, and machinery, and it too generated demands for transportation services.

Partly as a result of rising productivity, population grew, further contributing to economic development by increasing the density of markets. From the invention of agriculture to the end of the eighteenth century, world population had grown gradually, roughly doubling every thousand years. But now, population more than doubled in the nineteenth century alone. In 1800, Europe contained about two hundred million people, double its population in 1650 and almost four times the population of the Roman Empire. By 1900, the continent held four hundred million people. During the same hundred-year period, the population of England and Wales alone expanded from a little over nine million to about thirty-three million people, despite the emigration of millions to North America and elsewhere, where their numbers also multiplied. Population also became more concentrated in towns and cities. Whereas about 30 percent of England's people lived in towns of two thousand inhabitants or more in 1800, over half did by 1850, and more than three-quarters by 1900. Other industrializing countries including Germany, France, and the Netherlands were also at least 50 percent urban by the end of the nineteenth century.

EXPANSION AND CONQUEST

The idea that some group of people is indigenous to a certain region is one that can have only relative validity, at best. Humans began fanning out from eastern Africa and the Middle East into Asia, Australia, and Europe more than one hundred thousand years ago. From northeast Asia, they migrated to the Americas; from southeast Asia, to the islands of the Indian and Pacific oceans. The ancient civilizations of Egypt and

Mesopotamia are believed to have been peopled in part by relatively recent migrants from neighboring regions. Even East Africa, the cradle of humankind, has seen successive waves of migration sufficient to erase any claim by its inhabitants to being more aboriginal to their area than are the peoples of later-inhabited zones. Large-scale migrations, spilling of blood, and intermixings of populations have been the norm, not the exception in history: from the Bantu migration across Africa to the movement of the Han people into the southern half of China to the invasions of Indo-European speakers into Europe and India to the arrival of the Magyars and Turks from central Asia to Hungary and Asia Minor. The expansion of western Europeans, which laid the groundwork for globe-spanning empires, was not a new departure, then, except in one respect: it brought into contact the peoples of continents who had not known of one another's existence, setting in motion a chain of events that would lead for the first time to a more fully interconnected world.[32]

The main colonizers, the Spanish, Portuguese, Dutch, French, and British, by the eighteenth century controlled all of North America, large swaths of Asia, and many outposts along the African and Asian coasts. To this they added, by the end of the nineteenth century, the African interior, Australia, New Zealand, New Guinea, and much of remaining Asia and Oceania. Even unconquered lands like Japan and China were forced to westernize. That Europe, once launched on this course, would conquer so many lands was largely the result of such technological advantages as the superiority of its ships, cannons, guns, and horses. The nature of the conquest, however, varied significantly, depending on the balance of populations, and the balance of germs.

The Americas offer a perfect example. In 1492, they contained a few densely populated regions and many areas of sparse population in which shifting agriculture and hunting were practiced. Roughly 14 million people lived on the two continents, compared with about 81 million in Europe and 280 million in Asia.[33] Although the Europeans' larger overall

32. Although the Mongol Empire, which brought China, the Near East, and much of eastern Europe under common rule in the thirteenth century, was history's largest, it ruled over peoples who had known of one another's existence and who, over long periods of time, if sporadically, had already diffused to one another their crops, domesticated animals, technologies, and even religions. It was also far shorter lived and less lasting in its effects than was the later overseas expansion of Europeans.

33. Population estimates (those given above are from McEvedy and Jones, 1976)

population and technological advantages, especially possession of horses and gunpowder, might have allowed them to dominate the Americas with enough effort within a few years, the balance was tipped early on by the diseases they brought with them. The organisms causing these diseases had been breeding in Old World populations for thousands of years, leading to a degree of resistance among their surviving descendants. But they were previously unknown to the Amerindians, whose post-contact populations in some cases fell to as little as a tenth of what they had been, due to the resulting epidemics. Relatively small numbers of colonists, aided by horses and guns, were able to subdue the surviving residents of large parts of the continent in short order, and when conflicts between them arose, the members of entire tribes were frequently slaughtered.

Continuing immigration allowed much of these two continents, then, to be resettled by essentially European societies, although the demography varied from case to case. The much larger numbers of native peoples in what would become Mexico, for instance, contributed significantly to that country's gene pool. Elsewhere, including the southeastern section of the future United States and parts of Brazil, settler aspirations to generate wealth through plantation agriculture combined with the decimation of the natives and the unwillingness of European workers (who could fairly easily obtain land elsewhere in the New World) to bring about the importation of large numbers of slaves from Africa. Trade in slaves became an important element in growing trans-Atlantic commerce, making fortunes for some traders, dividing Africans, and adding a large African component also to the population of the Americas.

On its home ground, Africa provides a very different case. It was almost certainly more densely populated than the Americas (with its total in 1500 estimated at forty-six million), though less populous than Europe and Asia. But more important than absolute population is the fact that here the balance of disease worked in the other direction, making ventures into its interior deadly to Europeans who lacked tolerance for its tropical

---

are especially unreliable for the indigenous population of the Americas in 1492, not only because of the absence of anything like modern censuses but also because of uncertainty about just what proportion of the pre-Colombian population died from the diseases brought by Europeans. Conceivably, the total population of the Americas stood in larger ratio to that of Europe than these particular estimates indicate, although there is little question that population densities north of Mexico and south of Peru were much lower than were European averages.

diseases. Being less hospitable to plantations than the New World and less endowed with the spices that Europeans sought in the East, the continent was circumnavigated and dotted with an occasional coastal outpost, but the European scramble for the bulk of its territory waited another four hundred years, until better technology and medical measures were available. With the major exception of its southern tip, then, Europeans and their emerging industrial-age technologies came very late to Africa, and European settlers were relatively few and concentrated in the handful of climatic zones considered by them to be hospitable.

Although colonial regimes were imposed on sub-Saharan Africa for but a short period of time, however, they had a profound effect, for they came by and large as an overlay on a complex mozaic of tribal and language groups that had lacked large-scale states, so that the national entities that emerged lacked linguistic cohesion or a cadre of experienced administrators. These late colonies sought to extract economic benefit by exploiting the continent's untapped minerals and establishing plantations of tropical and semitropical crops like cocoa and palm oil. When independent Africa later entered the world economy, it did so as an exporter of primary products par excellence.

Asia, the most populous of the continents, was affected in equally distinct ways by Europe's expansion. Long-distance commerce was an established business of Muslim, Chinese, and other traders long before the Europeans began sailing in the Indian Ocean. Indeed, international commerce was far livelier in East than West at the time of the Crusades, and it was the desire for better access to that trade that spurred Europe toward its own outward stance. Beginning in the sixteenth century, superior ships and cannon allowed the Portuguese, then the Dutch, British, and French, to begin muscling in on Asian trade and relegating local traders to smaller-scale and more local activities. Much of Asia was already densely populated and hence not a likely zone for European settlement. But more direct control of the production of crops like rubber and tea, whether under contract with local landowners or by establishment of their own plantations, was attractive. The balance of germs in this case was more evenly matched: perhaps because of prior diffusion of communicable diseases across the Eurasian land mass, neither Europeans nor Asians were especially at risk from new contacts.

Where local rulers were weak or political elites disunited, special trading privileges eventually gave way to colonization. By the mid–nineteenth century, India and Indonesia, two of Asia's most populous countries, were under the direct rule of Britain and the Netherlands. Indochina followed, under the French. Giant China and neighboring Japan granted Europeans only limited presence in certain ports, but China's efforts to limit European influence at least partially backfired. First, an expanding Russian empire whittled away its territory from the north; then Britain and Portugal claimed enclaves on the coast. Eventually Japan, once a small country in the Chinese political sphere but later an assiduous borrower of Western technology, would seize large chunks of Chinese territory.

Western Europe's overseas expansion and subsequent industrialization created an interconnected economy spanning Old and New Worlds. Complex trade webs included those in which Europeans and North Americans sent goods and money to Africa, brought back slaves for southern plantations, and in turn sent the resulting cotton to Europe for production of exportable textiles. Crops from the New World became both staples (maize in Africa) and bases of plantation economies (rubber in Indonesia, sugar cane in the Philippines). Consumption habits changed, as Europeans, for example, became accustomed to tea, coffee, chocolate, tomatoes. North America became an exporter of wheat and, with the advent of refrigeration, South America an exporter of meat. Colombia grew coffee, Honduras bananas, Ghana cocoa, Sri Lanka (Ceylon) tea.

Economic theory, as we have seen, shows that increased trade can benefit all parties due to the benefits of specialization and comparative advantage. But trade imposed by force is inherently suspect, and trade, however initiated, need not benefit all individuals within a given country, as when exports of European cloth destroyed competing domestic industries in countries like India. Even less likely to benefit were those whose own persons were sold as slave laborers. That there must be at least some losers is implicit in the fact that it took gunboats to force open so many ports.

One source of the unevenness in the benefits from trade was inequality in the level of development, including technological capabilities. The new international trade linked economies at various stages of industrialization to agrarian and handicraft economies, horticultural economies, economies composed predominantly of nomads, and even economies of stone-tool-using hunters. The least developed economies could not trade with the most developed on very advantageous terms, and even relatively developed agrarian economies might see little benefit from trade if they exported mainly crops and minerals in exchange for the industrial countries' manufactures, with their own handicraft industries collapsing from this competition. The challenge that less developed countries faced in attempting to emulate the industrial leaders will be the topic of Chapter 4.

Movements of capital and especially of skilled labor could allow industrial capability to spread from country to country over time. Such a process of diffusion started in Europe itself and spread outward, first to countries where large numbers of Europeans had settled. Northern Europe, including France, Germany, and the Scandinavian countries, was the first to follow England into industrialization in the nineteenth century, with the United States following close behind. Parts of central and southern Europe, Canada, Argentina, Chile, South Africa, and Australia followed as well. Russia — an increasingly important if politically and socially regressive power whose imperial expansion into the Caucasus, central Asia, and Siberia rivaled the sea-based expansions of the Atlantic countries — also took initial steps toward industrialization. Only one country outside the European cultural sphere made significant strides toward industrialization before the twentieth century: Japan. That country had kept the Europeans at a distance, but then successfully embarked on a concerted effort to master their technologies and join the industrial world. By the beginning of the twentieth century, it would become an imperial power in its own right in Korea, Taiwan, and the Chinese mainland.

The benefits of trade and industrialization were unequally shared *within* nations, too, owing to internal economic differentiation. Although the old inherited statuses and feudal ties to land had been dissolved, few from the common rank of peasants and craftspeople amassed the capital or managerial acumen to escape dependence on wage employment in the emerging industrial societies. In nineteenth-century England, Charles Dickens, as well as Karl Marx and Friedrich Engels, wrote distressingly of the horrors of the factories and the poor living conditions of the workers. They described the enclosure movement as a mass dispossession of the old peasant class, driving those who constituted it into urban destitution as workers locked in dark and dangerous factories for fourteen-hour days, or members of the "reserve army of the unemployed." Radical anti-capitalism would appeal to many urban workers in the United States and other industrialized countries in the late nineteenth century and the first decades of the twentieth.

It is worth noting, finally, that the world that emerged with European expansion and industrialization was one consisting of somewhat novel entities, namely modern nation-states. They were marked by considerable centralized power, but also by bureaucracies partly free of the vagaries of politics, and by substantial countervailing power in economic and civil institutions standing apart from the state. Although nation-like entities had certainly existed before, much of Europe lacked such structures when the Atlantic countries began their overseas voyages. Neither Germany nor Italy had coalesced in their modern forms, for instance, and it was not unusual to find widely scattered parcels of territory treated as private possessions of one monarch or another. Moreover, most of the New World, Australia, New Guinea, and Africa lacked large-scale political units, and these areas were first forced into such structures by colonial rule. By the late nineteenth century, most of the Americas had adopted the nation-state form, being the first of Europe's colonies to break free, albeit under the dominance of descendants of Europeans. With the completion of the decolonization process elsewhere, in the next century, the making of a world of nation-states would itself be completed.

Although a guiding principle of the emerging economies was that states should leave most economic decisions to households and firms, modern states were to have important functions and impacts on their nations' economies. The impetus that competition among western European nations gave to their outward expansion is one consequence of the existence of states that had immense economic ramifications. Debates over tariff policy largely account for the rise of economics as a science, as will be seen in the next chapter, while arguments over taxation significantly contributed to the American Revolution, among other events. The role that progressive state policies played in extending the benefits of capitalism and increasing its political palatability will be discussed briefly below and more extensively in Chapter 3. Governments also made critical investments in infrastructure without which industrialization would have proved impossible. In many of the countries that followed England in industrialization, tariffs and other measures, including state involvement in banking or the financing of investment, played important roles, as will be seen in Chapter 4.

There were also large economic costs of the coalescing of nations, and of the competition among them. National boundaries and identity might not emerge without conflict, and the sorting out of problems of ethnicity and nationality is a process that continues to exact large economic and human costs to the present day. Also, competition among nation-states was rarely limited to the friendly or exclusively economic kind. The world wars of the twentieth century illustrated, on unprecedented scales, the immense economic and human costs of competitive nationalism. They raised clouds over the progress of the industrial market economies for a considerable part of that century.

INDUSTRIAL ECONOMIES INTO
THE TWENTIETH CENTURY

Technological improvements, specialization, and trade eventually delivered large gains in living standards for the core industrial countries, if not for their less developed trading partners and dependencies. By the late eighteenth century, Adam Smith was already remarking that "in a civilized and thriving country . . . the accommodation of [a] prince does not always so much exceed that of an industrious and frugal peasant, as the accommodation of the latter exceeds that of many an African king, the absolute master of the lives and liberties of ten thousand naked savages."[34] Differences in living standards among the European countries to which Smith traveled or of which he heard first-hand accounts encouraged him in the belief that economic development hinged importantly on differences in institutions and policies, and that development could make a difference to all ranks of society. Yet three-quarters of a century after Smith wrote, not all agreed that the common people were better off under industrial capitalism. The wretched condition of many working people in the mid–nineteenth century was what impressed pessimists and critics.

By the late twentieth century, however, the anticipation of a permanently impoverished working class put forward by nineteenth-century critics of capitalism would be hopelessly overtaken by events. Recent historical research suggests that the average per capita income of western Europeans and North Americans grew by a factor of ten or more between the 1820s and the late 1980s.[35] Average wages grew by a factor of four or

34. Smith, 1985 [1776], pp. 13–14.
35. Maddison, 1991, p. 10, estimates that average incomes in western Europe, Australia, Canada, and the United States grew by a factor of almost five between

more in France, Germany, Sweden, the United Kingdom, and the United States between 1860 and 1960.[36] Nor were the advantages of improving productivity material ones only. Life expectancy in England in 1920 was only thirty-eight years; by 1992, it had grown to more than seventy-five years. Access to education and the franchise also dramatically expanded.

Despite the ultimately favorable outcome for so many, the economic story of the twentieth century is a complex one, even if our attention is restricted to the industrialized world. Its earlier decades found industrial capitalism still an embattled and fragile system, with its gains concentrated mainly in a few countries, and with a considerable proportion of wage earners still skeptical of its benefits. Socialists and radical labor organizers still attracted followings in America, and Communists and Social Democrats who as yet advocated the nationalization of industry were major political forces in Europe. The steady growth of international trade was interrupted first by World War I, then by mounting protectionism, and finally by a wave of financial crises and economic depression that put vast numbers of people out of work even in the United States, the country left ascendant by the war. The burden of war reparations led to hyperinflation and political instability in Germany. While Germany and other countries opted for military expansion and totalitarian government, the United States turned to a program of public works and fiscal stimulation to hobble through the decade before the full economic mobilization of World War II returned it to vigorous economic growth. Only with that war's end did the cloud that had descended over industrial capitalism in the 1920s begin to lift convincingly.

Before this could happen, a large part of Europe and Asia took a detour from the mainstream of capitalist economic development. Karl Marx, whose economic writings will be discussed in Chapter 2, had predicted that the "internal contradictions" that capitalism suffered due to the conflict of interest between the laborer and the owner of capital would lead to the system's eventual demise. Although there were not yet signs of that demise in the most industrialized societies, followers of Marx in some less developed countries were not content to wait for it to happen. One such group captured political power in Russia, withdrew the country from

---

1820 and 1950, and by nearly three times more by 1989, for a total increase of almost 1400 percent.

36. Phelps Brown, 1968, p. 344.

participation in the First World War, and, after a relatively chaotic decade, designed a new economic mechanism wherein the government owned most capital and land and dictated production through an administrative hierarchy, without market competition or a free price system. In the West, Russia's early successes with forced-draft industrialization encouraged radical workers and struck fear in the hearts of some capitalists. The approach would be copied by revolutionaries in other poor countries, and imposed on Eastern Europe when Soviet troops occupied it after World War II. Yet the successes of the approach in building heavy industries in formerly agrarian countries were never extended to more sophisticated technologies or to industries that could satisfy modern consumer demands.

Meanwhile, war exacted a heavy toll on the industrial economies. While the most important human costs are incalculable, a few costs lend themselves to financial accounting. A recent careful analysis estimates, for instance, that war deaths among their working populations destroyed 6 percent, 9 percent, and 18–19 percent, respectively, of the "human assets" of Japan, Germany, and the Soviet Union. Germany lost 17 percent of its fixed industrial assets, Japan 34 percent, and Italy 10 percent; the Soviet Union lost 25 percent of its national wealth. And while it was being fought, the war consumed the bulk of the productive capabilities of the main participants. In 1943, for instance, 42 percent of American, 55 percent of British, 61 percent of Soviet, and 70 percent of German national income went into the war effort.[37]

As the end of the Second World War closed the curtain on three decades of misfortune, the lessons from the aftermath of the preceding war were remembered. Rather than retreating into economic isolation and attempting to punish the aggressors, the victors invited them into the international trading system, and the country that emerged strongest from the war, the United States, helped rebuild the economies of former allies and enemies alike. World trade recovered to the levels seen before the First World War and then continued to grow. Even the destruction of physical facilities had its silver lining, as those who suffered the greatest losses were able to rebuild the most rapidly, putting in place capital stock and infrastructure of a vintage that might otherwise have taken decades to be

37. Harrison, 1998, pp. 21, 37.

adopted. Germany and Japan grew rapidly in per capita income, surpassing the United Kingdom, which had been roughly equal to the United States in per capita GDP before the war but now fell significantly behind.

The form of capitalism that emerged in the post–World War II era was not quite the same as its early-twentieth-century antecedent. Mixed economies, with large roles for both government and market, had begun to develop in the United States, Britain, Sweden, and elsewhere before the war — in part, some have argued, as a response to the threat posed by socialism.[38] After the war these became the norm throughout the industrialized world. The ideal of laissez-faire, or a "hands off" approach to the economy by government, gave way to a new consensus that it was a government's duty to react to macroeconomic imbalances and provide its citizens with a variety of social protections. The organization of workers into labor unions was legally recognized and protected throughout the industrial capitalist world, and in some countries tripartite cooperation between organized labor, corporations, and government emerged as a stabilizing force.

The organization of production had also evolved in new directions. Large, diffusely owned corporations, with shares traded on stock exchanges and with the ability to marshal huge quantities of finance from retained earnings, new share issues, and borrowing, accounted for substantial portions of industrial employment and output, especially in the United States. Similar large companies with more concentrated financing by banks existed in Germany and Japan, countries that rose rapidly from military defeat to industrial big-power status. The inefficiency of marrying dispersed outside ownership to insider professional management, which Adam Smith had seen as vitiating the corporate form, appeared to be abated by complex interplays of financial market surveillance, check-and-balance supervision between managers and boards of directors, and improved accounting and communications.[39] The efficiencies of the large corporation led one prominent business historian to declare that the

38. While such suggestions are often made about America in the New Deal era, they may also apply to the origins of the welfare state a generation earlier, as will be seen in Chapter 3.

39. Theoretical views of the complex contracting relationships that mark modern corporations can be found in Milgrom and Roberts, 1992, Putterman and Kroszner, eds., 1996, and Williamson, 1985.

"invisible hand" of the market had been partially eclipsed by the "visible hand" of the corporate manager.[40] Yet the system retained diversity and fluidity, as enterprises of many different scales continued to coexist, and various corporations jostled one another and battled for prominence. The heating up of international competition that became more noticeable beginning in the 1970s played an especially important role in checking the arrogance and potential slothfulness of the larger corporations.

Beyond the institutional innovations of more active macroeconomic management and an expanded welfare state, the key force powering capitalism's astonishing dynamism in the twentieth century was the unleashing of technological changes even more remarkable than those of the first century and a half of industrial revolution. Already in the late nineteenth century, a "second industrial revolution," rooted increasingly in science, was introducing such technologies as the use of electrical power, petroleum and diesel fuels, and new chemicals and artificial fibers. By the mid–twentieth century, still more technological developments were being generated by the joint influences of markets, governments, and a rapidly advancing understanding of the physical universe. Capitalism vigorously displayed its tendency to promote technological advances, a tendency attributable to the fact that the producer who can get a jump on his competitors enjoys a period of monopoly profits, whereas one who fails to keep ahead may well go out of business. And the governments of the industrialized nations complemented this dynamism with lavish expenditures on military and basic science research and weapons procurement, as well as through the provision of infrastructures for rapid communications and transportation. Scientific research did its part with an explosion of knowledge in chemistry, biology, physics, and other fields that led to a myriad of economic applications in areas such as electronics, information processing and communications technology, and medicine. The accelerating pace of technological change that capitalism made possible also seemed to make capitalism indispensable, since a continuous stream of consumer comforts and gadgetry had become the expected norm, and only competition and the profit motive seemed able to deliver it.[41]

40. See Chandler, 1977.

41. As economist Joseph Stiglitz wrote, "This may then be the ultimate irony: Marx may have been right in his theory of economic determinism, in his view that technology determined the nature of society, the economic and social systems that

Improvements in technology went hand in hand with a steady increase in the amounts of physical capital available in the forms of production equipment, buildings, infrastructure, and means of transportation. In the United States, capital per worker rose from about $16,000 in 1890 to about $48,000 in 1950 and $85,000 in 1987, all in constant dollars; comparable figures for the United Kingdom in the same years are $8,000, $14,000, and $58,000, respectively.[42] Basic economic theory and common sense predict that as workers are equipped with more capital goods, their output rises, as is reflected in the wage and average income figures mentioned above. Moreover, capital accumulation is almost inseparable from technological change, as new technologies are in practice incorporated in new capital goods. What economists call "human capital," or the stock of skills that a worker builds up by way of education and experience, also grew explosively. Differences in capital stocks per worker and in the skill levels of the workforce explain much though by no means all of the income gap between developed- and developing-country populations.

The centrally planned economies that followed the model established in the Soviet Union in the late 1920s also experienced rapid economic growth in the early postwar decades, keeping pace with the quantitative rate of output growth in the capitalist economies until the 1970s. By then, however, cracks in their abilities to generate technological improvements, or to deliver growth commensurate with its costs, were becoming more visible. Those costs included the lower consumption levels needed to attain growth by investing in more rather than better physical capital, and the sacrifice of economic and political freedoms and human rights that went along with one-party dictatorship. With industrial capitalism delivering an abundance of material goods along with a broad range of political liberties, most of the Marxist regimes were faced with popular revolts once their leaderships signaled an end to suppression of dissent by force in the late 1980s. As repression dropped away, the desires of most people in those countries turned toward adopting the economic system of the industrialized West. The institutional features of planned socialism

---

would prevail. Where he erred was in his ability to forecast how technology would evolve. . . . It is these changes, in the end, that doomed socialism." Stiglitz, 1994, p. 205.

42. Figures are rounded and calculated at U.S. prices of 1985; from Maddison, 1991, p. 66.

and of capitalism will be compared in Chapter 3; the initial period of the transition from socialism in the former Communist countries will also be discussed there.

GLOBALIZATION IN A POST-INDUSTRIAL ERA?

By the late twentieth century, advances in communications, transportation, and methods of information processing and transmission had given rise to levels of global specialization and economic interaction unimaginable in earlier times. With incredible rapidity, by comparison with rates of change in earlier epochs, the railroads and steamships that had revolutionized transportation and communications at the start of the industrial revolution were overtaken by still more modern technologies. Highways and fast-moving automobiles and trucks augmented the railroads. Communications speeds increased many times over, first with the telegraph, then the radio and telephone, then the Internet and electronic mail. Jet aircraft collapsed the physical distance between the continents to a few hours of travel.

The shrinking of the economic globe can be illustrated by numerous examples: for instance, how the American entertainment giant the Walt Disney Company prepared to launch its latest animated feature film, *Mulan*, in 1998. Nearly seven hundred artists, animators, and technicians worked on the production of the film in a newly built two-hundred-thousand-square-foot animation studio in Florida. Simultaneously, a range of toys and decorated food boxes and clothing was being prepared for promotional campaigns, including one coordinated with some of the twenty-three thousand McDonald's restaurant franchises around the world. Most of the toys and other items used in this campaign were designed in the United States, contracted for in Hong Kong, and subcontracted to small-scale manufacturers in China. Design specifications and orders moved from America to China in seconds by phone, fax, and electronic transmission, while "Happy Meal" boxes and toys were sent mainly in well-coordinated sea shipments but with potential refilling of orders to the United States and other countries in just half a day by air transport. The film was seen by tens of millions of paying viewers in theaters around the world, earning Disney over a hundred million dollars in its first month alone. Compare this with the era of the character the film depicts, a maiden-turned-soldier named Hua Mulan who would have taken weeks to gallop across China on horseback to meet the Huns around A.D. 600. Compare it, too, with the modest local character of entertainment in the ancient world, or in Shakespeare's time, just a few centuries ago!

The integration of such chains of design, production, promotion, and distribution across countries and regions of the world led in the 1990s to the popular use of the term "globalization." The facts, as we have seen, show that international trade and the nation-state itself had been growing hand in hand over the course of several centuries, and that the linking together of the world's economies had been going on in earnest at least since the overseas expansion of Europe's economies began in the fifteenth century. Although linkages were indeed closer than ever, the process of linkage was still far from complete even at the beginning of the twenty-first century. The "global economy" had only indirect influences on the lives of hundreds of millions of people living beyond the hotbeds of export processing, out in the hinterlands of Africa, Asia, and Latin America. Indeed, it was only because of the vast differences in levels of economic development, education, and infrastructure that a global division of labor, incorporating design in Florida with contracting in Hong Kong, assembly in southern China or Indonesia, and merchandising in Buenos Aires, Melbourne, and Johannesburg, embodied a certain economic logic.

The example also illustrates how the gains of globalizing production and distribution were often reaped disproportionately by large corporations able to integrate production and marketing stages within vast internal networks of managerial command and control. To be sure, globalization did not assure an easy ride for large companies, since it also meant increasing competition. Japan, South Korea, and Taiwan, among others, perfected postwar mass production and marketing techniques and, with their initially lower labor costs, spurred a new round of organizational restructuring and technological modernization in American and European companies. Large companies in all countries relied on smaller companies to play supply roles, and in technologically dynamic fields like computer software and consumer electronics, smaller, newer companies could still edge out competitors and emerge as major players. The economic organization of modern capitalism was one in which the internal bureaucratic coordination of operations *within* companies was continually competing with flows of goods *among* companies, making for a constantly changing symbiosis among companies of different scales and between managerially coordinated and market-mediated transactions.[43]

The ownership of assets also frequently changed hands through mergers, spin-offs, and takeovers and through the constant reshuffling of equity holdings in the world's stock markets. Improved communication and information processing technologies permitted millions of shares of companies' stocks to be bought and sold each day, with money actively moving among the financial markets of different parts of the world, and with new instruments permitting investors to tailor their portfolios to their own hunches, risk tolerances, and preferred time paths of consumption. Although wealth holding remained concentrated in the top few percent of households, a significant fraction of developed-country households began putting their money into play in the financial markets, with the combined assets of workers' pension funds and other investments accounting for about 40 percent of all stock shares in some countries.

The intensified globalization of financial markets made for increasing linkage of interest rates, inflation trends, government deficits, and exchange rate movements among the world's economies. Dollars earned by oil exporting countries, which had successfully raised world market prices by cutting back production in the 1970s, fattened the ledgers of the Western banks in which many of them were deposited. The banks in turn lent vast amounts of money to government and private ventures in middle-income countries like Mexico and Brazil. An upward shift of interest rates due to inflation in the late 1970s made it difficult for the borrowers to refinance their debts, causing a crisis of indebtedness in Latin America and Africa beginning in the 1980s (see Chapter 4). In the late 1990s, financial globalization also contributed to economic distress in the new industrial giants of Asia, where a boom fed by speculative investment using short-term foreign capital inflows went bust in a domino-like crisis of confidence. The interconnectedness of economies across the globe was underscored when large declines in Tokyo and Hong Kong stock market values during hours when London and New York slept had big impacts on the latter's stock markets the next morning day after day in the late

---

43. The role of the corporation in resource allocation and management is emphasized by Chandler, 1977. The view of the market economy as a mix of intrafirm and interfirm coordination will be discussed again in Chapter 3.

summer and autumn of 1997. By the end of the century, round-the-clock trading was being inaugurated to close one more gap in the network of global financial transactions.

Still another trend much in evidence by the 1990s was the emergence of services and information and the decline of manufacturing as dominant sectors in the richest economies, a trend that prompted some observers to dub the age "post-industrial." Though steel, automobiles, and machinery continued to be manufactured in the United States, Britain, and Germany, increasingly the world's physical workshops were being located in lower-wage economies like Korea, Brazil, and China, with the highest-income economies focusing more on knowledge generation and transmission, as well as services and entertainment. Among the many impacts of this trend was the rise to prominence of firms in electronic information processing and transmission, biotechnology and medicine, and financial services. While old manufacturing unions declined in membership and influence, an occupationally mobile technological elite emerged at the high end of the labor force, and earnings inequalities widened dramatically. Meanwhile, barriers to international trade continued to fall, and economic integration became the watchword in Europe in particular, but also in North America and elsewhere.

On the whole, industrialization and the emerging "post-industrial" era saw rising incomes in Europe and its overseas offshoots, in East Asia, and for certain segments of the populations of countries like Mexico, Brazil, and even India. But the benefits of modern technology and of a global economy remained far from universal. By the mid-1990s, with world population about to surpass six billion, more than three billion people still lived in countries with per capita incomes below seven hundred dollars, less than one-fiftieth of the average income in the industrialized world. And because incomes within the poor countries were themselves unequally distributed, the situation of the world's *poorest* people was far worse than this implies: more than a billion people were probably surviving on household incomes of less than a hundred dollars a year (twenty-seven cents a day). Thus, while industrialization had raised incomes in the nations where it had taken hold, and while its spread had been quite rapid when viewed in terms of the long scale of human history, after two centuries it had still registered decisive successes for only a minority of the world's population. An important question, then, is whether industrialization can in fact spread successfully to the rest of the world, or whether there are impenetrable barriers to this, such as resource constraints and population pressures.

An equally important question concerns the environmental sustainability of the gain in living standards achieved by the industrial world in the past two hundred years. The end of the twentieth century saw serious concerns about a potential global climatic catastrophe triggered by industrial pollution, with signs of significant climate change beginning to multiply. Large "First World" cities struggled to find places to dump the mountains of garbage they generated every day. The atmosphere showed a thinning of ozone, ice cover receded near the poles, and climate seemed increasingly prone to extremes and instability. The world grew ever more dependent on chemical fertilizers to support high agricultural yields for a still rising population, working soils dangerously depleted of organic nutrients. Despite encouraging indications that population growth tends to slow with successful economic development, world population was still growing rapidly, having increased by four billion in just seventy-five years after taking a hundred thousand years to reach the first two billion. In this setting, some suggested that the attempt to export developed-country lifestyles to the billions of people in the developing world might render the earth uninhabitable by future generations.

CONCLUSION

Human beings like ourselves lived in small hunting and foraging bands for tens of thousands of years, and their near ancestors had done so for over a million years more, before the first agricultural settlements triggered accelerated population growth and increasing specialization. Before agriculture, population growth was slow and population was sparse; the entire world probably had no more than ten million people in 10,000 B.C. Within a few thousand years of the spread of agriculture, large-scale states with taxation, priests, and armies appeared in a number of regions, their combined populations reaching a hundred million or more. These agrarian civilizations developed writing, mathematics, metallurgy, and shipbuilding, but their top-heavy social structures and limited technological gains made their progress unsustainable and of uncertain virtue to the majority of their inhabitants. In much of the world, hunting and gathering or small-scale herding and agriculture remained the norm, and it was to the latter that the Western world itself returned before a new wave of change beginning in the sixteenth and seventeenth centuries permitted the surpassing of its classical economic and technical achievements. Modern industrial economies in which the majority of people enjoy distinctly higher living standards than their peasant and forager ancestors have existed only in the past century, a mere moment in history's long sweep.

The new economic epoch — ushered in first in northwestern Europe and spreading thereafter to other parts of Europe, its overseas offshoots, and East Asia — benefited from the quantum leap in specialization made possible by reduced transportation costs and a new social order under which merchants and manufacturers exerted strong influence within democratic polities. By increasing the returns to innovation, the emerging institutional system of private property rights and decentralized markets stimulated waves of productivity-enhancing technological change, paralleled by explosive gains in the natural sciences. Struggles over the distribution of the benefits from industrialization led to the growth of labor unions, universal suffrage, and welfare states, in the advanced economies, and to the foray into state-controlled industrialization in the less-advanced economies spanning the eastern half of the Northern Hemisphere. Meanwhile, industrialization was uneven in Latin America and Asia, and largely lacking in Africa. Only at the end of the twentieth century did the majority of the people of the southern continents and the East appear convinced that the capitalist model could and should be emulated.

By that time — our own time — world population had grown sevenfold since 1800 and by a factor of six hundred since the first agrarian villages. The benefits that denser populations had earlier conferred, by fostering more complex divisions of labor, more market activity, and technological change, now appeared to many to have been exhausted. Human beings, busily removing fossil fuels and other resources from the earth's crust and covering ever more of its land surface with concrete and pavement, had begun to notice their impact on their planet's climate and on the shrinking diversity of its biosphere. Whether industrial civilization can be generalized to the billions still in poverty and whether such a system can be made sustainable for more than a few generations are among the most important questions we face as we begin a new millennium.

REFERENCES

Bergstrom, Theodore, 1996, "Economics in a Family Way," *Journal of Economic Literature* 34:1903–34.

Boserup, Ester, 1965, *Conditions of Agricultural Growth: The Economics of Agricultural Change Under Population Pressure*. New York: Aldine.

Brower, David, 1995, *Let the Mountains Talk, Let the Rivers Run*. New York: HarperCollins.

Butzer, Karl, 1976, *Early Hydraulic Civilization in Egypt: A Study in Cultural Ecology*. Chicago: University of Chicago Press.

Cameron, Rondo, 1993, *A Concise Economic History of the World*. New York: Oxford University Press.

Cavalli-Sforza, L. Luca, and Francisco Cavalli-Sforza, 1995, *The Great Human Diasporas*. Reading, Mass.: Addison-Wesley.

Chandler, Alfred, 1977, *The Visible Hand*. Cambridge: Harvard University Press.

Crone, Patricia, 1989, *Pre-Industrial Societies*. Oxford: Basil Blackwell.

Diamond, Jared, 1998, *Guns, Germs, and Steel: The Fates of Human Societies*. New York: Norton.

Fehr, Ernst, and Simon Gächter, 1998, "Reciprocity and Economics: The Economic Implications of Homo Reciprocans," *European Economic Review* 42:845–59.

Finley, M. I., 1973, *The Ancient Economy*. Berkeley: University of California Press.

Harrison, Mark, 1998, "The Economics of World War II: An Overview," pp. 1–42 in Mark Harrison, ed., *The Economics of World War II: Six Great Powers in International Comparison*. Cambridge: Cambridge University Press.

Kaplan, Hillard, and Kim Hill, 1985, "Food Sharing Among Aché Foragers: Tests of Explanatory Hypotheses," *Current Anthropology* 26:223–46.

Landes, David, 1998, *The Wealth and Poverty of Nations: Why Some Are So Rich and Some So Poor*. New York: Norton.

McEvedy, Colin, and Richard Jones, 1978, *Atlas of World Population History*. New York: Facts on File.

Maddison, Angus, 1991, *Dynamic Forces in Capitalist Development: A Long-Run Comparative View*. New York: Oxford University Press.

Milgrom, Paul, and John Roberts, 1992, *Economics, Organization, and Management*. Englewood Cliffs, N.J.: Prentice Hall.

Morgan, E. Victor, 1965, *A History of Money*. Harmondsworth, England: Penguin.

Phelps Brown, E. H., 1968, *A Century of Pay*. London: MacMillan.

Pomeranz, Kenneth, 2000, *The Great Divergence: China, Europe, and the Making of the Modern World Economy*. Princeton: Princeton University Press.

Putterman, Louis, and Randall Kroszner, eds., 1996, *The Economic Nature of the Firm: A Reader*. New York: Cambridge University Press.

Ridley, Matt, 1996, *The Origins of Virtue: Human Instincts and the Evolution of Cooperation*. New York: Viking.

Sanders, William, and Joseph Marino, 1970, *New World Prehistory: The Archeology of the American Indian*. Englewood Cliffs, N.J.: Prentice-Hall.

Smith, Adam, 1985 [1776], *An Inquiry into the Nature and Causes of the Wealth of Nations*, ed. Edwin Canaan. New York: Modern Library.

Smith, Vernon, 1975, "The Primitive Hunter Culture, Pleistocene Extinction, and the Rise of Agriculture," *Journal of Political Economy* 83:727–55.

Stiglitz, Joseph, 1994, *Whither Socialism?* Cambridge: MIT Press.

Trigger, Bruce, 1993, *Early Civilizations: Ancient Egypt in Context*. Cairo: American University in Cairo Press.

Veblen, Thorstein, 1908, "Professor Clark's Economics," *Quarterly Journal of Economics* 22:147–95.

de Waal, Frans, 1996, *Good Natured: The Origins of Right and Wrong in Humans and Other Animals*. Cambridge: Harvard University Press.

Williamson, Oliver, 1985, *The Economic Institutions of Capitalism*. New York: Free Press.

Wittfogel, Karl, 1957, *Oriental Despotism: A Comparative Study of Total Power*. New Haven: Yale University Press.

Wright, Robert, 1994, *The Moral Animal: The New Science of Evolutionary Psychology*. New York: Random House.

SUGGESTIONS FOR FURTHER READING

Deane, Phyllis, 1979, *The First Industrial Revolution*, 2d ed. Cambridge: Cambridge University Press.

Elvin, Mark, 1973, *The Pattern of the Chinese Past: A Social and Economic Interpretation*. Stanford: Stanford University Press.

Engerman, Stanley, and Robert Gallman, 1966, *The Cambridge Economic History of the United States*. New York: Cambridge University Press

Gerschenkron, Alexander, 1962, *Economic Backwardness in Historical Perspective: A Book of Essays*. Cambridge: Harvard University Press.

Habakkuk, H. J., and M. M. Postan, eds., 1966, *The Cambridge Economic History of Europe*, 3d ed., 2 vols. Cambridge: Cambridge University Press.

Johnson, Allen, and Timothy Earl, 1987, *The Evolution of Human Societies: From Foraging Groups to Agrarian State*. Stanford: Stanford University Press.

Kuznets, Simon, 1965, *Economic Growth and Structure: Selected Essays*. New York: Norton.

Landes, David, 1969, *The Unbound Prometheus: Technological Change and Industrial Development in Western Europe from 1750*. London: Cambridge University Press.

Landes, David, 1983, *Revolution in Time: Clocks and the Making of the Modern World*. Cambridge: Belknap Press of Harvard University Press.

Mitchell, Brian R., 1982, *International Historical Statistics: Africa and Asia*. New York: New York University Press.

Mitchell, Brian R., 1993, *International Historical Statistics: The Americas, 1750– 1988*. New York: New York University Press.

North, Douglass, 1981, *Structure and Change in Economic History*. New York: Norton.

North, Douglass, and Robert Thomas, 1973, *The Rise of the Western World: A New Economic History*. Cambridge: Cambridge University Press.

Parker, William, 1984, *Europe, America, and the Wider World: Essays on the Economic History of Western Capitalism*. New York: Cambridge University Press.

Patrick, Hugh, ed., 1976, *Japanese Industrialization and Its Social Consequences*. Berkeley: University of California Press.

Sahlins, Marshall, 1972, *Stone Age Economics*. Chicago: Aldine-Atherton.

ECONOMIC
THOUGHT
IN
PERSPECTIVE

It is probably no exaggeration to say that economics developed mainly as the outcome of the investigation and refutation of successive Utopian proposals.
—F. A. von Hayek,
   "The Trend of Economic Thinking"

Pure logical thinking cannot yield us any knowledge of the empirical world. All knowledge of reality starts from experience and ends in it.
—Albert Einstein

It is 1848, nearly forty years since John Stuart Mill, at the age of three and under the tutelage of his father, had begun his studies of Greek. By age seven, the younger Mill had read Plato, by twelve, all of the main classics of Greece and Rome. Never having been permitted a child's time to play or have friends, he had experienced a nervous breakdown in his twenties but emerged, strengthened by poetry and a newfound friendship, to become the accomplished philosopher, social theorist, and master of political economy of his day. Now, he is contemplating the future of the economy and of economic science. For the economy, he sees change: capitalist establishments will one day be replaced by partnerships of workers. Our understanding of how the economy works is, however, already more or less complete. "Happily," he writes, "there is nothing in the laws of value which remains for the present or any future writer to clear up; the theory of the subject is complete."[1]

Elsewhere in London, about a dozen years later, Karl Marx, the German doctor of philosophy turned radical journalist who has been expelled from half the capitals of continental Europe, settles into his favorite chair in the library of the British Museum on Great Russell Street to begin another day's work on his magnum opus, *Capital*. Marx too thinks that capitalism is due for a change, but he sees it coming by revolution, a much sharper break from the past. As for political economy, it needs a thorough rewriting to purge it of the pernicious influence of bourgeois apologists like Mill, and to expose the fact that profit is nothing but the unpaid labor time of the working man and woman. Unlike the comfortable and established Mill, Marx has no steady source of income and tries to live on payments for an occasional contribution to the *New York Tribune* and on subsidies from his collaborator Friedrich Engels, who draws income from a family business in Manchester. Living in poverty, Marx and his wife have had to bury two children. Today one of Marx's own ailments, a persistent case of painful boils, afflicts him as he pores over his notes. When he returns in the evening to the two-room apartment he shares with his family, he will write in his diary: "I hope the bourgeoisie as long as they live will have cause to remember my carbuncles."[2]

1. Mill, 1929 [1848], p. 436.
2. The quotation and elements of the story are given in Heilbroner, 1999, p. 150.

Economics, like other social sciences, did not emerge as a distinct discipline until the nineteenth century. Philosophers like Aristotle and medieval scholastic writers such as Thomas Aquinas gave some attention to the subject matter now studied by economists, and by the late eighteenth century some writers were devoting increasing portions of their energies to it. But Adam Smith's only professorial posts, held between 1746 and 1762, were chairs in logic and moral philosophy, and the free-trader par excellence ended his life as a customs commissioner in Edinburgh, Scotland. Even in the nineteenth century there were few full-time teachers of economics at universities in Europe and North America, much less elsewhere. Today, economics is among the most popular subjects taught at colleges and universities throughout the world, with about thirty thousand students earning bachelor's degrees with a major in economics and eight hundred new Ph.D.s being awarded in economics each year under the tutelage of more than twenty-five thousand professors of economics in the United States alone.[3]

The number of students getting some exposure to economics is much greater, with about a million undergraduates taking an introductory course in the subject each year in the United States. Comparable training is now offered in most other countries at least at the undergraduate level, and in several at the graduate level.

The main line of development of the economic thought taught in most of the world today begins with Smith and other English writers known collectively as the classical school of political economy. The heirs to the classical economists as the mainstream of modern economic thought are known as neoclassical economists. The neoclassical approach can be traced back to the 1870s, when the idea that prices are determined by marginal utility (see below) was independently hit upon by writers in England, Switzerland, and Austria. For many decades, however, neoclassical economics coexisted with competing approaches including the historical school (centered in Germany) and the institutional school (centered in the United States). Around 1920, the institutional school boasted as many followers at U.S. colleges and universities as did the competing neoclassical approach.

After World War II, neoclassical economics achieved decisive dominance in the universities of the developed Western and especially the

---

3. Estimates from Klamer and Colander, 1990.

English-speaking countries. An anti-capitalist alternative to economic orthodoxy, first offered by Karl Marx and his followers in the late nineteenth century, became the orthodox economics of the Communist world following the accession to power of the Bolsheviks in Russia in 1917. But Marxian economics was also replaced by the neoclassical approach in the former Communist countries in the 1990s, although some Marxian economists continue adapting its analysis in the West and elsewhere. Other alternative approaches, some of them also influenced by Marx, were common in developing countries until the late 1970s, but they too subsequently lost ground to neoclassical economics. Both the mathematical formalism of the neoclassical school and its compatibility with the social philosophy underlying capitalism helped to increase its influence first in the industrialized West and then almost worldwide by the end of the twentieth century. As free market policy approaches gained ascendance over both the protectionist strategies of many less developed countries and the state-centered socialism of the former Communist nations, the intellectual dominance of neoclassical economics was cemented.

Although the intellectual landscape of economics teaching and scholarship is more unified around a shared core of ideas than was the case at any other time in the history of the subject, economics as a field of study may well exhibit more diversity today than at any other time in its history. Within what most economists would classify as the broad neoclassical mainstream, one can find numerous shadings and flavorings, some of them distinct enough to be viewed by their adherents as constituting opposing schools. This is true not only of macroeconomics, where the controversies among Keynesians, monetarists, new classical economists, and others are most visible to the newcomer to the subject, but also of many other areas of research. And through its very success and the resulting large numbers of its students and academic specialists, economics has come to be composed of subfields so distinct and narrowly focused that experts in one specialty often have difficulty understanding the research of experts in another.

There are a large number of relatively technical and complex models that even undergraduate students of economics are expected to master today, and the typical student begins to be exposed to such concepts as "marginal revenue," "consumer surplus," and "elasticity" early in their studies. Usually, such concepts are presented in much the same fashion as are the basic ideas of physics or chemistry — that is, as "natural laws" of the world, objectively there to be understood and mastered. That much of economic theory consists of analytic conveniences that have at times been controversial, tools the use of which may be colored by a variety of assumptions, is rarely noted. Compounding this is the fact that courses in the history of economic thought and the methodology of economics, once required of most economics majors, have to a large extent moved into the optional column, if they are offered at all. Students at many schools are more likely to encounter criticisms of economics in their sociology courses or in off-campus bookstores than under the auspices of their college economics department. This chapter's brief overview of the evolution of economics as a field is aimed at offering the reader a basic perspective on where economics came from and on its current diversity.

We begin our discussion with the two mainstream schools — classical, followed by neoclassical. We will then talk about approaches outside the mainstream, and differences of viewpoint within it. We end with an overview of the specialized subfields that constitute economics today.

ADAM SMITH

Classical political economy began with publication of *An Inquiry into the Nature and Causes of the Wealth of Nations* by a Scottish political philosopher named Adam Smith. This book, published in 1776 (the same year the American colonies declared their independence from Britain), achieved enormous influence in Europe as a tract in social and political philosophy. It was in England, however, that it gave rise to an organized body of economic thought that would hold sway until the late nineteenth century. Although neoclassical economics was to replace the classical approach by the late 1890s as the most influential school in Britain, the neoclassical approach is essentially a continuation and renovation of the classical one, and the two are alike in many respects.

Both classical and neoclassical economists have assumed that people act in their personal interests, and that those interests are mainly to increase their pecuniary wealth and to minimize the effort expended in doing so. Each school attempts to show that when individuals act in this fashion without any organized guidance by the state, church, or other bodies, the society as a whole is made more prosperous. The schools' methods of analysis thus begin at the level of the individual, the family, or the firm — an approach known as "methodological individualism." Based on the belief that uncoordinated selfish acts redound to the general interest of society, members of both schools have argued for the merits of a private enterprise system in which government intervention is limited to particular instances where markets demonstrably fail. The philosophy of minimal intervention shared by leading figures in the two schools is known by the French term *laissez-faire* (meaning "allow to do").

Before considering the formal theories of classical and neoclassical economics, it is worth pausing to notice the important departure from earlier thought that the laissez-faire philosophy represents. Historians of economics refer to the school of thought characterizing the writers who immediately preceded Adam Smith as "mercantilism." Mercantilist writers were not professional scholars but rather merchant pamphleteers (hence the name) who advocated government policies that they believed would profit their private interests. For example, unlike classical and later neoclassical economists, who would advocate free trade, mercantilists called for a protectionist approach that would favor domestic producers in the home market while also facilitating the growth of exports. They also openly favored policies to keep wages low as a way to force industriousness upon the working people and to foster high profits, which would support the accumulation of capital. They courted the favor of the kings who then held the reins of government by arguing that such policies would enrich the monarchs' treasuries and enable them to enhance their military and naval forces. The idea was that protecting domestic markets and promoting exports would generate a favorable balance of trade, which would lead to a net inflow of gold and silver. It was understood that not every country could achieve a favorable trade balance — one could do so only at the expense of another — but mercantilism was not meant to provide a universal policy prescription. Nor did mercantilism pretend to suggest a policy that would be best for the common man, as suggested by the observation above regarding wages. Rather, it amounted to advice to one's own sovereign regarding a way for him to increase his power and wealth at the expense of his rivals in other countries and without regard to the well-being of his subjects as such.

Adam Smith's economics broke with that of the mercantilists by arguing for a policy that would be universally applicable, and by rejecting the mercantilist argument that trade could or should be rigged in one's own country's favor. According to Smith, in arguments that would be greatly strengthened by the formalism of his follower David Ricardo, each country achieves maximum economic benefit by pursuing a policy of free and unregulated internal and external trade. And when countries trade freely with each other, each one specializing in products in which it has a comparative advantage (that is, where its costs of production are low, as compared with its costs of producing other goods), the people of all countries can consume more of all goods than in a situation with limited trade (see Chapter 1). The argument was not that each king should give up protectionism to serve some common moral interest, but rather that any given kingdom would be better off under a free trade regime than under one that attempted to encourage exports and discourage imports. This idea would become a mainstay of economics, yet it is still far from universally accepted by the common person or the politician.

Smith not only disagreed with the mercantilists on the nature of the facts about trade. He also disagreed at a more fundamental level about the goals of economic policy. For the mercantilists, the aim of policy was to enrich and strengthen the monarch, even if this was done at the expense of his subjects. This is why the mercantilists could favor policies that would keep down the wages of a country's workers, on grounds that poorer workers are forced to work longer hours and will produce more and cheaper goods. Of course, the idea that low wages are good for business has been seductive to business owners in every time and place. But some thinkers have noted that such a policy is shortsighted, as poor workers make for more limited markets and for a more poorly educated and motivated workforce. Smith not only recognized such factors but also argued for a whole new outlook on the economy, one that viewed the wealth of the nation as being measured not by the amounts of bullion in the king's coffers but rather by the prosperity of the people as a whole. In line with this, he viewed economic progress as going hand in hand with improvements in productivity, living standards, and thus the wages of the ordinary working man.

The key to prosperity, and the reason for its intimate relation to trade, according to Smith, was what he termed the "division of labor." We have already seen much evidence of this principle from economic history, as discussed in the previous chapter. The idea is that as a society develops economically, its people become more specialized to specific occupations and tasks. Instead of blacksmiths making horseshoes, nails, rivets, and pins, we find specialized factories making each item, and within these factories, the overall production of an item becomes subdivided into numerous differentiated subtasks.

Specialization among and within lines of production increases productivity for several reasons, Smith argued. First, workers can become very adept at tasks in which they specialize. Second, workers can sort themselves among jobs, with each specializing in one for which he or she is relatively well suited. Third, the subdivision of tasks leads to innovations both in the techniques of production and in the types of equipment used. Fourth, specialization can lead to savings of time otherwise lost on moving from task to task. As a result of such factors, argued Smith, the average output per worker in a specialized pin factory in eighteenth-century Scotland was already several hundred times that of a medieval blacksmith making a few pins as part of his more general occupation.

But the division of labor cannot exist in a vacuum. People can't eat pins, nails, or most other specialized goods, so a high degree of specialization is impossible unless there are mechanisms for exchanging the high-volume output of specialized enterprises for the goods made by other producers. Smith argued that the emerging capitalist economy was providing such a mechanism in the form of the social institution that we call "the market." Operating in a market setting, the owners of pin factories can sell their products for money, and they and their workers can use this money to purchase the goods that they want from other producers. The great virtue of a market, Smith pointed out, is its ability to facilitate specialization, making it possible to have enterprises producing huge quantities of specific goods that can end up in the hands of tens of thousands of consumers scattered over large distances, without requiring that these consumers coordinate their plans with one another.

Not only did Smith's economics exhibit a fundamental shift from the prior body of writings that were concerned with enriching monarchs and toward a new economics concerned with increasing the general prosperity of nations. Even more fundamentally, perhaps, it embodied a distinctively modern, secular, and optimistic worldview by virtue of its contention that the good of society could be served by letting people pursue their private and selfish interests. Prior to Smith's time, a common view of the human condition was that people are at root inclined toward evil and misdeeds, and that a civilized social order therefore requires institutional and moral checks, such as a hierarchical class structure, powerful lords and monarchs, and strong religious institutions and sanctions. In Smith's view, people are indeed self-interested, but the world has been so arranged, perhaps by a Divine Providence, that their pursuit of their private interests does not wreak havoc but on the contrary works out to the general advantage of all. It is because the butcher, the brewer, and the baker are interested in filling their own pockets, argued Smith, that they go so industriously about the business of supplying us with good meat, ale, and bread in the hopes of keeping us their loyal customers. The rationale for a strong government to keep watch over an untrustworthy populace was thus set aside by a revolutionary new philosophy that was essentially echoed in Thomas Jefferson's famous phrase "That government that governs least governs best." The need for moral restraints to curb the inclinations of the selfish individual, an idea entrenched in Western thought for the previous millennium and more, now also seemed to be called into question.

This is not to say that Adam Smith saw no role for government, or that he saw the outcome of profit seeking as universally desirable. He warned that businessmen in a given industry tend to conspire against the public by forming cartels and trying to raise prices above competitive levels. He was also concerned that market forces alone would tend to push the division of labor to the point at which the common working person would be a civic "idiot," unable to play a role in the life of the increasingly democratic polities that were just beginning to emerge. To offset this tendency, he favored public provision of basic education.

As to morality, Smith argued hopefully that its basic foundations lay in human nature, which exhibited a natural concern for being regarded well by others, as well as a degree of natural sympathy. "How selfish soever man may be supposed, there are evidently some principles in his nature, which interest him in the fortunes of others, and render their happiness necessary to him, though he derives nothing from it except the pleasure of seeing it," he wrote in his first book, *The Theory of Moral Sentiments*.[4] Although arguing that self-interest was the more reliable motivator of basic economic behavior, then, Smith assumed common foundations of decency that would curb temptations to steal and cheat in business by exposing people to a disdain that most would seek to avoid.

4. Smith 1971 [1759].

THE CLASSICAL SCHOOL
AFTER SMITH

Following the innovations of Smith, a number of English writers began to flesh out a theoretical framework for understanding the workings of a capitalist economy. Along with Smith, these writers assumed that society contained three categories of persons (workers, landlords, and capitalists) supplying three types of inputs to production (labor, land, and capital). Also like Smith but unlike the neoclassical economists who would follow, they explained the prices of goods by reference to the average cost of producing them, namely the wage, land rent, and interest or profit required to attract resources into an industry. These successors to Smith made some headway in developing the theory of price and resource allocation, which he had treated somewhat less formally, but all eventually reached an impasse that could be overcome only through the later introduction of a more mathematical and microanalytic approach by the neoclassical school.

A thumbnail history of the period can begin with Thomas Robert Malthus, a one-time English parson who became famous for arguing (initially in an essay published in 1798) that population growth tends to outstrip resources, thus condemning the mass of people to a life on the margins of subsistence. Malthus's argument, while debatable on a variety of grounds, contained the seeds of what would later be known as "the law of diminishing returns." This law states that as one adds more and more of some productive factor (say labor) that is available in expandable quantities to some other factor (say land) that is available only in fixed quantity, the additional output per unit of the variable factor will be declining with each further increment. The application to population theory was that as the numbers of persons and hence laborers grew while the cultivable land area was constrained by the limited endowment of nature, the output per worker would decline to the point at which no more could be supported. Wages could not permanently remain high, Malthus reasoned, since a high wage will spur an increase in population, which will cause wages to fall until they settle at the subsistence level.[5] Malthus was to revise his

5. In Malthus's analysis, equilibrium will be restored in the event that population growth *overshoots* the point at which the average output exactly supports the survival

arguments, originally written to refute his father's attraction to utopian ideas, and become a contributor to economic theory, an avid compiler of statistics, and a seminal influence on population studies and even biology.[6] In 1805, he became one of the first professors of political economy, which he taught (along with modern history) at the college of the East India Company.

David Ricardo, a successful financier turned political economist who was Malthus's contemporary, became the greatest of the classical economists from the standpoint of both professional influence and analytical insight. Ricardo further developed both Adam Smith's theory of trade and specialization and Malthus's theory of diminishing returns. He proved that two countries could benefit from trade even if one produced every good at lower absolute cost than the other, provided only that the *relative* costs of production differed between the two for at least some pairs of industries. This argument, which continues to defy the commonsense understanding of the man in the street, is still taught in courses on the economics of trade. It is the only piece of classical analysis so widely included in contemporary economics books.

Ricardo's main analytical project, though less enduring in its impact, was no less influential in its time and no less intellectually ambitious. Although the ideas he put forth here would be substantially superseded by the work of the neoclassical school, his approach so impressed his contemporaries that it became the bedrock of economic analysis for the next half century, and it was even borrowed by Marx and other socialists to further their radically counterposed projects. Ricardo's goal was to build a general theory of prices and the distribution of income. That theory was built on two preexisting pillars: (a) Malthus's concept of wages tending toward the subsistence level, and its basis in the diminishing returns of variable factors of production, and (b) Smith's idea that by shifting their capital to that occupation in which its return is highest, capitalists will tend to bring about a more or less uniform rate of return on investment.

In Ricardo's theory, land rents were determined by relative fertility and

---

of the working population, through such checks on population as outmigration, war, famine, and disease.

6. Both Charles Darwin and Alfred Russel Wallace, co-discoverers of the theory of evolution, credited their reading of Malthus's *Essay on Population* as the key to their realization that natural selection must operate on organisms that typically reproduce in far larger numbers than their habitats can sustain.

by the total amount of land needed to meet a society's demand for food. As population expands on a given base of land, either less and less suitable parcels have to be cultivated to satisfy the growing demand for food, or more and more capital and labor have to be invested in the parcels already cultivated, or production had to be expanded along both of these "margins." Given their ability to produce more output than the inferior plots with a given expenditure on capital and labor, land of superior quality would come to command a large market premium, called rent. Ricardo assumed that wages tend toward the level required for workers' subsistence, and that the value of a product just equals the sum of wages, rents, and profits earned in producing it. Thus profits, seen as the portion of value left over after deducting wages and rents, would fall as rents rose. Since laborers had to receive at least a subsistence level of wages, argued Ricardo, profits could not be restored simply by having capital flee from agriculture to other sectors: the resulting decline in farm output would raise food prices and wages, thereby lowering profits throughout the economy. Given this law of equal rates of return, implying that profits would ultimately be the same in all sectors, Ricardo's model could predict the profit rate of an entire economy by focusing on its agriculture alone. With this theory in hand, Ricardo went on to advocate (eventually as a member of Parliament) the importation of lower-cost grain to England from continental Europe, the idea being that such imports would permit workers to cover their subsistence needs at a lower money wage to the employer. By reducing the demand for produce from England's own farm land, the cheap imports would also lower land rents. Thus, profits would rise, and there could be more creation of capital and hence more economic growth.

One thing that Ricardo's model did not account for was the possibility of technological progress. Once opportunities like that of importing food from poorer countries were exhausted, world economic growth had to come to a standstill, in Ricardo's scheme, because population growth would eventually raise food costs and land rents, squeezing profits and leading to a decline in investment. The prediction of both Ricardo's and Malthus's analyses, on this point, is what gave economics its reputation as "the dismal science." While the predictions of static wages and stalled growth have thus far been belied because technological progress has stayed ahead of population growth at least in the successfully industrializing countries during the century and a half since they wrote, one can find numerous ecological thinkers today who would assert that "the jury is not yet in" on the larger question of the sustainability of unlimited economic growth.

But it was not so much the failure of Ricardo's analysis to predict the long-term trend of productivity or wages as its analytical incompleteness that caused it ultimately to be superseded. In the Ricardian model, as has been mentioned, the cost of a good was determined by the average cost of producing it. This framework used only the most primitive notion of *demand,* and it failed to recognize the mutual interaction between cost to the producer and value to the consumer, an interaction that was only fully appreciated after the introduction of the concept of the margin. The model also ran into difficulties because it abstracted from changes in market value associated with changes in the time that elapsed between the undertaking of an investment and the receipt of its returns (that is, it overlooked modern time discounting and associated issues).

Despite these limitations, Ricardo was viewed as a prodigious innovator by his contemporaries, and his contributions were as important for their method of reasoning as for their substantive conclusions. While it was Adam Smith who set out the philosophy of laissez-faire and made a convincing case for the virtues of the market, his theory of prices and of wages, rents, and profits was rudimentary. Smith's enduring influence lies in his economic philosophy and his conceptual intuitions, and he brought a broad knowledge of economic history to bear upon his arguments. Ricardo, by contrast, is often considered the father of economic *analysis*—that is, of the practice of using abstract reasoning and mathematics to demonstrate a point. Indicative of his more historical and hence realistic bent, for example, Smith had noted that the principle of a uniform rate of return on capital had many exceptions, such as those relating to differences in risk. It was indicative of the flair for simplification that powered Ricardo's drive for formal elegance that such exceptions were brushed aside in his own analysis.

Ricardo's example exerted a profound influence on the economists who were to follow. His successors in classical political economy were so impressed by his reasoning that they believed it necessary only to fill in a few details, proclaiming that the principles of political economy had been worked out once and for all. This was certainly ironic, because Ricardo would provide but a small foretaste of the push toward abstraction and formalization that would come to dominate economics in the late twentieth century.[7] Nevertheless, the difference of method within the classical school well illustrates the conflict between the inductive or historical approach, on one hand, and the deductive and abstract approach on the other. Because the tension between these two approaches has been a continuing theme in the evolution of economics in every generation that has followed Ricardo's, it may be worth pausing here to explain their nature.

A DIGRESSION ON
METHODOLOGY

Induction means drawing general conclusions from specific cases, examples, or events, while deduction means reaching specific conclusions from general statements or principles. If we observe many episodes in which producers' costs rise and then the prices of their goods go up, we may reach the conclusion that cost increases are in general followed by price rises, an example of induction. If, instead, we know it to be a general principle that cost increases are followed by price rises, then we can infer that the occurrence of some specific cost increase will be followed shortly by a price rise, an example of deduction.

Although the two processes seem at first blush to be mirror images, many philosophers have argued that they are not. Deduction, they argue, is a strict logical procedure, which is guaranteed to reach true conclusions if carried out according to certain rules and if based on a true premise. Induction, on the other hand, involves a leap of faith that cannot be assured of success. To use our example, if the principle that all cost increases are followed by price rises is true, then it must also be true, by deduction, that today's cost increase will also be followed by a price rise.

7. Interestingly, the mathematics actually used by Ricardo is quite basic. He developed the idea of the margin in his analysis of rent, foreshadowing later economists, but he stopped short of using the calculus, though its application seems almost unavoidable today. Indeed, when a few mathematicians hit upon the idea of applying calculus to the study of market demand in the 1830s, they were overlooked by the English economists. This might seem surprising given that Sir Isaac Newton had developed the calculus and applied it to the study of celestial bodies and mechanical laws almost a century before *The Wealth of Nations*. But it clearly illustrates that economics was as yet a new field of inquiry, and that the idea of applying mathematics to social studies had occurred only to some isolated and unappreciated individuals.

However, the fact that all cost increases that were observed in the past happen to have been followed by price rises does not in itself prove that "every cost increase is followed by a price rise" is a true, general principle. Examples do *not* prove that a rule is true, but a true rule *does* logically apply to each of its instances.

In the eighteenth and nineteenth centuries, science was thought by most practitioners to be an inductive process, in which numerous close and careful observations are made, with useful general conclusions then being drawn from them. However, the growing realization that induction is not a strict logical procedure led to a desire in some quarters to de-emphasize reliance upon it. The approach that evolved was one in which deductive logic played a more central role in science. A key criterion in the appraisal of a scientific theory was that its logical structure should be internally tight and consistent. Internal logical structures consisted of deductive statements of the form "all A's are B, X is an A, therefore X is B," and of the logical inferences that follow from strings of mathematical statements. Concordance between the theory and observations of the phenomenon in question was also important, but checks for such accord were to be done as the final step in a progression that started with theory building, moved to the derivation of testable implications or predictions, and only after that led to the comparison of observations with those predictions. The old notion that good theories are based on careful initial observations of facts was downgraded or even repudiated in the new deductive approach.[8]

When turning to the evolution of the discipline of economics, we find that Adam Smith's historical approach was relatively inductive in character, whereas Ricardo's approach had more of the flavor of the emerging deductive approach. Indeed, Ricardo's followers so emphasized logical

8. For a more detailed discussion of these issues, see Blaug, 1992, where it is argued that the very concept of "induction" as a logical process is illusory, and thus a separate term "adduction" is used for "hunch formation" or "leaps of faith." Another influential idea discussed at length by Blaug is the notion that a theory is more scientific the more possible it is to state what set of conceivable observations would force it to be rejected. The more clearly such conditions can be set forth, the more the theory is said to be "falsifiable," and thus the more scientific it is deemed. A theory can never be proven true, according to this view. Rather, a good theory is one that is eminently falsifiable but repeatedly fails to be falsified when subjected to empirical tests.

structure that they did not think it very important to subject the theory to testing, as will be remarked below. On the whole, mainstream economics after Ricardo was to move increasingly in the deductive direction. Unlike the late classical economists, twentieth-century neoclassical economists tended to place roughly equal weight on both internal coherence and empirical testing, although the two aspects were often not balanced due to the bifurcation between theoretical and empirical research. Meanwhile, influential critiques of mainstream economics, and alternative schools, often favored a more inductive approach, thinking it more realistic and better grounded in the world as it really is. How this controversy played out, and the roles of theory and observation in contemporary economics, will be noted at a number of points in the remainder of this chapter.

J. S. MILL AND
LATE CLASSICAL ECONOMICS

The classical approach prevailed in England until roughly the end of the nineteenth century. At mid-century, its leading expositor would be John Stuart Mill, a towering intellectual figure who also made major contributions to social philosophy and the philosophy of knowledge. Mill's father had been in the intellectual circle of both Ricardo and the political philosopher Jeremy Bentham, the founder of Utilitarianism (see Chapter 5), and the younger Mill was trained from an early age to master the works of these and other social thinkers. J. S. Mill published the first edition of his *Principles of Political Economy*, which would remain the standard text on the subject for almost fifty years, in 1848.

One of the main distinctions between classical and neoclassical economics, as we will see, is the failure of the former to deal with supply and demand in a rigorous manner. Adam Smith and his predecessors understood well enough that when the supply of a good increased with everything else unchanged, its price would fall, since it would take a price cut to persuade purchasers to buy more units of it. Likewise, when there was an increase in demand for a good, but no other changes, then the price of the good would tend to rise, because, being unable to purchase the additional units they now wanted at the going price, purchasers would compete for the available supply by offering more for each unit. But the classical economists did not integrate these intuitions into their formal analysis of "the theory of value." Instead, they viewed prices, as has already been indicated, as being determined only by the average cost of producing a good in terms of the land, labor, and capital that went into it.

Why did the classical economists ignore changes in supply and demand when developing their theory of value? One reason is that their focus was on prices in a long-run equilibrium, after short-term fluctuations in an economy had finished working themselves out. Beginning with Adam Smith, the classical economists were looking for explanations of the relative prosperity of nations, a long-run phenomenon, rather than trying to provide a theory that would hold over very short time frames and at the level of individual firms. It was their view that in the long run costs of production or supply alone determined prices, while demand affected only the quantity produced. The supply of a good (or at least of any producible good, as opposed to a natural resource) would tend, as they saw it, to expand so long as consumers were willing to pay more than the cost of production, but it would contract whenever the price consumers would pay fell temporarily below the cost of production. Thus, adjustments in supply would cause prices to settle at average costs of production.[9]

However, their long-run orientation was not the only reason that the classical economists refrained from a more formal treatment of demand. A second cause of this neglect is that they saw a logical problem with the idea of connecting prices with the value that consumers attach to a good, what they referred to as its "use value" and what would later be called "utility." It seemed to them that a number of examples could be offered of goods having great utility but low prices (water, for instance), as well as of goods having little utility but high prices (such as diamonds). This paradox convinced classical economists that it was best to think of use value or utility as something that a good must surely have before it could command a price, but not as a direct determinant of that price in any quantitative sense. The apparent disconnect between value and utility would be seized upon by Marx in his critique of capitalism.

9. In modern terms, the long-run supply curve of an industry was understood to be horizontal because changes in demand would lead to changes in the number of firms, or other changes in industry capacity, until a new equilibrium was reached at the average cost of production. This classical view is in fact consistent with the modern economic analysis of long-run equilibrium, provided that there are constant long-run average costs.

Mill viewed himself as a loyal follower of Ricardo, and hence accepted the view that value is basically determined by cost. But he began to fill in the gaps left by Ricardo's theory with respect both to supply and demand and to the role of time in price determination. Mill distinguished three types of goods: goods whose cost of production remains constant at any quantity, goods whose quantity is fixed and not expandable, and goods whose output can be expanded but only at an increasing cost. The first type is that generally assumed in earlier classical economics, which he associated with manufacturing. The second is an exceptional category that includes such things as works of art and rare books, but also unique locational value. The third can be identified with agriculture for the sorts of reasons noted by Malthus and Ricardo. Mill recognized that only the first type of good should have the classical feature of having an equilibrium price that is independent of demand. Because the supply of the second type of good is fixed, its price is determined entirely by demand. For the third type, both supply and demand play a role.

Perhaps influenced by Bentham, Mill and a contemporary, Nassau Senior, also began integrating considerations of psychic utility into their thinking about price formation. Neither the cost of labor nor the cost of capital, they suggested, could be understood without reference to subjective considerations, namely the disutility the worker attaches to providing labor and the disutility that the saver attaches to forgoing consumption. Because the disutility of waiting several periods must outweigh that of waiting only one period for a return on one's investments, time must also play a role in determining the cost of capital and hence variations in the prices of products produced using technologies with longer or shorter gestation periods, too.

Although Mill followed Smith and Ricardo in his advocacy of free trade and markets, his social and political philosophy was distinctly progressive. Though treated as yet another apologist for capitalism by his radical contemporary, Marx, Mill was an early champion of equality of the sexes, universal suffrage, and labor unions, and in his own way an advocate of socialism. He argued that an educated working class would reject traditional capitalism in favor of a system of worker-owned cooperatives, the main requirement being the promotion of universal education and the freedom of workers to associate. He also foresaw the use of the political process to help the poor and ameliorate social injustices. But he saw the free market as the best way to allocate resources, and he did not think the transition to a system of producer cooperatives required legislative action. It was Mill who first argued, in a move anticipating liberal and social democratic thought a century later, that a democratic society might use taxation and other mechanisms to redistribute the riches produced by markets and competition, and hence that *production and distribution can be conceptually separated.*

Methodologically Mill was eclectic, making use of both the analytical method of Ricardo and the historical method of Smith. Unfortunately for his later reputation as an economist, though, he tended to treat Ricardo's theoretical framework as inherently true and immune to empirical contradiction, arguing that economics is by its nature a "hypothetical deductive science." As remarked by historian of economics Mark Blaug, this position was especially ironic because, in a work on the philosophy of knowledge that was considered definitive in his day, Mill had taken the position that induction and testing for verification are the bases of the scientific method.[10] He felt that economics was an exception because economists could not employ the experimental method (a contention that has begun to be seriously questioned only recently, as explained below). It was Mill who first defined economics as an inquiry into human behavior that operates on the hypothetical assumption of an "economic man," interested in wealth and effort avoidance only. The task of political economy, in Mill's view, was to show how and where the theory could be applied, not to test whether the theory is sound. After all, the bases of the theory are known to be sound by any reasonable person on the basis of introspection and common experience.

THE BIRTH OF
NEOCLASSICAL ECONOMICS

The direction that Mill had begun to take by giving greater recognition to demand and utility considerations was pursued more fully in neoclassical price theory, which would ultimately provide for a complete integration of supply and demand into price theory. Unlike the classical economists, neoclassical economists are as interested in the short run as in the long. They believe that the influences of both supply and demand, of both cost

10. See Blaug, 1992.

of production and value to the consumer, need to be recognized and taken into formal, quantitative account. The breakthrough that allowed them to do this in a more thoroughgoing manner than was open to Mill was the departure of looking at both cost of production and value to the consumer as changing functions of the quantity of each good that is produced and consumed. The neoclassicals, that is, began to look at cost and value *at the margin*, or with reference to the last unit. The cost of that unit to the supplier is labeled "marginal cost"; its value to the consumer is called "marginal utility." Translated into dollar terms, marginal utility lies behind the price that the consumer is willing to pay for the last unit, and is therefore the vertical coordinate on the consumer's demand curve.[11] Already in dollar terms, marginal cost becomes the vertical coordinate on the seller's supply curve. Where supply and demand curves, aggregated over all relevant sellers and buyers, meet, marginal cost and marginal utility are equal. This point of intersection identifies the equilibrium price and quantity of a competitive market.

The neoclassical approach was not born overnight, nor did it catch fire immediately upon being introduced. Indeed, the idea of linking demand or prices to marginal utility by use of differential calculus had actually been suggested several times in earlier decades, including the 1830s, without even being noticed by the influential economists of the day. Further slowing general acceptance of the approach was the fact that one of the three expositions that finally won wider attention, that of William S. Jevons in 1871, became steeped in controversy because the young Jevons sharply criticized Ricardo, contending that *only* demand determined prices, with production cost playing no role.[12] This misunderstanding is probably due to the fact that the idea of focusing on the margin and applying the differential calculus to economics was applied by the first generation "marginalists" only to utility, perhaps because the omission of

11. The translation into dollar terms is required because utility itself is viewed as a subjective variable not directly measurable in money terms.

12. Carl Menger of Austria and Léon Walras of Switzerland are credited with hitting upon the marginal utility idea independently of Jevons in the same decade, the 1870s, so the three are conventionally listed as the idea's co-discoverers. Menger's innovation resembled that of Jevons, but he opposed the use of the calculus and favored a more introspective and naturalistic approach. Walras's main project was modeling the general equilibrium of the economy. Both are discussed later in the chapter.

demand from the classical model provided more stimulus to innovate on that side of the microeconomic equation. Even though Ricardo had come rather close to a marginal approach in his treatment of production costs and land rents, it was only in the 1880s that marginalism and the calculus were applied to the understanding of costs and supply.

Ultimate acceptance of the neoclassical approach awaited not only the integration of the supply and the demand sides of markets as viewed through a marginal lens but also the integration of the marginal approach as a whole with the ideas of the classical economists. The synthesis was carried out by Alfred Marshall, a professor of political economy at Cambridge from 1885 to 1908. It was Marshall who, in his *Principles of Economics*, first published in 1890, brought the upward sloping supply curve and the downward sloping demand curve together in a clear exposition of the marginal approach to price determination.[13] He laid out the distinctions between the short run, in which the amounts of capital that firms have to work with is fixed, the long run, in which firms can vary both capital and labor, and the very long run in which there is also entry and exit of firms to and from industries. Further developing the line of thought begun by Mill, he showed that supply curves are less elastic, and demand thus more determinative of prices, the shorter the period of analysis under consideration. In this connection, he noted that the classical theory of prices determined by long-run average costs was often a correct depiction of long-run tendencies.

Hardly one to act the scientific revolutionary, Marshall criticized Jevons for an unwarranted emphasis on utility. He argued that to say that utility (demand) rather than cost (supply) determines prices is like claiming that one blade of a pair of scissors, not the other, does the cutting of a piece of cloth or paper. He defended Ricardo by insisting that this approach is no more than an elaboration of the classical model, with a more complete treatment of the short run.

Although he was a contributor of important technical innovations,

13. Walras's general equilibrium approach also brought together demand and supply. However, he initially modeled demand on the assumption of constant average costs, which means that average and marginal cost are equivalent. Because his work was so mathematical, and perhaps because he wrote in French, it was not fully appreciated by the predominantly Anglo-Saxon world of economic scholars until well into the twentieth century.

including the concept of the price elasticity of demand,[14] Marshall es-
chewed the use of mathematics in his exposition, saving it for his appen-
dices and judging that if a mathematical theorem in economics doesn't
translate well into words, it is unlikely to be of much importance. He
showed an interest in the historical aspects of economic institutions, and
saw a kinship between economics and biology. His moral concerns, eclecticism of method, and interest in history were reminiscent of Adam Smith
and J. S. Mill; he had shifted to economics from an original attraction to
the ministry because of "strong humanitarian feelings about improving
the quality of life of the poor."[15]

Although Marshall's exposition was sufficiently convincing to wean
most remaining adherents of the old classical economics to the new marginal approach, the appeal of "mainstream" economics was still limited to
a small circle of academics. While a modest number of American, Swedish, Austrian, and Swiss economists were at work developing neoclassical
economic analysis by the end of the nineteenth century, other scholars
interested in studying economic phenomena found the approach of this
school unappealingly mathematical and abstract. These scholars, who
preferred to deal with the complexity of actual economies without an
elaborate formal structure that seemed to them unrealistic, are today
treated as "heterodox" or non-mainstream, and their contributions will
be discussed below.

During the first half of the twentieth century, neoclassical economics
continued to develop. Following the lead of late-nineteenth-century theorists including the French economist Léon Walras, who taught at Lausanne, in Switzerland, and the English economist Francis Edgeworth,
theorists modeled the economy as an interconnected system, concep-
tualizing the simultaneous equilibrium of many markets. They provided a
theory not only of the supply and demand of final goods but also of the
pricing of inputs to production, including capital, and thus of the distribution of income. They began venturing into other areas as well, including the economics of imperfect competition and regulation and the

14. This measures the responsiveness of quantity demanded to a change in price
by looking at the ratio of the percentage change in quantity to the percentage
change in price.

15. Landreth and Colander, 1994, p. 285.

analysis of goods and services, like national defense, that are provided through collective action rather than decentralized markets. Walras's successor at Lausanne, Vilfredo Pareto, and an English economist, Arthur Pigou, were among those making important contributions to the formalization of concepts of economic welfare and ways of measuring the welfare costs of monopoly and other market imperfections, suggesting how economic outcomes could be improved by selective government interventions. By the 1940s, the basic skeleton of neoclassical microeconomics as it continues to be taught to today's undergraduates was fully in place, although refinements about uncertainty, imperfect information, and strategic interactions remained to be developed. It was not until the 1950s, though, that more substantial numbers of students with strong mathematics backgrounds would flock to graduate schools to earn advanced degrees in the subject and to contribute to an eventual explosion of a highly technical literature in economics. In the meantime, neoclassical economics faced serious competition from other approaches.

CRITICS OF THE CLASSICAL AND
NEOCLASSICAL SCHOOLS: MARX

Both classical and neoclassical economics had critics. Classical economics had arisen in large part to argue against the advice that monarchs should put the accumulation of gold and silver reserves above all other objectives, and in favor of putting first the common welfare, which they asserted represented the true wealth of a nation. But whereas Adam Smith could view himself as a populist advocating economic liberty and the basic equality of persons, classical economics took on a more conservative appearance in the hands of his successors. This is in part because economists like Malthus and Ricardo were more pessimistic about the prospects for economic growth, predicting that wages could not for long rise above a subsistence level. More important, however, was the fact that an outlook like Smith's, though it had been on the cutting edge of the fight against feudalism and constraints on trade in the eighteenth century, came to look like a defense of the emerging capitalist status quo as more radical thinkers began to champion the interests of those with little property or education. Classical economics seemed to treat a world of unequally distributed wealth and capital as "natural," and to gloss over the conflict

between workman and capitalist with its doctrine of a harmony of interests. Where in Smith's time it was the conflict between the traditional
aristocracy and the new commercial class that was on the front burner of
social change, by the mid–nineteenth century it was the conflict between
the capitalist class and the working class that was coming to the fore as a
result of advancing industrialization and the decline of agriculture.

Smith, Ricardo, and the other classical thinkers had grounded their
theories of price or value not only on the cost of production generally but
on the amount of labor with which goods were produced, in particular.
While Smith toyed with several versions of a "labor theory of value,"
Ricardo developed a nearly complete labor theory, suggesting, for instance, that the value imparted to final products by capital could be converted to labor used based on the amount of labor that went into making
the capital. Ricardo's departure provided an opening to several writers,
the so-called Ricardian Socialists, who argued in the early nineteenth
century that that portion of the produce of labor that did not end up as
compensation to the laborer must be seen as an unjust expropriation of
output by the landlord or capitalist. At the same time, various thinkers,
often referred to as Utopian Socialists, were developing blueprints for,
and in some cases setting up experimental versions of, more egalitarian —
and in their views more ideal — economies.[16]

The most influential socialist thinker was Karl Marx, who borrowed
much of the structure of Smith and Ricardo's economics but embraced a
radical view of history and social change based in part on the then popular
ideas of the German philosopher G. W. F. Hegel. Hegel had offered an
interpretation of history as an unfolding evolution of "Spirit"; Marx suggested "turning this view on its head" in favor of a "historical materialist"
conception of social evolution. He argued that one social order gives way
to another in a revolutionary upheaval as changes in society's technological and resource base render the old social system unsuitable. Just as the
societies of antiquity had given way to feudalism and feudalism had been
replaced by capitalism, he then predicted, so would capitalism itself be
overturned in favor of a worker-dominated society and economy.

Many who have not read his economics think of Marx primarily as a
philosopher and social critic. Some feel he should have kept to those
fields! Marx, however, spent years studying classical economic theory and

16. Heilbroner, 1999.

attempting to develop a consistent alternative to it. His own economic theory is as formal and mathematical in character as was that of Ricardo — though both are elementary in this respect compared with the later neo-classical school. Like the classical economists, Marx focused on long-run equilibrium prices and on conditions of perfect competition. The main difference between Marx's and the standard, classical economics was his attempt to show that labor is the sole source of value, and that profits accordingly are due to "surplus" labor. The latter refers to labor extracted by the capitalist when the worker produces more than his own requirements for living but earns an amount capable of purchasing those requirements only.

Although rejected by mainstream economists, Marx's economic theory is sufficiently coherent to have been the object of mathematical study by a number of respected theorists in the twentieth century. All agree that he ran into serious conceptual snags, such as the need to abandon his labor theory of value as a theory of prices in industries with divergent ratios of capital to labor costs. Even without these snags, his theory was quickly dated — like its classical cousins — by the marginal revolution that sowed the seeds of neoclassicism. More impressive than his formal value theory are his insights into technological change and into conflict within the workplace, which have commanded the respect of even some conservative-minded economists and have inspired much research in recent decades.[17]

Followers of Marx's approach became numerous not only because self-styled Marxists eventually captured political power in a swath of the globe stretching from central Europe to the Pacific. The approach won adherents in the half century before Communists took power in Russia, and it continued to appeal to some in non-Communist countries, including France, Germany, Italy, and Japan, through most of the twentieth century. Disenchanted with prevailing social arrangements, they viewed neoclassical economics as a poorly disguised ideological defense of an exploitive and corrupt economic system. Nor were Marxian economists in the West necessarily sympathetic with the actions of Marxist-run governments. Often they agreed with critics who saw in them new forms of

17. A careful appraisal of Marx's economics with useful references to relevant literature is provided by Blaug, 1983, chapter 7; a fascinating discussion by a respectful conservative is the chapter on Marx in Schumpeter, 1994 [1954].

exploitation, and many applauded the fall of totalitarian Communist states in 1989 and 1991. Western Marxian economists applied the analytical and critical approaches of Marx to the problems of inequality, class conflict, and politics in capitalist economies. At present, several hundred economists in the United States still view themselves as "radical political economists," with roots in Marx's approach. The proportion of economists taking a Marxian approach is larger still in some European countries and Japan.

OTHER HETERODOX ECONOMISTS

While Marx's is the most widely known challenge to the economic mainstream, it is by no means the only important one. Other heterodox schools have attracted at least as many academic economists to their ranks in particular countries and times. Classical and neoclassical economics were challenged not always or only from the standpoint of their alleged class biases — Marx called classical economists "hired prizefighters of the bourgeoisie" — but also for their attempt to put economics on the same mathematical footing as physics and other "hard" sciences. This trend toward deduction, formalism, and mathematics, which is first evident in Ricardo and is ironically shared by Marx, became pronounced with the introduction of the differential calculus into economics during the marginal revolution.

The early neoclassicists themselves differed somewhat with regard to the role of mathematics, with some, such as the French economist Walras (who taught in Switzerland), putting mathematics at the very center of their enterprise while others, such as Marshall, argued for a more minor role for mathematics. Nevertheless, the neoclassical school was on the whole more mathematical than its predecessors, and its "mathematical formalism" led to open rebellions in at least three major instances. The first of these might be regarded as something of a family squabble, as it began with one of the three economists (the others being Jevons and Walras) credited with the introduction of marginalism in the 1870s, the Austrian Carl Menger. Menger argued against the representation of marginal utility as a derivative, insisting that decisions are almost always made over discrete rather than continuous changes of quantity, and preferring to treat the concept as a psychological phenomenon that did not lend itself to excessive quantification.[18] Menger also pointed the way to a concern with knowledge that would be a hallmark of his intellectual heirs.

Some of the latter, including notably Ludwig von Mises and Friedrich von Hayek, who are collectively known (with Menger) as the "Austrian" school, went on to attack neoclassicism as erroneously focused on the idea of equilibrium. The genius of a market economy, they argued, can be recognized only when one looks at the forces that are driving the economy *in the direction of* an equilibrium, but that never come to rest because many conditions change before an equilibrium is ever reached. For instance, entrepreneurship, which is crucial to a capitalist economy, cannot even be depicted in a model of the economy at equilibrium, for it is nothing but searching for and risking bold responses to *out-of-equilibrium* opportunities for profits that constitutes its essence. Some Austrian ideas have enjoyed a resurgence of influence in recent years because they provide insights into the advantages of market over nonmarket economies (see Chapter 3), and because they contribute to the interest in problems of information that has marked the neoclassical mainstream itself in recent decades.

Two other important schools outside the classical and neoclassical mainstream were the historical school, centered in Germany, and the institutional school, centered in the United States. Members of these schools criticized the neoclassical school as overly abstract, unrealistic, and uninterested in economic history and the roles of the institutions that meld economic with social and other dimensions. Although differing somewhat on the virtues of capitalism, both schools were critical of the neoclassical assumption that free markets lead to optimal outcomes. Members of the German school argued vigorously against the mainstream postulate that free trade is in every nation's interest, favoring instead the idea that a country that is behind in the process of industrialization needs protection to allow its "infant industries" the time to get on their feet. Their views in this respect influenced German and American policies in the nineteenth century and the policies of many other countries in the twentieth (see Chapter 4). German historical economists also engaged in a lengthy methodological debate with Menger and other main-

18. As students who have taken their first course in calculus know, one can take a derivative of (or differentiate) a curve or function only where it ranges smoothly and continuously over a set of neighboring values.

stream economists. While some mainstream economists including Alfred Marshall proposed to resolve the differences with the historicists diplomatically, by favoring a methodological eclecticism, the debate probably sharpened the determination of others in the mainstream to forge ahead with abstract formalism.

Institutionalism became prominent in the economics profession of the United States in the early twentieth century, when it may have had more adherents than the neoclassical approach. Probably best known among the economists following this approach was the iconoclastic writer Thorstein Veblen, who advocated a unified and more empirically based social science that would include psychology and anthropology as well as economics. Veblen rejected the mainstream assertion that profit seeking serves social efficiency, arguing that in an era of large firms with substantial market power, it is more likely to lead to restrictions in output than to increases in productivity. For Veblen, the future of the economy would turn on whether engineers, who took productivity as their goal, or businessmen, who focused on profits, ended up in control of the enterprise system. Veblen also criticized the mainstream assumption that consumers are rational maximizers of given preferences, arguing instead that tastes need to be understood in terms of social psychology, that consumption is often driven more by competition for status than by the desire to satisfy intrinsic needs, and that demand can be manipulated by advertising.

While Veblen criticized the lack of attention to empirical detail in mainstream economics, he did little empirical research of his own. Two important successors probably better followed his admonitions in this regard, and each had substantial influence both on policymaking and on the economics profession. John Commons, who advocated a focus on the nature of transactions rather than on the private calculations of individuals, wrote several volumes on the history of labor in the United States and founded a long-lived empirical tradition in the economics department of the University of Wisconsin. He was an active advocate of various economic reforms, directly influencing legislation in Wisconsin and other states. His influence on the labor and welfare policies of the New Deal era was such that at least one influential economist would call him "the intellectual origin of the movement toward the welfare state."[19] Another institutionalist, Wesley Mitchell, advanced applied statistical studies in

19. Boulding, 1957, quoted in Landreth and Colander, 1994, p. 345.

economics both through his own applied research on business cycles and by founding the National Bureau of Economic Research, a nonprofit organization that is even more important today than in his own time.

Later Marxists, historicists, and institutionalists can be said to have shared a common complaint about neoclassical economics: that it had moved in the wrong direction from the economics of the classical era by narrowing the scope of the discipline. This narrowing, reflected in the change of name from "political economy" to "economics," was manifested in the further separation of economics from normative social and political philosophy, and in reduced concern with social and political context. For instance, whereas the classical economists had identified "labor," "land," and "capital" with distinct social classes having different behavioral orientations—capitalists were assumed to plow profits into capital accumulation, while landlords were assumed to use their rents for consumption—early neoclassical economists tended to treat the factors of production as symmetrical and highly abstract. Classical economists (and Marx) had been concerned about potentially conflicting interests among the classes—between landlords and capitalists, in the case of Ricardo, capitalists and workers, in the case of Marx—and had focused on the distribution of income and its relation to economic growth. Early neoclassical economists appeared less concerned with income distribution, and economic growth and long-run trends received far less attention from them than did momentary or static equilibrium. These relative deficits, as well as the inattention to the disequilibrium and knowledge issues that concerned the Austrian economists, began to be redressed in the final decades of the twentieth century. By drawing attention to them, the critics can be said to have made a lasting contribution.[20]

KEYNES AND MACROECONOMICS

Between the 1870s and the 1920s, the basic structure of neoclassical economics took shape and eclipsed classical economics as the mainstream of the discipline in Britain and among pockets of adherents elsewhere.

20. Readers ready to pursue the relation between institutional and neoclassical economics may be interested in a recent book with the suggestive title *The Struggle over the Soul of Economics: Institutionalist and Neoclassical Economists in America Between the Wars* (Yonay, 1998).

But a crisis struck the school when the Great Depression of the 1930s shook confidence in the self-regulating nature of the market system.

Adam Smith and those who followed him had believed that decentralized decision making by individual capitalists, workers, and landowners, unencumbered by government regulation, must automatically lead to the full and socially beneficial employment of a society's resources. A few economists of note, including Malthus and Marx, had questioned whether this was true on a national scale: what if income were so distributed, for example, that there was not enough demand to soak up the commodities being produced? The usual response to such questions had been that such a situation cannot persist, for in general supply creates its own demand. The argument here was that the value of each good produced will be fully offset by payments to the workers, landowners, and capitalists who were involved in its production, and that this must put enough purchasing power to buy all of the goods produced into the hands of all the workers, landowners, and capitalists of the economy as a whole. The fact that people may choose to save rather than consume some of their earnings is no problem as long as savings flow into productive investment, for then these funds too wind up going into the purchase of goods, namely capital goods. The mix of goods produced might temporarily fail to match the mix of goods that people want — for instance too many consumer goods and too few capital goods — but this should be only a temporary problem. Given the overall balance implied by the previous argument, goods that are in excess supply at any given time should be offset by other goods in excess demand. There should be no problem keeping all the available workers and machines employed.

Questions of aggregate balance received little attention in the early decades of the neoclassical school, since its focus was on working out the details of the theory of prices and resource allocation at the firm and market level. The weakness of the international economy in the aftermath of World War I, culminating in the Great Depression, changed this. John Maynard Keynes, a student of Marshall who had achieved early prominence in the field of monetary economics and had given prescient warnings about the consequences of imposing punitive reparations on Germany,[21] saw the depression as a threat to both economics and capital-

21. According to Cameron, 1993 (cited in Chapter 1), p. 351, Keynes, "an economic adviser to the British delegation at the peace conference, was so distressed

ism, and called for a rethinking of the economics of the macro level, or macroeconomics. He saw a number of reasons why price adjustments might not suffice to restore equilibrium to an economy entering a spiral of low demand, leading to layoffs and low returns on capital, leading to still further declines in demand. True, widespread unemployment should in the long run lead workers to offer to work for lower wages, and there might be some wage low enough that it would be profitable to employers to rehire all of the available workers. But there could be institutional or other obstacles to wage declines, and similar reasoning might apply to interest rates and to the demand for investment, as well as to other markets. Decisions to postpone consumption out of fear of economic crisis could be problematic, for instance, if people decided to hoard money as idle cash. In the long run, markets should equilibrate, but, Keynes famously quipped, "in the long run we are all dead." We can't wait for the long run to arrive, and must have policies to deal with macroeconomic disequilibrium now, when we are faced with it.

At the level of theory, Keynes introduced a new approach to the relations among macroeconomic, or aggregate, variables (such as national income and the general price level) that was intended to replace its precursor. He called his approach the General Theory, suggesting that it encompassed the conventional theory as a special case just as Einstein's theory of relativity encompassed Newtonian physics. At the policy level, he embraced government action to stimulate a depressed economy by spending in excess of its revenues — a so-called counter-cyclical approach, whose flip side would be low spending and high taxes to cool an overheating economy. Management of the money supply might offer another policy tool. Some of these policies had already begun to be used with partial success in Sweden and the United States, and Keynes's stature and reasoning helped give them added credibility.

Keynesian policies did not prove sufficient to restore full vigor to the depression-era economy — it took economic mobilization for the Second World War to complete the job. Following the war, nevertheless, his ideas were widely used as a basis for economic policymaking. Keynes's

---

that he resigned his position and wrote a book, *The Economic Consequences of the Peace*, in which he predicted dire consequences, not only for Germany but for all Europe, unless the reparations clauses were revised."

macroeconomic theory was given a more formal structure by mathematical economists including Britain's John Hicks and America's Paul Samuelson. Yet the same economists and others, such as Kenneth Arrow and
Gerard Debreu, were simultaneously furthering the formalization of
neoclassical microeconomics theory itself. Their successful refinement of
the ideas of predecessors like Walras, Edgeworth, and Marshall contributed to a decisive shift toward the mathematicization of graduate training
and research in economics, and to the increasing dominance of the neoclassical school of economics in most of the non-Communist world.

Rather than eclipse neoclassicism in the classroom, then, Keynes's
theory for some decades thrived alongside it, a slightly uneasy marriage of
different theories for the different domains of macro- and microeconomic analysis. The main challenge to it came from a group, led by
American Milton Friedman, known as monetarists, who argued that government cannot adequately time its responses to macroeconomic imbalances, and that the best rule to follow for a stable economy is simply a
moderate and stable rate of growth of the supply of money paralleling the
growth rate of the economy. In the 1980s, though, Keynesian macroeconomics was shaken by deeper theoretical criticisms and underwent a period of ferment as its practitioners scrambled to rebuild their theories on
neoclassical-style foundations of rational individual choice.

Although academic macroeconomics had found no real equilibrium as
the twentieth century ended, public approaches to macroeconomic policymaking by governments and international bodies did not tend to de-
part much from the Keynes-inspired approaches of the 1960s and '70s. At
the end of the 1990s, for instance, both the conservatively inclined International Monetary Fund and the more liberal U.S. government were
applauding the Japanese government's decision to use expansionary fiscal
policy to restart that country's stalled economy. And the notion that the
economy is self-regulating was belied repeatedly by the critical importance of decisions by the U.S. Federal Reserve Board, which was credited,
for instance, with averting a recession in 1998 by reversing its opposition
to low interest rates. At this level, at least, the intellectual revolution
launched by Keynes had been victorious, for the old assumption of a self-
regulating market had clearly been modified by a consensus that governments need to keep an eye on their countries' economies, and that their
helping hands can at least sometimes play an important auxiliary role.

MODERN ECONOMICS

While such events were unfolding in the field of macroeconomics, the core areas of economic theory, which continued to focus on individual agents and firms, were anything but stagnant. Although much of the basic microeconomics that would be taught to undergraduates was already in place, the successful elaboration of that theory by more mathematically oriented economists, and the explosive growth of university education during the twentieth century, fueled the enormous growth of economics as a discipline on both quantitative and qualitative levels. Quantitatively, there was a large increase in the number of new Ph.D.s and thus economics scholars, including increasing numbers from the non-Anglo-Saxon world and from outside Europe. The number of specialized fields in which active research programs were being undertaken, and the number of both general and specialized technical journals in which economists published their research, grew rapidly, and the demand for economists by both governments and the private and nonprofit sectors grew. Qualitatively, economists applied increasingly sophisticated methods to both theory and analysis of empirical data, even if the relevance and realism of their approaches continued to be questioned.

Criticism, to be sure, continued to develop and flourish both outside and within the economics profession. Radical economists continued to attack the mainstream paradigm as Marx had its classical precursors, viewing it as an intellectual apology for a capitalist system that caused a lopsided distribution of income, dehumanizing jobs, environmental degradation, and economic and military aggression.[22] Radical analyses viewing the underdevelopment of the Third World as the product of the subordination of developing countries within a world capitalist division of labor were popular among those nations' intellectuals, who developed a variety of "dependency" theories loosely linked to Marxism.[23] Within the industrialized countries, some economists challenged neoclassicism as insufficiently realistic and empirical, calling, for instance, for more "behavioral" approaches similar to those of psychology, or for "evolu-

22. An accessible and engrossing account of the debate between radical and mainstream economists is provided in Lindbeck, 1977.

23. For example, see Wilber, ed., 1979.

tionary" approaches based on analogies to biology. The mainstream was also attacked both from the ideological right, which challenged its assumption that governments could be assumed to act benevolently even though private individuals act on self-interest, and from liberal economists, who called for more attention by the discipline to problems of poverty, discrimination against women and minorities, and other social issues.[24]

Even as such criticisms were reaching the point at which many wrote of a "crisis" in economic theory, however, the momentum of professionalization and mathematicization of the economics discipline, whose academic practitioners in the developed world now numbered in the thousands, continued unperturbed. Although in some respects neoclassical economists seemed inclined to ignore their critics, their approach also showed a remarkable ability to respond to criticism with new growth. Partly in response to questions about conflicts between capital owners and workers raised by radical economists, for example, and partly in response to calls for increased institutional and behavioral realism, economists developed more complex analyses of the contractual relations between employers and employees and of the internal structures of firms. The assumption that economic agents act on perfect information, an obvious example of lack of realism, gave way to a massive outpouring of research on situations in which individuals act with different, or "asymmetric," information regarding the problems they face. Models in which each decision maker takes the actions of others as given became less dominant, and those in which strategic interactions play an important role more so. Although some contributors to the resulting literatures on organization, information, and so forth viewed their new ideas as *alternatives* to the neoclassical paradigm, it seems more appropriate to view them as part of that paradigm in its broadest sense, for they retained the central approaches of assuming rational individuals seeking to maximize attainment of their objectives, of the prominent use of mathematics — often including the calculus or marginal approach — to model the process, and of a common set of assumptions about objectives, such as the desire to consume more and to work less.

While the basic models of the era of Walras, Marshall, and Pareto, with

24. Some of the approaches and criticisms just mentioned are surveyed, and references given, in Landreth and Colander, 1994, chapter 14.

the central notion of optimal resource allocation in a competitive economy, remained at the core of economics education, the analysis of strategic interactions and asymmetric information issues brought changes important enough to be viewed by some practitioners as a revolution in
economics. Of particular importance was the development of game theory, a branch of mathematics used to study decisions made by agents
aware of the impact of their own decisions on the decisions likely to be
made by others. Its relevance was first recognized in the study of oligop-
oly, an industry structure in which neither the assumption that each firm is
so unimportant that it can take the behavior of the market as given (perfect competition) nor the idea that the firm can unilaterally dictate price
and quantity (monopoly) is appropriate. The calculating manager of a
firm in such an industry should consider the effects of his choices on the
choices that other large firms might make. From here, applications spread
out in many directions, including bargaining between employers and
unions, problems of collective action, and much more. The theory of
prices itself (general equilibrium theory) was recast in game-theoretic
terms. Game theory and the economics of imperfect information also
helped stimulate the study of economic behavior in the laboratory, where
subjects were enlisted in experiments simulating decision making under
various real-world situations.

Much as economics as a whole was once part of a more general body of
philosophy and later became a field unto itself, so the subfields within
economics became increasingly distinct and specialized. This process of
intellectual division of labor is quite closely analogous to the division of
labor affecting other sectors of activity, as discussed in Chapter 1 and
above. In both cases, an increasing division of labor is partly occasioned
by larger markets and larger populations (in the present instance, by an
ever growing demand for higher education and hence ever growing numbers of professional scholars), and in both cases, it is propelled by productivity gains that come with specialization (here, because the scholar can
command a deeper knowledge of a narrower field, and each can apply
herself to an area of comparative advantage). A brief survey of the terrain
may be helpful.

As a first cut, economic study is often broken up into three broad
divisions. These are microeconomics, which studies prices and resource
allocation at the level of individual consumers, firms, and industries; macroeconomics, which studies national income, employment, the overall

price level, and other aggregate variables; and econometrics, which is the application of statistical methods to the study of economic data. Within each field are found a great many specialties: for instance, microeconomic theory includes models of the general equilibrium of the economy, models of interaction between principals (such as employers) and agents (such as employees), game theory, and other specialized fields. Econometrics includes approaches focusing on changes over time (time-series analysis), others studying differences across contemporaneous units (cross-sectional analysis), the study of data with both time-series and cross-section dimensions (panel data), and other specialized fields.

A finer subdivision of economics also requires the enumeration of subfields further distinguished by subject matter. Labor economists study labor markets, unions, and the evolution of wages; development economists study the economics of less developed countries; trade economists study the economics of international trade, and so on. In some cases, the approach of a subfield fits mainly into one of the three broad divisions or another. The theory of international trade, for instance, is primarily a specialized branch of microeconomic theory, as is the theory of industrial organization, which analyzes the effects of monopoly and of other market structures, and finance theory, which studies capital markets and the financing of investment. Monetary economics has traditionally been studied as a branch of macroeconomics. It is just as common, however, for a topical subfield to span all three of the broader divisions. Among labor economists, for example, one finds some who specialize in micro-level analyses, for instance developing theories about the impact of varying payment arrangements on the incentives and effort provided by workers. But one also finds labor economists who work on the macroeconomic determinants of an economy's rate of unemployment or of wage inflation. And applied labor economists use econometric tools in their empirical studies. Development economics similarly includes micro, macro, and econometric studies.

Although there are too many specialties within contemporary economics to be discussed in this brief treatment, a few of the others attracting large numbers of researchers ought at least to be mentioned. Public choice studies the theory and practice of collective decision making, especially with respect to the provision of public goods, such as defense and public transport systems. Public finance studies the design and impact of tax mechanisms. Welfare economics studies theoretical aspects of normative questions, such as those regarding the efficiency and fairness of outcomes of a competitive economy (issues touched on in Chapter 5). Urban and regional economics look at the spatial and locational dimensions of an economy. The economics of organizations looks at the structure of incentive schemes and of the contractual arrangements among the parties to an organization, such as a modern business firm. Comparative economic systems and transition economies looks at the effects of different types of property rights assignments and of assigning different roles and levels of importance to the state as compared with the market. Environmental and resource economists (who will appear in Chapter 6) study problems of natural resource depletion, policy responses to pollution, and related issues. Health economists study the organization and functioning of the health care industry. Agricultural economists study the special problems of agriculture, demographic economists study economic aspects of migration and fertility decisions. Economic historians study past economies and the historical development of the present economy. Historians of economic thought specialize in the subject to which this chapter provides a brief introduction.

The division of labor among specialties has borne fruit in enormous outpourings of specialized literatures on all the topics just enumerated, and more. Among the most recently emerging fields, one could list feminist economics, which studies problems of discrimination and of measuring the economic contribution of unpaid work in the household, and experimental economics, which, as already mentioned, applies laboratory methods to undertake controlled studies of economic decision making. In each of these fields, new theories and findings are constantly being disseminated in specialized periodicals, contributions to which undergo a process of peer evaluation before their acceptance for publication, and in books and edited collections of papers. The *Journal of Economic Literature*, a publication of the American Economic Association, lists the contents of some 210 periodicals mainly on economic topics, most of them published in quarterly issues. This list leaves out periodicals too specialized or not sufficiently influential to be included, including 450 other periodicals (some of them multidisciplinary) that are indexed in the association's electronic publications database, EconLit. Although some have suggested that the average published paper in this vast literature will be read by only two or three economists aside from the author and the periodical's editor and peer reviewers, papers in the most influential publications, like the *American Economic Review,* are studied carefully and often are placed on the syllabi of graduate courses even before their publication (when they circulate as working papers). Their influence is routinely gauged by the number of times they are cited by authors of other papers in the same and similar periodicals.

As with the division of labor in general, however, specialization in scholarship also has its downside. It was Adam Smith who wrote, "The man whose whole life is spent in performing a few simple operations . . . becomes as stupid and ignorant as it is possible for a human creature to become."[25] Although the operations of the specialized economist are hardly simple, a critic of modern academic economics wrote in 1985 about the discipline that had grown from Smith's work: "Departments of economics are graduating a generation of *idiot savants,* brilliant at esoteric mathematics yet innocent of actual economic life."[26] A significant number of economists and still more academics in fields like sociology and history tend to agree with this assessment,[27] and many voice doubts that economics is a true science. The neoclassical approach is criticized for being overly deductive, for drawing conclusions from careful chains of reasoning but without adequate criticism of the assumptions used or testing of the implications drawn. Empirical research has expanded, but often at one remove from model building, and with as much interest in pure methodology as in the substance of the issues under investigation.[28] Yet despite these concerns, those earning the Ph.D. degree in economics from top universities continue to be sought after not only for teaching and research positions at academic institutions but for work in government, international organizations, and large companies, banks, and investment firms.

25. Smith, 1985 [1776]), p. 445.
26. Kuttner, 1985.
27. For example, see Klamer and Colander, 1990, which takes off from the Kuttner quote into an investigation of actual graduate training in economics through an analysis of surveys and interviews in leading economics departments.
28. A serious discussion of the methodology of science and the respective roles of model building and deductive logic versus empirical observation and model testing is beyond the scope of this book, but the interested reader may begin with Blaug, 1992.

CONCLUSION

The discipline of economics as taught today in most colleges and universities follows an approach usually called neoclassical. Like the classical economics of Adam Smith and David Ricardo, it views the market system as a largely self-regulating mechanism for the decentralized allocation of resources in a manner serving the overall interest of society. Also like classical economics, it assumes that people are basically self-interested and rational in their behavior, and it predicts social outcomes on the basis of individual actions. Neoclassical economics departs from its classical precursor in its more thoroughgoing use of mathematics, especially the differential calculus, which allows it to integrate both demand and supply considerations into its model of price formation and resource allocation. Although the basic framework of neoclassical economics was put in place between the 1870s and the 1920s, the approach has continued to evolve in the ensuing decades, giving rise to numerous specialized subfields and developing theoretically as well as in its empirical methodology.

Both the sanguine appraisal of markets and the deductive and abstract method employed by mainstream economics have had their critics. Radical economists, members of the German historical school, and American institutional economists were among those who bemoaned the narrowing scope of mainstream economics and its further turn from empiricism in the transition from the classical to the early neoclassical period. Austrian dissenters criticized the mainstream's preoccupation with equilibrium and its abstraction from information problems. While nonorthodox approaches flourished in Europe and North America until the Second World War, Marxism became orthodoxy in the Communist world and heterodox schools were active in many developing countries. The still growing neoclassical economics, however, expanded its scope and methods. Empirical research obtained a new lease on life, and theorists began to tackle issues like incompleteness of information, and even class conflict, that had been raised by the critics. The free market orientation of the mainstream was also leavened by an increased awareness of market imperfections and the corrective roles of government.

With the fall of Communism in the East and the ascent of pro-market ideologies in much of the developing world in the 1980s, neoclassical economics attained a position of intellectual dominance over most of the globe. Although dissatisfaction with the neoclassical school remains widespread in many quarters, it shows considerable resilience and no sign of relinquishing its grip on the main centers of economics teaching throughout the world. Those who wish to propose or develop alternative viewpoints within the professional realm of the economist are therefore left with little choice but to first master the tools and the vocabulary of this school.

REFERENCES

Blaug, Mark, 1983, *Economic Theory in Retrospect,* 3d ed. Cambridge: Cambridge University Press.

Blaug, Mark, 1992, *The Methodology of Economics: Or How Economists Explain,* 2d ed. Cambridge: Cambridge University Press.

Boulding, Kenneth, 1957, "A New Look at Institutionalism," *American Economic Review* 47:1–12.

Hayek, Friedrich A. von, 1933, "The Trend of Economic Thinking," *Economica* 1 (2):121–37.

Heilbroner, Robert, 1999, *The Worldly Philosophers: The Lives, Times, and Ideas of the Great Economic Thinkers,* 7th ed. New York: Touchstone.

Klamer, Arjo, and David Colander, 1990, *The Making of an Economist.* Boulder, Colo.: Westview.

Kuttner, Robert, 1985, "The Poverty of Economics," *Atlantic Monthly,* February, pp. 74–84.

Landreth, Harry, and David Colander, 1994, *History of Economic Thought,* 3d ed. Boston: Houghton Mifflin.

Lindbeck, Assar, 1977, *The Political Economy of the New Left: An Outsider's View,* 2d ed. New York: New York University Press.

Mill, John Stuart, 1929 [1848], *Principles of Political Economy with Some of Their Applications to Social Philosophy,* ed. Sir W. J. Ashley. London: Longmans, Green.

Schumpeter, Joseph, 1994 [1954], *History of Economic Analysis,* edited from manuscript by Elizabeth Boody Schumpeter, with a new introduction by Mark Perlman. New York: Oxford University Press.

Smith, Adam, 1971 [1759], *The Theory of Moral Sentiments.* New York: Garland.

Smith, Adam, 1985 [1776], *An Inquiry into the Nature and Causes of the Wealth of Nations,* ed. Edwin Cannan. New York: Modern Library.

Wilber, Charles K., ed., 1984, *The Political Economy of Development and Underdevelopment,* 3d ed. New York: Random House.

Yonay, Yuval P., 1998, *The Struggle over the Soul of Economics: Institutionalist and Neoclassical Economists in America Between the Wars.* Princeton: Princeton University Press.

SUGGESTIONS FOR FURTHER READING

Barber, William, 1967, *A History of Economic Thought*. Harmondsworth, England: Penguin.

Bell, Daniel, and Irving Kristol, eds., 1981, *The Crisis in Economic Theory*. New York: Basic.

Blaug, Mark, 1985, *Great Economists Since Keynes: An Introduction to the Lives and Works of One Hundred Modern Economists*. Totowa, N.J.: Barnes & Noble.

Deane, Phyllis, 1978, *The Evolution of Economic Ideas*. Cambridge: Cambridge University Press.

Dobb, Maurice, 1973, *Theories of Value and Distribution Since Adam Smith: Ideology and Economic Theory*. Cambridge: Cambridge University Press.

Friedman, Milton, 1953, *Essays in Positive Economics*. Chicago: University of Chicago Press.

Fusfeld, Daniel, 1998, *The Age of the Economist*, 8th ed., Reading, Mass.: Addison-Wesley.

Heilbroner, Robert, and William Milberg, eds., 1996, *The Crisis of Vision in Modern Economic Thought*. New York: Cambridge University Press.

Hirschman, Albert, 1977, *The Passions and the Interests: Political Arguments for Capitalism Before Its Triumph*. Princeton: Princeton University Press.

McCloskey, Donald, 1985, *The Rhetoric of Economics*. Madison: University of Wisconsin Press.

Myrdal, Gunnar, 1961, *The Political Element in the Development of Economic Theory*, translated from the German by Paul Streeten. Cambridge: Harvard University Press.

Roemer, John, 1988, *Free to Lose: An Introduction to Marxist Economic Philosophy*. Cambridge: Harvard University Press.

Silk, Leonard, 1976, *The Economists*. New York: Basic.

Spiegel, Henry William, 1991, *The Growth of Economic Thought*. Durham, N.C.: Duke University Press.

ECONOMIC
SYSTEMS

Year by year the role of Western governments in the economy rises. . . . Capitalism retains the stimulus of private property, free enterprise, and competition, and produces a rich supply of goods; high taxation, falling heavily upon the upper classes, enables the government to provide for a self-limited population unprecedented services in education, health, and recreation. . . . the fear of socialism has compelled capitalism to increase equality.
— *Will and Ariel Durant,*
    The Lessons of History

The nine most terrifying words in the English language are "I'm from the government and I'm here to help."
— *Ronald Reagan*

Can it be said that, after the failure of Communism, capitalism is the victorious social system, and that capitalism should be the goal of the countries now making efforts to rebuild their economy and society? Is this the model which

ought to be proposed to the countries of the Third World which are searching for the path to true economic and civil progress? . . . if by "capitalism" is meant a system in which freedom in the economic sector is not circumscribed within a strong juridical framework which places it at the service of human freedom in its totality and sees it as a particular aspect of that freedom, the core of which is ethical and religious, then the reply is certainly negative.
— *Pope John Paul II,*
    Centisimus Annus

When . . . co-operative societies shall have sufficiently multiplied, it is not probable that any but the least valuable work-people will any longer consent to work all their lives for wages merely; both private capitalists and associations will gradually find it necessary to make the entire body of laborers participants in profits.
— *John Stuart Mill,*
    Principles of Political Economy

Bob and Diane Gorman are a typical American couple who live in a medium-sized midwestern city. After graduating from high school, Bob found a job in a local factory belonging to a large manufacturing concern. His plant was unionized and Bob enjoyed good job security, a paycheck that increased a few steps ahead of inflation throughout his first fifteen years of work, and benefits including three weeks of paid vacation. Diane held some clerical and secretarial jobs but left the workforce for ten years when their first child was born, to be followed in turn by two others. By the early 1980s, Bob and Diane were in their thirties, held a mortgage on a home in a middle-income suburb, and were able to afford two cars, eating out once or twice a week, and other trappings of a comfortable lifestyle.

But Bob's company began to encounter stiffer competition. In the late 1980s, he was temporarily laid off several times, and in 1990 the company shut down its local operation, leaving him unemployed. Bob has never been able to find an equally well-paying job, and he now works in a sales job at a retail store for about 60 percent of his former paycheck. They have managed to maintain their lifestyle by having Diane reenter the labor force.

At the beginning of the new millennium, the Gormans are not bitter but instead remain staunch believers in the American dream. They believe their incomes to be average, and they are largely unaware that the top 20 percent of Americans, measured by income, saw their earnings rise by 1.6 percent a year in the 1980s and '90s, while their own real household income and that of the bottom 60 percent of households overall remained unchanged. They like the idea of a simple "flat" tax, with each family paying an equal share of its income, and they favor cuts in government spending and social programs from which they don't benefit. But there are several from which they do benefit. Bob has collected unemployment insurance from the government on several occasions, and he is anxious about Social Security remaining solvent. And they would be unable to see their children off to college without the availability of government-backed loans.

Chen Jianming and his wife, Wang Mei, live in the city of Harbin in northeast China. Mr. Chen, age fifty, has been a worker in a state-owned factory since leaving high school, and Ms. Wang, one year younger, has a job in an urban collective enterprise that the city government helped establish. When economic reforms came in the early 1980s, the couple benefited because the job security, heavily subsidized housing, and access to medical care that they already enjoyed thanks to Chen's job were now augmented by their first pay increases since they started working in the 1960s. With the onset of reforms, they were also eligible for bonus payments and experienced dramatic improvements in the quality and variety of food and consumer goods that were available.

After a dozen years of reform, however, Mr. Chen's factory switched to part-time operation. These days, the factory still pays him half of his old salary, although there is little work for him to do, and there are rumors it may be shut down. The enterprise of Ms. Wang is also struggling in the face of competition from more efficient private enterprises in the city's suburbs and in other provinces. With their incomes cut back, Chen and Wang face an imminent crisis, because the city is now experimenting with housing reform that will cause their rent to rise to the full market rate, or by a factor of seven, over the course of two years.

One ray of hope comes from their twenty-eight-year-old son, who studied computer science at the university and is now working in a new private venture. If it succeeds, the younger Chen could become wealthy. But it may not succeed, as there are more such startups in other provinces where the level of technology is more up to date and there is a steadier inflow of foreign capital. At the moment, too, he is without significant income and depends, along with an infant son, on his wife's modest earnings as a teacher in a public school.

The elder Chen and his wife came of age in the era of radical Maoism. They were loyal socialists who watched the early reforms with uncertainty, despite its evident benefits. Now they see their government as turning its back both on them and on the old socialist ideals. Their son is more enthusiastic about the reforms, but as he discusses the impending housing crunch with his parents, he feels acutely aware that there are few guarantees for his own or his parents' futures.

In a world in which private property and market exchange are the dominant institutions of economic life, most economics teaching takes a mixed market economy as its setting, assuming the institutions of such an economy to be given and natural. We have seen, however, that economies with relatively unfettered private ownership of capital and land, in which most people earn the greater part of their livelihoods by exchanging their labor services for wages, have been prominent for only a few of the many thousands of generations of human history. Nor have such economic institutions been the only ones observed even in recent times. For nearly seven decades of this century, one of the world's largest countries, the Soviet Union, attempted to operate its economy with little private ownership of resources. State planning substituted for markets as the main coordinator of resource allocation. This economic system was imposed upon or copied by a dozen other countries containing, with the Soviet Union, well over a quarter of the world's population. One Communist country, Yugoslavia, developed a radical variant of the system in which markets played a greater role and state companies were at least nominally controlled by their workers. Still other countries, notably Hungary and later China, experimented with other decentralized forms of socialism.

Although centrally planned economies have now all but disappeared from the world's stage, the capitalist world itself continues to be marked, as it has always been, by considerable variety. Some countries, such as France and Germany, have had substantial government ownership of enterprises while others, like Sweden and the United States, have had little. Some countries, like those of Scandinavia, the Netherlands, and Germany, have large welfare states that redistribute substantial portions of their national product, while others, like the United States and Japan, have undertaken less redistribution of income, although the U.S. government's involvement in welfare and other programs is still great by the standards of the nineteenth century. In the developing world, millions of rural people have lived until recently under semifeudal conditions, and massive protectionism and regulation has marked most economies in Asia, Africa, and Latin America until the present decade. Economic systems thus retain considerable variation.

ECONOMIC SYSTEMS DEFINED
AND ILLUSTRATED

The term "economic system" refers to a set of institutions, routines, or social arrangements under which resources are managed and goods and services are produced and distributed. "System" connotes a set of elements that interact with one another to form a unified whole. Institutions, such as the *laws* that specify the rights of persons over things ("property rights"), organizations, such as business firms, labor unions, cooperatives, and governments, and procedures, such as contracting, auctions, and voting, are all elements of an economic system. In an economic system, people, resources, and goods might also be viewed as participating or constitutive elements. The system is *economic* to the extent that through it people attempt to meet their material needs and wants, and in it the basic economic functions of production and distribution take place.

The major economic systems of the twentieth century can be distinguished by identifying the ways in which the interactions among participating and constitutive elements display different regularities, rules, and procedures. In a capitalist economy, individuals hold rights to determine the use of such resources as land, equipment, and money, to possess the output or revenue that those uses generate, and to agree to the use of their resources by others in exchange for some kind of compensation. This bundle of rights, called ownership, can be transferred from one person to another by gift or by sale. Groups of individuals can also jointly own entities such as firms that engage in exchange and own property as if they were persons in their own right.

Although the rights to use of resources are generally tradable in a capitalist economy, one resource, human labor power, is not a legally transferable commodity, being ownable only by the person who supplies it. In modern capitalism, the right to determine labor's use and to possess its products can be transferred to others through a wage contract, but no person can be owned by others or can, even voluntarily, contractually commit her labor services to others for more than a limited period of time. This makes labor *inalienable*, distinguishing modern capitalism from feudalism, under which the serfs who were the majority of the population owed uncompensated labor to the lords, and in which serfs could even be transferred with their manor from one lord to another.

It also distinguishes capitalism from the ancient economic systems of Egypt, Mesopotamia, or Greece, and from the plantation economies of the eighteenth and nineteenth centuries, where slavery was a common institution.

The voluntary exchange of goods and services at prices determined only by the mutual agreement of the transacting parties gives rise to the basic coordinating mechanism of a capitalist economy: the market. As resource owners seek to earn a good livelihood from their labor and property holdings, resources flow toward activities in which they have a high return. As individuals or households then use their incomes to purchase finished goods and services, signals of demand are spontaneously transmitted throughout the production sector. Thus, resources are allocated and reallocated in an ongoing fashion in response to the indications of demand and scarcity that are encoded in and transmitted by prices. Under an idealized, or pure, capitalism, there is a government, but rather than being charged with running the economy it has limited economic roles, consisting of the securing of property rights, the enforcement of contracts, the issuing of currency, and the provision of goods and services — "public goods" — that cannot be profitably and efficiently supplied by business firms for reasons that will be discussed shortly. Not only is the government not charged with achieving overall economic coordination; neither is any other collective body constituted for this purpose. The economy is said to be "self-regulating."

Some contrasts between capitalism, feudalism, and ancient slaveholding societies were mentioned above. The most dramatically different economic system of modern times was the centrally planned socialist economy that existed from 1928 to the 1980s in the Soviet Union, and after World War II in many other countries as well. As in capitalism or any other economic system, people and resources formed participating and constitutive elements, and it was through the economic system that people satisfied their material needs and wants insofar as that proved possible. But the regularities, rules, and procedures marking the system distinguished it from capitalism. Individuals were permitted to own consumer goods, for example, but the means of production, such as land, structures, and equipment, were the property of the state, which theoretically owned them on behalf of the nation's people. The roles of government and those filled by business enterprises in a capitalist economy were merged. In a sense, the government ran an all-embracing monopoly business,

"U.S.S.R. Incorporated," or "Poland Incorporated." Most production took place in state-owned enterprises, so most workers were state employees. Enterprises existed as distinguishable entities, but they had little autonomy, being more like branch factories or workshops of the overall government monopoly than like separate business firms.

In the Soviet system, price signals and profits were to play no role in coordinating the economy. Instead of reacting to profit opportunities, an enterprise was supposed to produce whatever it was told to produce by the government ("headquarters"), using whatever inputs were assigned to it for that purpose. In principle, then, all major production activity was determined by a state plan, which dictated how the society's productive resources would be utilized. Intermediate goods, such as the iron needed by steel mills and the steel needed by machine makers, were also allocated by planners, and thus were to move from the state enterprise that produced them to the state enterprise that used them in accordance with a national economic plan. Final goods were mostly allocated by a more conventional sales system: citizens taking their earnings from state employment, along with pensions, subsidies, and other forms of income, could spend it as they wished, subject to the availability of goods, and sometimes also to rationing schemes. But the sales outlets were state-owned stores. In principle, the aim of the planners was supposed to be maximizing the societal welfare or some articulated set of national goals, with no particular regard for profit or other financial indicators.

It is worth noticing that planning and bureaucratic coordination are not unique to centrally planned systems. They are common in the private sectors of market economies as well. This is true in the sense that the individual enterprise or factory is quite often a branch of a larger company, being evaluated and following instructions provided to it by higher-level managers. Likewise, a considerable proportion of movements of semifinished components, raw materials, and so on take place in a market economy not through decentralized responses to price signals but under the management of large companies. As a component of some final product moves from one work station to another, from one division to another, or down a conveyer belt, it responds to a manager's directives or a company production plan, and is thus only indirectly influenced by market forces. Often the transfer of that component from one division to another takes place at an internal accounting or transfer price that has little or no relation to supply and demand. Indeed, resources frequently move within a firm without being priced at all. The assignment of workers to tasks within the workplace and over the course of the working day, to give another example, is also managed by companies not by bidding and negotiating a wage for each task but under the regulation of a workplace hierarchy.

If the allocation of resources by managerial hierarchies is not unique to the centrally planned systems, what was in fact distinctive about them? One answer is that it was both the extent of hierarchical centralization — binding an entire national economy under one comprehensive center — and the fact that this extent was determined not by market competition between firms of differing sizes but by government determination that there would be but one overarching "firm."

A market economy can be said to be one in which hierarchical organizations compete with one another and with smaller organizations, independent contractors, and other organizational forms. The sizes of the "planned economies" — General Motors, I.B.M., Citicorp, Joe's Sub Shop — that emerge as a result of the process reflect the relative efficiencies of operations on different scales in different lines of business. In centrally planned economies, on the other hand, the entire economy was to operate as an integrated business as dictated by law, constitution, and the ideology and authority of the ruling party.[1] Such centralization proved difficult to make work in practice, and it also turned out to have clear disadvantages from the standpoint of productive and allocative efficiency.

CRITICS AND DEFENDERS
OF CAPITALISM

Critics of capitalism point to the existence side by side of great wealth and great poverty, to the insecurity of people's jobs, to the wastefulness of companies duplicating one another's research and advertising outlays, to the disregard of producers for the environmental impacts of their

1. The idea that both centrally planned economies and capitalist companies allocate resources by command, and that the two differ in that competition determines the scope of commands in the capitalist system but political fiat does so in the centrally planned system, was first stated by Ronald Coase, 1937. Coase's depiction of capitalism as a mix of planning and markets is further developed by Oliver Williamson, for instance in Williamson, 1985.

activities, and to other drawbacks. But in the early twentieth century, at least, the most fundamental assertion of such critics was that these and other problems were not surprising because capitalism encourages people to follow the dictates of private greed while it gives no individual or institution the responsibility for guaranteeing the rationality or coordination of the system as a whole. When no one is in charge and it is "every man for himself," good results can hardly be expected, the critics said. This makes it useful to review the arguments for an economy in which people are left to do as they will, and where nobody at all is responsible for the overall outcome.

One case for capitalism is constructed on the intrinsic value of freedom itself. This type of argument is called *libertarian*. A pure libertarian argues that economic freedom is desirable regardless of its consequences for narrowly economic or material well-being. The fact that liberty and a strong economy go hand in hand, in the libertarian's view, is just a bonus, not a major reason for advocating economic freedom.[2] Notice that to most libertarians, freedom includes importantly the right to own and dispose of property. Some socialist critics have argued that exclusive private property ownership and unlimited checks on inequality actually *narrow* the domain of economic freedom for the majority of people. To grant one person the exclusive freedom to use a thing, they suggest, is to deny every other person the freedom to use it. And in a world of finite wealth, the accumulation of wealth and the resulting opening of choices to some might imply the reduction of wealth and the resulting constriction of choices to others.

A different kind of argument for capitalism asserts that economic freedom is desirable because of its *consequences* for output and consumption. This approach is known as a *utilitarian* one. Standard economics is utilitarian in that it rests its case for capitalism only in small measure on the intrinsic value of liberty. Its main argument is that capitalism actually achieves good results in terms of material well-being. In short, economists argue that capitalism achieves both coordination and prosperity without a coordinator, thus saving on costs of coordination and delivering liberty, along the way, as an added bonus.

Economists from Adam Smith on have recognized that the fundamental paradox of a decentralized economy is that individual actors are guided

---

2. See Rothbard, 1973.

by self-interest, with nobody in charge, and that the overall result is nevertheless favorable, judging from the relative prosperity of capitalist societies. Smith used the term "invisible hand" to describe the coordination mechanism that acts without central direction in a market system. He argued that such a system achieves better coordination *without* a coordinator than would be possible *with* one, a position that was elaborated in the twentieth century by Friedrich von Hayek. The invisible hand is the working of supply and demand, which modern economists see as generating *price signals* that reflect the relative scarcity of resources and goods, and also the levels of demand for these by consumers. In response to the prices shaped by the forces of supply and demand, owners steer their resources into high-return uses, and producers select techniques requiring the least input of costly resources to produce the highest-valued products. Because the prices that consumers are willing to pay reflect their valuations of the goods and services to be produced, decentralized production, which leads to the provision of a set of products having the maximum attainable money value, is argued to be the optimal way of using society's scarce resources.

Modern economists have provided proofs of the intuitions of Adam Smith that are far more rigorous and mathematically elegant than were the arguments that Smith himself made in the eighteenth century. But these proofs are essentially theoretical ones, and they require numerous, somewhat specialized, and in some respects unrealistic assumptions. They do not, therefore, dispense with all criticisms of capitalism. For one thing, the set of goods produced by a hypothetical perfectly competitive market system are optimal only in a particular sense, that is, in terms of whatever happens to be its distribution of income. This is because while the demand for goods reflects the value that consumers place upon them, there is nothing to assure that all consumers have an equal voice in the matter. Consumers having little or no purchasing power are disenfranchised in the "voting" over what should be produced and supplied, while those with great purchasing power get to cast their "dollar votes" over and over again. Thus, the system might be said to respond effectively (or in an ethically acceptable way) to people's needs only to the extent that there is a socially acceptable distribution of the money backing by which needs are translated into demand. But none of the proofs of capitalism's efficiency includes any guarantees about its distribution of income.

Another reservation about capitalism that retains its bite despite the modern "invisible hand" proofs concerns the effects that economists refer to as "externalities." Consider a firm that produces, say, aluminum, which is used to make soft-drink cans. Suppose that the aluminum production process releases pollutants that spread through the atmosphere and raise the incidence of lung cancer by a few hundred cases per year within its region. Suppose also that disposal of the cans in landfills is less expensive at market prices than is recycling the material into new cans. In principle, the costs of treating the cancer cases, the human toll upon the victims and their families, and the damage to the environment in nonbiodegradable trash should be included among the costs (to society) of producing the cans and consuming the soft drinks, alongside the wages paid to the factory's employees and the costs of its materials, energy supply, and machinery.

In an unregulated market system, however, the owners of the factory can treat the air in which it disposes of the pollutant as a free good. The factory includes among its cost per sheet of aluminum only those costs associated with the standard inputs, and it is thus only those costs that will be passed on to consumers and be reflected in the prices they pay. Neither the producers nor the consumers of aluminum cans may therefore put much weight on the cost of the additional pollution that aluminum production generates when deciding how many aluminum soft-drink cans to produce or to purchase. If pollution is an unavoidable by-product of aluminum production, and if, say, production of steel for soft-drink cans is less polluting, it may be socially preferable to produce fewer aluminum cans and more steel cans. Recycling of the cans may also be desirable, but might not take place without public action. In the unregulated economy, the mix of aluminum and steel cans and the degree of recycling will not reflect full costs, and if aluminum happens to be relatively inexpensive (when the pollution cost is ignored), too many aluminum cans will be produced.[3]

Another problem the "invisible hand" does not contend with by itself is the production of public goods. Public goods are goods that, once

3. An alternative view is that the producer would not overpollute if the local population has a "property right" to clean air and can force the firm to come to an agreement on and pay them for the right to pollute. With large numbers of people involved, however, informal collective action may not be feasible. The state in a democratic polity arguably solves this problem of representing the people's rights and dealing with would-be polluters on their behalf.

produced, are difficult to prevent people from consuming, even if they show no willingness to pay. And consumption of a pure public good by one more person does not reduce the amount available to be consumed by others. An apple is not a public good because either you eat the apple or I do, and it is relatively easy for you to deny me an apple that you possess unless I pay you for it. By contrast, national defense is a public good because citizens could not be induced to voluntarily pay a private provider for it. You will benefit from almost exactly the same level of national defense whether everyone except you contributes to it or everyone including you does so. Once you and your family are enjoying its benefits, it is nearly impossible to prevent me and my family from also doing so. Moreover, your enjoyment of an effective national defense in no way reduces the amount available for me to enjoy.[4]

The problem that the existence of public goods poses for a decentralized economy is that they will not be produced, or will be provided only at inappropriately low levels, by ordinary profit-seeking firms. Suppose that a private company tried to operate an air force and navy that effectively protected the borders of a country, turning to the citizens to get paid for its services. Unless the company has the unilateral right to impose charges on the citizens, large numbers of them might claim that they did not want so much defense, and they might refuse to pay anything to the company, or might offer only token amounts. Anticipating this, no company can be expected to enter such a business under ordinary market arrangements. The standard solution is for people to organize, through government or some other venue, to see to the provision of a public good by mandating contributions in the form of taxes.[5] Private companies can be hired by the government to be the actual suppliers of the public good

4. In other cases, such as highways and parks, it is possible to restrict consumption to those who pay a fee, but this changes the nature of the good (a highway or bridge with a toll booth is a different good than one without it, among other reasons because it is likely to take longer to get across it).

5. People can also organize voluntary associations that provide them with public goods, assuring the necessary contributions through within-group social pressure or by linking provision of certain private membership privileges to the payment of fees or dues that also finance the public goods. This kind of solution tends to work best on a small scale or with goods of interest to special subgroups of the general population. Public radio and television stations in the United States are examples of such goods, as are self-enforced agreements among fishermen to avoid the overfishing of a common fishing ground.

or to produce components for it, but the required revenues are collected by the government through taxation.

Now, in the most extreme version of the capitalist economy, where the government's only roles are enforcing contracts and printing currency, public goods would clearly be provided at insufficient levels. In our definition of capitalism above, however, we allowed the government a role in providing public goods. What complaint about public goods might critics of capitalism still make, in this case? Some critics have argued that even though the government can in principle step in to provide public goods, a capitalist economy tends to be biased in favor of the production of private goods, which can be profitable for private firms to produce without mediating action by government. The government, being disproportionately influenced by private companies and wealthy individuals, may, therefore, not provide satisfactorily for provision of many public goods, an expansive list of which might include certain kinds of education and information dissemination, cultural goods, and systems of public transportation and public parks. Capitalism overprovides the automobiles that get some of us to the parks and the fast-food restaurants and motels that surround them, but it underprovides the parks themselves, the public transportation to reach them, and the clean air to breath in them, the criticism goes.[6]

One reason public goods may be undersupplied is that wealthier individuals are often able to provide themselves with private alternatives to these goods (homes in the suburbs, automobiles, getaway vacations in Hawaii), and that large numbers of other individuals who would benefit from more provision of public goods lack the political clout to see that it occurs. On the other end of the political spectrum, however, one may encounter exactly the opposite argument, namely that *too many* goods are provided by government, because private companies and individuals benefit from the undisciplined purchasing habits that mark the government's dealings with defense contractors and other suppliers, because politicians play upon the ignorance of citizens who appreciate the benefits but not the costs of large government, or because government provision of goods, including some that fail the conceptual test for genuine "public"-ness, is a form of disguised redistribution from rich to poor.

One last major area in which critics of capitalism have questioned its

6. For an early influential critique along these lines, see Galbraith, 1978.

optimality is that of macroeconomic performance. As we saw in Chapter 2, mainstream economics has faced one of its greatest challenges in this area, with such economists as John Maynard Keynes arguing that "invisible hand" forces could not be counted upon to establish aggregate full employment or satisfactory stability of prices. Even though Keynes's model of the macroeconomy has been forcefully criticized by neoclassical theorists, few economists today assert that our economies are self-regulating from the standpoint of inflation and employment. From the point of view of a Keynesian, government interventions, such as increasing government deficits in times of rising unemployment and raising federal lending rates in times of rising inflation, are ways in which government can compensate for the inadequacies of the decentralized price mechanism where macroeconomic matters are concerned.

For a more radical critic of capitalism, however, the need for a government coordinating role proves the error of the very idea of a self-regulating market. The radical may argue, moreover, that reactive interventions by government are not good enough, for instance because they are inherently difficult to time, or because the interventions adopted reflect the interests of some (businessmen concerned with the stability of wages and interest rates, for example) more than others (working people concerned about job security and unemployment). A more active coordinating role for government might therefore be argued for.

SOCIALISM AND ITS DISCONTENTS

Given the potential problems of capitalism that have been spelled out above, it is fairly easy to see how proponents of central planning could have imagined that it would be able to improve upon a market economy. To an early socialist, it would have been sufficient to argue that capitalism was an anarchic system, lacking in coordination and governed by greed, and that those who controlled its resources were concerned only about profits, not about people's real needs. Under centrally planned socialism, they said, the means of production would be owned by the whole people in common, the government would act on their behalf and would see to it that these resources were used to meet their genuine needs, and the economy would be systematically planned, not left to the uncoordinated actions of individuals. Socialism would be the next logical step toward an economy under the democratic control of the common citizen.

More sophisticated socialists admitted that capitalism is not entirely anarchic—even Marx saw lawful regularities in the market forces of a capitalist economy. Their arguments for socialism therefore emphasized that the needs that capitalist producers satisfy are mainly those backed by spending power. They pointed to the unequal distributions of wealth in capitalist countries, and they argued that political democracy was not sufficient to prevent the wealthy from exercising disproportionate control over government. The association of wealth with political power implied to them that government interventions that might in principle contain macroeconomic instabilities, regulate pollution, see to the production of public goods in optimal quantities, and even engineer a more equal distribution of income (through progressive taxation, for instance) in practice took place only to the degree necessary for preventing a violent upheaval against the system, not to the degree that would be ideal from the standpoint of most individuals. By putting control over the means of production in the hands of the whole populace in common, they contended, a socialist system could in a single stroke see to the optimal use of resources to meet people's real needs, whether of public or private goods, taking fully into account the problems of externalities, and preventing macroeconomic imbalances from arising in the first place by the appropriate application of advanced economic planning. The contrast between the massive unemployment and economic dislocation marking the capitalist economies during the Great Depression of the 1930s and the successful execution of a crash industrialization program in the Soviet Union during the same period helped to convince socialists of the merits of their argument.

But things turned out quite differently than planned. As a witness to the rapid scientific progress of the industrial revolution, it seemed obvious to Karl Marx that if human intellect were brought to bear on the problem of coordinating the use of an economy's resources, society could then improve upon the resource allocation of an economy without planning. Hindsight shows that Marx grossly underestimated the complexity of planning an economy, as did his collaborator Friedrich Engels, who remarked that the problem of economic planning is one of "administration only." That, essentially, was the mindset under which the first centrally planned economy was brought into existence in 1928 under the rule of Soviet dictator Josef Stalin.[7] And the Soviet economy did score initial gains in output. The rapid industrial progress in the early decades of the Soviet economy seemed to provide proof, to many a Third World nationalist and some First World labor organizers, that a state-run economy offers superior features. Indeed, as late as the 1960s, some Western leaders viewed the contest between the Communist and capitalist systems as one of economic might versus political freedom — as if the economic advantages of the Soviet system were incontestable![8]

Within mainstream economics, a quiet debate had brewed for some years about the feasibility of a centrally planned system. One group of economists had argued that the efficient allocation of a society's resources was impossible without the guidance offered by market prices. A second group had argued on the contrary that planners could identify an efficient allocation of resources by means of equation systems embodying the standard efficiency criteria of neoclassical economics. The first group, led by the Austrian economists Mises and Hayek, suggested that such computations were beyond the practical capabilities of any real-world planning bureaucracy, and that the difficulty of merely collecting all the information that would be required to solve a complex economy's planning problem would overwhelm the planners. These economists also emphasized that the conditions underlying the resource allocation process are constantly evolving, and that only a market economy can in practice approach efficiency in production. In such an economy, prices can adjust freely, thus providing instantaneous signals regarding the changes that are taking place unbeknownst to any one individual. Moreover, entrepreneurs motivated by the potential profits to be earned can respond quickly to opportunities without awaiting the outcome of new bureaucratic deliberations, thus quickly and flexibly channeling resources where their results are most valued.

Interestingly, in the years after Mises and Hayek made their arguments, theoretical economics found their case unconvincing. Some economists

7. The Bolshevik faction of the Russian Communist movement under V. I. Lenin seized power in 1917, but it is Lenin's successor who is usually credited with initiating the fully centralized economy.

8. The notion of Soviet economic superiority derived from the country's high rates of economic growth, rather than any absolute advantage, which never did appear. Close students of the Soviet economy were already aware of the problems to be discussed below.

proved theorems showing that a hypothetical economy in which the resource allocation problem is solved centrally by an omniscient and benevolent planner is equivalent to one in which the same problem is addressed through the decentralized profit seeking of entrepreneurs responding to price signals. Even if it were the case that real planning bureaucracies would have to make do with much cruder methods than were used in the theoretical models, their methods could be improved upon in the future by adopting more of the features of those models and by making use of the emerging capabilities of high-speed computers. The idea that the market could be imitated by planners using incomplete information was also advanced by a number of economists, including Oskar Lange and Abba Lerner.

Today, most economists look back on the writings of Mises and Hayek as remarkably farsighted. The high growth of early Soviet decades was achieved from a low industrial base, utilizing resources previously underemployed in a semifeudal economy, harnessing powers of command heightened by an iron fist of terror, and emphasizing the production of simple producer goods such as steel beams and cement. Although the Soviets were also able to achieve some advances when they concentrated resources on such sectors as military and space technology, the overall rate of growth of their economy flagged when more advanced stages of the industrialization process were reached, when underutilized resource pools (peasant labor, untapped mineral deposits) began to dry up, when terror was partially relaxed, and when the focus shifted to raising the material living standard of the population. In an age of more sophisticated technologies, the economy strained to update the industrial methods it had borrowed from depression-era Germany and America, and it proved unable to come close to the quality and cost improvements in Western and east Asian computer, consumer electronics, and other industries. It is probably fair to say that the system was ultimately rejected by the peoples subjected to it, not because they preferred freedom to economic growth, but because they were convinced that it held advantages in neither of these respects.

Mises and Hayek correctly saw that the burden of gathering the information needed to devise instructions to the thousands of enterprises that compose a complex economy would overwhelm planners. Unable to develop plans covering the production of each of the hundreds of thousands of distinguishable products of a modern industrial economy, Soviet planners dealt with coarsely aggregated categories — numbers of nails, rather than numbers of each of several hundred varieties of nails, for instance. This left the details of production to be worked out at lower levels. Offered incentives to meet production targets in the form of bonuses and promotion opportunities, enterprise managers naturally focused on output quantity and neglected quality, product assortment, spare parts and service, and innovation. Rather than work hard to find cheaper and better production methods, the incentive system prompted managers to improve the skills and connections with which they could bargain for more inputs, making output targets easier to achieve. Bonus schemes also failed to elicit full output potential, since managers were reluctant to suggest, by producing more today, that their factories could be given still more ambitious targets in the future.

Another element of the planning problem, and one that Mises and Hayek probably underestimated, is the problem of motivating managers to provide planners with true information. As Hayek had emphasized, central planning would need to make use of information that is scattered at local sites of production throughout an economy. Hayek focused on the difficulties associated with the sheer volume of such information, suggesting that the superiority of a decentralized system lies in the fact that most of this information need not be gathered into one place, since dispersed resource owners and entrepreneurs can simply act on what they know while responding to the information about "global" conditions that is automatically encapsulated and communicated through the price mechanism. In addition to having a need for information gathering and for an associated planning bureaucracy that is not required under capitalism, however, central planning faced the further difficulty that enterprise managers would have had incentives to deceive their superiors whenever doing so would help them to obtain more easily achieved targets. Thus, managers would systematically tend to understate their production capacities and overstate their need for inputs, leading to a chronic bias toward inefficient production techniques.

Of course, planners were not entirely unaware of the interest of managers in being assigned more inputs and less ambitious output targets. To counter it, they set targets at levels more demanding than those argued for by managers, and they left few resources in reserve to meet unforeseen production requirements. After all, any slack seemed intolerable in a system bent on maximum economic growth. Only capitalism is wasteful of resources! But the ambitiousness of plans strengthened managers' incentives to hide their production capacities, and the caution with which the state doled out input supplies encouraged them to hoard whatever inputs they could get hold of. The unreliability of input supplies from the state also led enterprises to undertake such activities as the building of their own equipment under their own roof, at low efficiency, so as to reduce reliance on and hence vulnerability to the caprices of the planning bureaucracy. Studies showed that relatively more machines were built by their ultimate users, and relatively fewer by specialized machine makers, in the Soviet Union than in the United States. Economies of specialization are likely to have been forfeited.

It may be true that the supply system could have been made more reliable, and planning might have been rendered more efficient, through improvements in the planning process itself. Although planners were forced to work with crude accounting methods when the process began in the Soviet Union in 1928, they might later have drawn on various mathematical programming and planning techniques developed to formulate more sophisticated plans. What prevented them from doing this was in part the fact that economics and its use in the policy arena in the Soviet Union was dominated by forms of Marxism that put ideology ahead of science, and that were averse to the use of methods developed in the West. But it seems almost certain that the Mises-Hayek critique of the difficulty of dynamic adjustment to changing circumstances under central planning would have held much truth even under maximum openness to such methods and with the most effective use of available computing power. Even today, it remains impossible to solve complex systems of hundreds of thousands of simultaneous nonlinear equations with existing computing capacities. And even if this problem could be solved, the machinery of instantaneous data collection, processing, and plan dissemination would use real resources for which there is no parallel requirement in a market system. The hurdle of providing incentives to give accurate information would also remain.

In sum, while the coordination of a complex economy by planning instead of markets is conceptually feasible, it faces the major real-world problems of (a) massive information collection, (b) a computationally demanding planning process, (c) the difficulty of motivating managers to provide accurate information, (d) the difficulty of motivating managers to strive for cost reduction, technological improvements, quality, and appropriate product assortments, parts, and service, and (e) the wasteful and underspecializing responses of managers to an unreliable, bureaucratic input supply system.

All of this abstracts from social and political dimensions that may well have been more important than economic performance in determining the system's fate. Those dimensions also interacted in complex ways with the economic aspects of the planning problem. No Soviet-type system was established by a democratic process, and in every case state planning went hand in hand with totalitarian control of political life, education, and culture by political oligarchies having little basis for claiming to rule in the name of their nations' people. Motivation at all levels would have been affected by the chilling political atmosphere and the arbitrary power held by superiors. Political checks on the free flow of ideas and information could not have advanced technical progress. And instead of serving as a vehicle for governing the economy in the service of the "true needs of the people," the state-controlled economy was put at the service of the maintenance of internal power. Planners showed little concern about pollution and other costs of production, for example, registering a far worse environmental record than did capitalist industrial economies. Last but not least, the perceived need to compete with capitalist countries both directly, in military and geopolitical domains, and indirectly, by demonstrating achievements with respect to growth of output, severely warped the goals of the system.

As measured by economic growth alone, the Soviet system does not appear to have performed badly in its early decades. A representative estimate suggests that output in the Soviet Union grew at 5.5 percent per year during 1928–66, compared with a rate of 3.3 percent during roughly the same period in the United States, and 3.3 percent in Russia itself during the four decades prior to the Bolshevik seizure of power.[9] Similarly, after negligible growth of per capita income and low rates of capital formation in the century before Communist rule in China, that country devoted more than 20 percent of its national product to investment and achieved growth rates of 6 percent or more, or about 4.5 percent in per capita terms, from 1952 to 1978. Soviet output growth exceeded that of

9. Gregory and Stuart, 1998, pp. 230 and 225. The first two growth rates are for GNP, with the period covered for the United States being 1929–69. The pre-Communist estimate for Soviet Russia is for the years 1885–1913.

the United States in the decades of the 1950s, 1960s, and 1970s, dropping below it only in the 1980s.[10] But the Soviet Union and other centrally planned economies grew mainly through the tapping of underutilized resources or their transfer from low productivity agriculture into higher productivity industry, not by increasing the productivity of inputs by way of technological advances. This spelled trouble, as the pools of untapped resources gradually dried up or could not be squeezed further because of inefficient organizational structures.

Figures on output growth in the Soviet-type economies need to be viewed cautiously, because output was heavily skewed toward producer goods like steel that contributed little to the welfare of the people, and the quality and assortment of consumer goods were low. Comparisons with more developed economies need also to be treated with care: growth, when the conditions for its occurrence are present, tends to be more rapid at lower than at higher levels of development. What the historical comparisons reveal clearly, however, is that the initial introductions of the central planning system in Russia and China led to periods of industrialization at paces significantly faster than those countries had been experiencing prior to the accession of the Communists to power. But growth eventually stalled in Russia, and it accelerated still more in China after that country's adoption of market-oriented economic reforms.

OTHER ECONOMIC SYSTEMS

So far, we have discussed only two sharply contrasting systems. The opposing social philosophies supporting these systems dominated much debate of the past century, and the economic, political, and military contest between the camps embracing them was a central part of that century's drama. But the two by no means cover the spectrum of actual economies. Indeed, the pure capitalist market economy is an abstraction not seen in practice, a model only imperfectly descriptive of any of several real-world economies. For their part, models of socialism also vary enormously, with some self-styled socialists even viewing that term as inapplicable to the Soviet system.[11] The form of planned socialism that de-

10. Gregory and Stuart, 1999, pp. 374–75.

11. The terms "centrally planned socialism" or "centrally planned economy" were used above because the term "socialism" has no universally agreed-upon defi-

veloped in Russia metamorphosed into other forms before its eventual demise. For a more complete overview of the diverse forms of economy, we consider some of these variants of capitalism, socialism, and other forms of economic organization in the following sections.

Variants of Capitalism

We can classify as capitalist all those economies in which most resources are owned privately, most prices are freely determined by the parties to exchange, the market is the main mechanism connecting consumers and producers, and labor is inalienable from the worker. Under this heading belong a broad spectrum of economies, from the relatively laissez-faire systems of nineteenth-century Britain or post–World War II Hong Kong, to the elaborate welfare states of contemporary Western Europe, as well as the economy of postwar Japan, with its powerful government-industry partnership and massive industrial conglomerates. Much but not all of the variation concerns the roles that governments play in capitalist economies. Even state ownership of some industrial firms or sectors has played a role in some countries having mainly private enterprises and market economic coordination.

During most of the period since World War II, the government of France has owned about 20 percent of that country's productive assets. Government ownership has at times been important in the United Kingdom, Germany, and other countries, but it has always had little role in the United States and Sweden. State ownership was in some cases intended to give the government strategic leverage over the economy or influence over sectors perceived to be of central importance to its growth and prosperity, for instance some national airlines and research ventures. It has also come about through happenstance, as when France's government confiscated the properties of Nazi collaborators or Nationalist China those of Japanese owners.[12]

The "welfare state," a dimension of the capitalist economy present in all of the most industrialized countries today, involves a major government

---

nition. Although it usually refers to a system in which most means of production are controlled by the state or by relatively large collectivities of individuals, it is sometimes interpreted differently, for instance as a philosophy of egalitarianism, or of the control of wealth by the community.

12. The last-mentioned factor helps account for the surprising fact that the Chinese government already owned a hefty share of the country's industry when the Communists came to power in 1949.

role in determining the distribution of income through taxation and spending. At least some taxes, such as those on personal earnings, are by intent progressive, meaning that those with higher incomes pay not only a larger absolute amount but also a higher proportion of their earnings to the government. There are also sharply progressive taxes on bequests, although the intended effect is often undercut by loopholes. The government supplements the incomes of low-wage earners, supplies public insurance to those who lose their jobs, and provides payments to retirees, along with a variety of other programs, sometimes including publicly funded health care. These programs and policies may be considered a response to the concern discussed earlier that while unfettered capitalism may be the best alternative approach for instilling dynamism and efficiency in production and resource allocation, it does not guarantee socially acceptable distributive outcomes. Alternatively, the welfare state has been argued to arise because the forms of insurance that it offers are feasible only when coverage is made universal, for reasons economists refer to as problems of "adverse selection."

When we speak of amending an "unacceptable" distribution of income (or consumption or wealth), "unacceptable" can be understood either as a moral term or as having mainly pragmatic reference to questions of social and political stability, or both. In his book on the welfare state, economist Nicholas Barr suggests that "the German government under Bismarck . . . created a broad system of social insurance" (the ancestor of the modern welfare state) "largely as a counter to socialist agitation," and that "the scheme was investigated by [British prime minister David] Lloyd George, and had a major influence on the form of the [British] National Insurance Act of 1911."[13] The architects of West Germany's postwar economic system built on this tradition in their concept of the "social market economy."

Barr, however, prefers the insurance-based explanation of public support for the welfare state. The key idea is that there is a failure of ordinary markets because, were private insurance companies to offer coverage for the possible loss of a job, for instance, they would have more applications from those who privately know their chances of job loss to be high. Since the insurance company would not have access to as much information about personal particulars and circumstances as would its applicants, it

---

13. Barr, 1987, p. 15.

would have to raise the rates charged as the applicant pool became more biased toward likely job losers. "Adverse selection" is said to operate because poor prospects differentially self-select into the system. The higher prices required to insure these poorer prospects would make the insurance unattractive to those with more modest probabilities of job loss, who would then opt out of coverage. A private market equilibrium would therefore involve only very expensive insurance policies taken out by a few people with high chances of job loss. Those with modest or low chances of job loss and those with high chances of job loss who are unable to afford the very high rates would be squeezed out of such a system. A universal unemployment insurance scheme operated by government could insure everyone at a lower cost, on average, because it is not subject to this "adverse selection" problem.[14]

The extent of intervention varied in the mid-1990s from the relatively modest level of the United States, which devoted about 12 percent of its gross domestic product to government health, housing, social security, and welfare programs, to the high levels of the Netherlands and Sweden, which spent 33 and 28 percent, respectively, of their GDPs on such programs.[15] Large social welfare programs need not imply a government role in the *production* sector: in Sweden, for example, state ownership of industry never exceeded 1 percent of assets, which is why comparative economists typically resist the tendency of some social commentators to label Sweden's economy as "socialist."[16] Even the state-funded services in

14. Mandating universal coverage but letting people choose among private insurance providers can achieve much the same effect. None of this is to say that public insurance is without problems of its own. All insurance schemes generate problems of "moral hazard," which means that people who are insured against a certain risk have less incentive to take measures to prevent the occurrences in question. Overly generous unemployment coverage, for example, could make workers more willing to take actions that risk their being fired, thus leading not only to a higher incidence of unemployment but also to poorer average performance on the job! Insofar as people do not act exclusively on self-interest but are at least sometimes motivated by social concerns or ethics, the long-run viability of public welfare policies may require a better understanding of how a work ethic, personal responsibility, and empathy for the less fortunate can be sustained in the face of moral hazard's eroding influence.

15. World Bank, *World Development Report, 1997*, p. 241. Figures are for 1995.

16. Although state ownership per se was low, the economic systems of Sweden, Norway, and a few other countries, especially prior to the 1990s, were often seen as

question may be supplied by private, nonprofit, or other nongovernmental providers, as is commonly the case in Sweden.

The Swedish case exemplifies the extent of social welfare benefits at their most generous. In Sweden in the 1980s, either parent was guaranteed leave at 90 percent of pay for six months upon the birth of a child, up to sixty days per year for the illness of a child, and any additional three months before the child's eighth birthday. Parents received child allowances of about four hundred dollars per year, and primary, secondary, and university education was free. Virtually all medical costs were covered by the government, which also paid all dental fees to age sixteen, and 50 percent of those fees thereafter. Workers enjoyed a guaranteed five weeks of paid leave per year on top of twelve paid holidays, 90 percent of pay in the event of illness, and generous pensions at retirement. These programs were largely financed by payroll taxes, which added about one-third to employers' payroll costs, by highly progressive personal income taxes, and by taxes on corporate profits.[17] Sweden and other countries halted the growth of their tax rates and welfare benefits in the mid-1980s for reasons discussed further in Chapter 5, but both taxes and benefits remain much higher in these countries than in others like the United States and Japan.

Almost every modern capitalist economy departs from the pure "hands off" philosophy of laissez-faire where macroeconomic policy is concerned. Rather than let the market alone solve problems of unemployment and inflation, that is, governments have attempted to help, for instance by spending more and taxing less during recessions, and by tightening money and credit supply during economic booms. Keynesian-type fiscal policies were instituted by Sweden's government during the depression era, even before Keynes wrote. During the postwar era, governments of major industrial nations have often attempted to stimulate their econo-

going beyond "welfare state capitalism" toward a distinctive system termed "social democracy." In this system, federations of employers and labor unions bargained over wage increases at the national level, the union federations advocated narrowing of wage differentials across industries and even skill levels, and government, unions, and employers worked successfully to maintain very high levels of employment (with unemployment rates running below 2 percent in most years). A discussion of the system's features and an analysis of its decline is provided in Moene and Wallerstein, 1993.

17. The information here is taken from Zimbalist, Sherman, and Brown, 1989.

mies out of recessions by increasing government spending, the latest example being that of Japan in the late 1990s. They have similarly attempted to reduce inflation by reducing spending and budget deficits. Throughout the 1990s, the U.S. Federal Reserve Board adjusted the rate at which funds were lent to banks, making money more expensive in order to counter anticipated inflation, and lowering rates when inflation expectations were low.

Some governments have gone further than using fiscal and monetary policies to affect aggregate economic activity and inflation rates. They have attempted to influence economic decisions at the sectoral or firm level through approaches known as "indicative planning" and "industrial policy." France pioneered the indicative planning approach after the Second World War. Unlike the command planning of the Soviet Union, these plans were not binding orders to the economy's firms. Indicative planners attempted to project trends in the economy and provide inducements for firms in selected sectors to expand or to contain expansion in ways the planners believed would be conducive to overall growth, industrial modernization, a desirable regional distribution of development, or the achievement of other goals. The industrial policy of Japan used similar measures, as well as agreements between firms and government ministries, to influence the economy's progression from the exporting of textiles and other simple manufactures, in the immediate postwar years, to the production and exporting of automobiles, heavy machinery, and sophisticated electronics and other equipment in later decades. Interventions in credit markets, exchange rate management, and controls over imports also contributed to Japan's state-encouraged program of private enterprise growth.[18]

Capitalist countries also vary in their economic organization at the microeconomic level. American and British corporations get much of their financing by issuing equity shares traded on stock markets, whereas German and Japanese companies have tended to rely more heavily on bank credit, with investment banks playing leading roles in financing and in company oversight. In Japan, companies attached to a common "main bank" form strategically linked groups called *keiretsu*. Sweden has a consumer-owned cooperative sector handling about 5 percent of the

18. A classic work on French planning is Cohen, 1977. An influential study of the Japanese system is Johnson, 1982.

country's national product, while Italy has worker-owned production co-operatives accounting for 2–3 percent of nonagricultural employment. Producer cooperatives play major roles in agriculture, transportation, and other sectors in Israel, and the main labor federation there owned companies that employed about 10 percent of the industrial workforce in the 1980s and larger shares still in earlier years.

Variants of Socialism

Socialist economies also admit of numerous variants. In the nineteenth century, social thinkers including Robert Owen, Charles Fourier, and Count Henri de St. Simon drew up blueprints for what they felt would be more ideal societies based on social equality and mutual responsibility.[19] Some of them, or their followers, established socialist experimental communities, which have had counterparts throughout the past two centuries. Karl Marx dubbed Owen and the others "utopian" and "unscientific," contending that the socialism of the future would arise by the workings of objective historical laws that could be neither predicted with precision nor altered by human will. However, he noted approvingly instances of functioning worker cooperatives, and in a famous letter to German socialists known as the "Critique of the Gotha Program," he himself predicted that society would one day attain a state of pure communism, in which "society [can] inscribe on its banner: From each according to his ability, to each according to his needs!"[20]

In this letter Marx also argued that a communist society would not be attained without a long transition through a less radical "socialist" period, in which inequalities would persist because the worker would be paid in accordance with his or her labor. A more capable worker would accordingly earn more than a less capable one, and these differences would be accentuated because some workers would have to support more dependents than others due to differences in household demographic structures. This distinction between "communism" (identified with "to each according to his needs") and "socialism" (identified with "to each according to his work") was embraced by Marxist states like the Soviet Union and China. Stalin, for example, would denounce egalitarianism, and the leftist faction in China's Communist Party, led by the wife of Mao Zedong, was crit-

19. A good discussion is found in the chapter "The Visions of the Utopian Socialists," in Heilbroner, 1999.
20. Tucker, ed., *The Marx-Engels Reader*, p. 531.

icized by more orthodox party members for trying to achieve communism prematurely.

Not all who were attracted to communist or communal ideals were inclined to wait, however. One example arose when thousands of young eastern European Jews who were inspired by the ideals both of socialism and of settlement in Palestine established kibbutz communities, where agricultural production was undertaken collectively and consumption was strictly communal and egalitarian. These communities prospered for more than three generations, becoming the homes and workplaces of more than one hundred thousand citizens of modern Israel, and retaining their radical egalitarian characters into the late 1980s. In the early decades of the Jewish state, they formed a dynamic force not only for national defense but also for increasing productivity and technological progress.[21]

The kibbutzim and other ultra-egalitarian communities have practiced communism on a local scale while operating within market economies, to which they sold their products and from which they obtained many of their needs. Where Communist parties captured state power, as in the Soviet Union, they typically declared "full communism" to be only a long-term objective. A partial exception was China under its first Communist leader, Mao Zedong, who showed his penchant for egalitarianism by promoting "people's communes" in which initially there was communal work on a massive scale and free supply of food in communal mess halls. The mass mobilization and poor management of these involuntary and regimented communes contributed to short-run economic collapse and mass starvation — more than twenty million are believed to have died, history's largest single famine. Although Mao would try again with his Cultural Revolution, in which he heaped praise upon an egalitarian farm production brigade called Dazhai, soon after his death his followers were purged by more pragmatic members of the Chinese Communist Party. Another ultra-left Communist was the Cambodian leader Pol Pot, whose desire to eliminate all traces of "bourgeois" thinking was taken to the extreme of mass executions of the educated and evacuations of cities, leading to the deaths of as many as a third of that country's people. Idealists like Owen and the founders of the kibbutzim would have shrunk with horror at such uses of terror and execution in the name of egalitarianism.

Unlike left-socialists like Mao and Pol Pot, those wanting to modify

21. See Barkai, 1977.

Soviet-type socialism usually advocated making more, not less, use of elements of capitalist economies such as markets, material incentives, and competition. These pragmatic reformers, who were to be found in every Communist state by the 1950s, argued that it was impossible for a government to run a vibrant economy by issuing and enforcing detailed instructions to tens of thousands of enterprises. By judging enterprise managers on narrow criteria such as output, they said, the planners might induce increases in quantities produced, but they could not induce appropriate cost cutting, technological improvements, or even a better mix of products. The reformers argued that firms strive for efficiency in market economies because there is a high correlation between efficiency — a broad concept that would be reflected in productivity, innovation, and quality — and profits, the bottom line sought by owners and hence managers of enterprises. Their reform proposals therefore called for giving managers more discretion and control over state enterprises, and encouraging them to strive for profitability.

But there was a fundamental problem with profit-focused reforms in Soviet-type economies. Profit, which is the difference between product price and product cost, will not lead to appropriate resource allocation if product and input prices are set arbitrarily by planners. One product might be profitable, another unprofitable, simply because of their differing arbitrary configurations of input and output prices. A possible response would be to adjust prices administratively with the express aim that they should signal social valuations and scarcities. But realistic reformers felt that this too lay beyond the limited capabilities of the planners. In the end, planned socialist countries undertaking economic reforms therefore allowed their state-owned enterprises to engage in some transactions at partially freed prices. Enterprises were to seek profits, rather than simply meet state output targets. As an inducement to profit seeking, individual state enterprises could retain a portion of their profits for distribution as bonuses, and for purposes of expansion. Smaller enterprises were permitted to be privately operated, in agriculture, retailing, and other sectors.[22]

22. Agriculture had been a somewhat special case throughout the histories of these economies, with most farming done by collective farms in the Soviet Union, China, and most Eastern European countries, but by private farmers in Poland and Hungary.

In Hungary of the 1960s through the 1980s and later in China, whose post-Mao reformers took a similar direction, such changes produced favorable results from the standpoint of improved quality and variety of consumer goods. But in Hungary at least, they did not improve measured economic growth, a fact that Hungarian economist Janos Kornai attributed to the continued availability of government assistance to state enterprises.[23] The Soviet Union and several Eastern European countries were experimenting with similar reforms when their leaders were overtaken by political events at the end of the 1980s. China, on the other hand, remained under Communist rule and eventually went beyond its forerunner in "market socialism," Hungary, with apparently superior results.[24] Although in the early 1990s state-owned enterprises still produced over 45 percent of industrial output, with enterprises owned by local rural governments and urban collectives producing another 38 percent, most prices were already then determined by market forces, and the country became a major consumer goods exporter, as well as attracting a large inflow of foreign investment. Between 1980 and the late 1990s, China's economy registered unprecedented output growth rates averaging around 9 percent, exceeding those of virtually all other countries.[25]

Cooperatives and Worker Self-Management

From the 1950s through the 1980s, Communist-ruled Yugoslavia (which at the time included the later independent nations of Slovenia, Croatia, Macedonia, and Bosnia) adopted a system resembling that of the Hun-

23. According to Kornai's theory of the "soft budget constraint," the managers of state firms in reforming socialist systems could benefit from high profits, but they suffered little from large losses, because the government would routinely bail out loss-makers with subsidies, tax forgiveness, low-price inputs, and other devices. Firms accordingly saw no reason not to attempt risky expansions, so the economies in question came to be marked by insatiable appetites for investment goods and production inputs, but low growth of real output and hence of consumer incomes and demand. (See, for instance, Kornai's overview of the entire Communist economic experience in Kornai, 1992.)

24. The term "market socialism" has a variety of uses, generally referring to a combination of market coordination with either state ownership of property or a mechanism for sustaining a highly equal distribution of property. For a history of the term and recent proposals, see Bardhan and Roemer, eds., 1993.

25. Botswana grew faster than China in the 1980s but not in the 1990s. World Bank, *World Development Report, 1997*, pp. 234–35.

garian socialist reforms, in which state enterprises operated with a degree of autonomy from government planners. A significant difference was that in Yugoslavia, formal control of a state enterprise was in principle in the hands of its workers. The workers elected an enterprise council, and the council in turn chose the enterprise director. Thus Yugoslavia became, on paper at least, the first worker-run national economy, although its form of worker self-management was mixed with public ownership and Communist Party dictatorship. The Yugoslav economy registered an "economic miracle" of rapid growth in the 1960s, but afterward it encountered structural crises resembling those of other middle-income countries in the 1970s and '80s (see Chapter 4 on import substitution industrialization). Observers noted that worker control of enterprises was limited by local Communist authorities, and that the economy was lacking in financial discipline, with a mass of inter-enterprise debts piled atop political loans from insolvent state banks.

Despite its failings, the Yugoslav experiment captured the imagination of economic systems analysts, whose attentions turned to the concept of an economy of worker-run firms. Western economists constructed theoretical models in which firms, in all other respects depicted as in standard microeconomics textbooks, are run by their workers but interact in free markets. The predictions of these models varied depending on their assumptions. In particular, a hypothetical competitive economy composed of "labor-managed firms" will, in the long run, behave identically to a competitive economy in which firms are owned by capitalists. This is the case even though the labor-managed firms are assumed to have the goal of making as much profit per worker as possible, while the capitalist firms are assumed to seek maximum profits, plain and simple.[26] But in the shorter run, or when competition is imperfect — for instance because unemployed workers may be unable to set up new firms quickly — the hypothetical labor-managed economy exhibits some peculiarities, including sometimes reducing rather than increasing output in response to increasing product demand. Empirical studies were also done, looking at such examples as worker-owned plywood cooperatives in Washington state in the U.S., industrial and other cooperatives in Spain, Italy, and

26. It makes no difference whether a firm tries to maximize total profit or profit per worker if the number of workers is a given, but if the number of workers is variable the two goals can lead to different behaviors.

France, and companies instituting profit-sharing, employee-stock own-ership plans and works councils in North America and Europe. The results of these studies suggested that when workers share in profits and participate in decision making, productivity is frequently enhanced, in part because the need for supervisors goes down.[27]

Why worker-controlled firms are relatively rare, despite this produc-tivity advantage, is an interesting economic puzzle. One hypothesis is that collective decision making is more difficult when those in charge are the workers, who may differ among themselves about ideal pay differentials, working conditions, and other dimensions of job design, rather than in-vestors, who are likely to have similar preferences focused on the returns from their investments. Others suggest historical accident and inertia. Probably the most frequently espoused hypothesis on why people work for others rather than being collectively self-employed, in modern econo-mies, is that most workers prefer a relatively fixed payment for work and are unable or unwilling to bear the risks of ownership.[28]

Although pure cases of worker-owned firms, such as the plywood co-operatives, the kibbutzim, or Spain's Mondragon cooperatives (which include among them a major exporter of consumer durables), are a tiny segment of the production sectors of the major market economies, to look at such cases alone is to seriously understate the importance of worker participation. Many law and medical firms are partnerships with long probation periods for potential partners and with hired nonprofessional staff. Most universities are faculty governed to an important degree. Ger-many's co-determination laws require that employees elect half the mem-bers of the company boards of large firms, and similar legislation exists in a number of other European countries. Large Japanese firms cultivate long-term employment relations with their employees, who receive a substantial part of their compensation in the form of bonuses. In those firms, teamwork is emphasized, workers are involved in production deci-

27. Some of the data are summarized in Blinder, ed., 1990, and Bonin, Jones, and Putterman, 1993.

28. To be sure, many workers in richer countries have sufficient wealth to finance joint firm ownership. But the problem could be that owning the firms they work in entails the added risk of putting all their eggs in one basket (that is, forgoing portfolio diversification). Increasing wealth and ability to bear risk could explain the recent trend toward employee share ownership and profit sharing in high technol-ogy firms.

sions on the shop floor, and managerial decision making is said to be more collegial than in American companies. Profit-sharing and employee-ownership schemes have enjoyed considerable popularity in the United States and other countries in recent decades, and several major airline, rental car, and other companies were substantially employee owned as of the late 1990s. The prospect of workplace democracy as an element of a more ideal economy is discussed further in chapters 5 and 6.

TRANSITIONS FROM SOCIALISM

The end of the 1980s marked a watershed for the then Communist world. Partial reforms in the Soviet Union had begun to open up that country's political system, but parallel economic reforms failed to halt a rapid deterioration in economic performance. When political unrest in several countries was met by indications that the Soviet Union was no longer resolved to impose its preferences upon the region, a wave of popular revolts swept the Communist parties throughout Eastern Europe from power. The Communists abandoned power in the Soviet Union itself two years later after an attempt by political hard-liners to reverse the tide of reform met with a show of popular resistance. With the demise of the Soviet Union, its constituent republics became independent states. In China, economic reforms were not accompanied by political change, and a student-led democratization movement in 1989 ended with a crackdown by Communist hard-liners and the ousting of leading reformers from the government. But efforts to backtrack on economic reforms exacerbated a temporary economic slowdown, and the country's leaders soon resumed the course of reforms in the early 1990s, all the while retaining a tight grip on their power over the state. By the end of the 1990s, markets played as important a role in resource allocation in nominally Communist China as in post-Communist Russia. Indeed, China's markets may, ironically, have been far more effective than Russia's, which were notorious for their crime and corruption.

In retrospect, it seems unsurprising that countries emerging from decades of Communist rule would attempt to emulate Western capitalism. Several Eastern European countries had begun experimenting with market-oriented reforms, and a halfway house between socialism and capitalism could conceivably have been pursued under a post-Communist regime. In Poland, for instance, the Solidarity labor movement, which played a prominent role in bringing down the government and inspiring resistance to the Communists in neighboring countries, had, prior to coming to power, embraced a platform favoring worker control of enterprises. Yet popular sentiment in the post-Communist countries leaned toward the view that only Western-style capitalism held the promise of generating the kind of economic prosperity that the West enjoyed and the East longed for. "No more experiments" was an oft-stated slogan. With Western governments and Western-dominated multilateral institutions, such as the International Monetary Fund, offering assistance to those willing to adopt sweeping packages of reforms, the post-Communist governments of Eastern Europe and the former Soviet Union began to move quickly away from systems of state ownership and state-controlled resource allocation.

The nations in transition from socialism faced significant problems, however. Due to the old Soviet-type development strategy, their industrial structures were lopsidedly oriented toward the production of producer rather than consumer goods. Their international trade had been arranged through a political cooperation pact, rather than on the basis of mutual commercial benefit. The cessation of orchestrated intrabloc trade, the opening of borders to imports of superior quality, and the relaxation of governmental support for outmoded industries brought on a rapid and massive decline in industrial output. In 1991, real GDP is estimated to have declined by an average of 10 percent in Eastern Europe and 12 percent in the Commonwealth of Independent States (successor to the USSR). Further declines in the CIS's output in 1992, '93, and '94 were 19, 13, and 17 percent, respectively, but a smaller decline in Eastern European output in 1992 was followed by slowly resuming growth the next year. Employment had also been negatively affected, dropping in each consecutive year from 1989 to 1993, for total declines of 21, 16, and 31 percent, respectively, in Hungary, Poland, and Bulgaria. The region also suffered from high inflation, which exceeded 30 percent throughout Eastern Europe in 1991 and a far more severe 1,000 percent in countries of the CIS in 1992.[29] There was also a decline in life expectancy, especially in Russia, where it fell a full six years, from seventy in 1989 to sixty-four in

29. Data from statistical tables published in various issues of *Economics of Transition*, a journal of the European Bank for Reconstruction and Development.

1995, with especially great impact among men in their prime working years. Rough estimates put the national product of Russia at the end of the 1990s at about half what it had been at the beginning.

Post-Communist governments moved to privatize state enterprises in a number of different ways. In the absence of developed domestic capital markets and wealthy private industrialists, and in view of political distaste for selloffs to foreign firms at what might have to be bargain-basement prices, several governments let citizens buy low-cost shares of investment trusts or mutual funds that would manage former state assets during the early years of adjustment. An alternative approach was that of "insider privatization," in which a state firm was purchased at a low price by incumbent management groups and workers. Employee buyouts were especially common in Russia, although observers concluded that managers were the real power brokers and beneficiaries of these transactions. Government subsidies to the state-owned sector were slashed in Poland, the Czech Republic, and other countries, with encouraging effects for financial discipline. But such subsidies declined much more slowly in other countries, including Russia. Russia's privatization seemed incomplete in view of continued state aid to some formerly state-owned enterprises, and failure to privatize others.

With output down and populations suffering from declining living standards in early post-Communist Europe, some began to wonder whether the more gradual transition that brought China such high growth rates in the same period might not have been the wiser path to take. As mentioned, China's economy scored high rates of growth in the twenty years following the adoption of market-oriented reforms in 1978. Although China's reforms were more incremental and although the Communist Party retained a firm grip on power there, the share of industrial output attributable to state-owned firms dropped from 78 percent at the beginning of that period to 26 percent at the end, and the roles of state enterprises in agriculture and services were far smaller. The decline in state output share occurred not because of privatization of state-owned firms or (at least initially) because of any contraction in their scales, but because firms of other types simply grew more rapidly. Rural industrial enterprises, the most important of which initially were those run by the former communes (now called townships) and production brigades (now called villages), were the fastest growing sector in the economy. Fully private firms and joint ventures with foreign firms grew rapidly after 1992.

Agricultural land remained collective property, but by 1983 it was contracted out to households in a kind of fixed-rent tenancy that made possible unprecedented rates of output growth.

In contrast to the former Soviet bloc, the initial decades of reform in China resembled a "win-win" situation in which there were few if any outright losers. Some considered the Chinese case to have shown the relative unimportance of property rights, as compared with material incentives and market competition. Others wondered whether China should not be viewed as a showcase of "market socialism." China's output had doubled in the 1990s after doubling in the '80s as well, even as Russia, trying to shake off Communism, had seen a halving of its output. And China had become both a magnet for foreign investment and an export powerhouse, dimensions in which the Russian transition remained a dismal failure. By the late 1990s, however, China itself was saddled with loss-making state firms, the smaller of which it began to privatize rapidly. "Win-win" reform appeared to be over as substantial numbers of state-sector employees found themselves unemployed in China's old "rust belt" cities.

One clear feature of the reforms in ex-Communist countries was the absence of any real prospect of the restoration of state socialism. Although a political backlash prompted by the high economic costs of transition brought former Communists back to power in Poland and several other countries, the parties in question had switched to positions resembling those of Western European social democrats, including support for continued market reforms. One could thus foresee a long-term process of transition that would gradually eliminate vestiges of the old Communist systems. Indeed, a few countries with adequate commercial and industrial traditions — such as the Czech Republic — seemed poised to shrug off fairly quickly what had for them been only some forty years of centralized control, and to become modern European economies. Others though, including Russia itself, were growing sluggishly at best and were beset by enormous problems of crime, social tension, and instability.

One of the most important lessons of the early transition experience has been that concerning the importance of economic institutions. Advice that the economies in transition needed only to decontrol prices and to privatize enterprises in order to enjoy the benefits of a market economy came under criticism as economists increasingly realized the importance of building up institutional structures, such as those of credit and equity markets. The need for experience in organizing firms and markets was also recognized more and more. Insofar as the transition experience warned against viewing an economy in too abstract a fashion, it substantially strengthened the position of those who criticized neo-classical economics for a lack of attention to institutions and other real-world details (Chapter 2).

CONCLUSION

Economics textbooks often treat the market economy as a given. In this chapter we've seen that industrial economies can be organized in a number of different ways. The example of the now defunct Soviet type of central planning, for instance, shows that a complex, specialized economy can in principle exist without private ownership of resources and without the coordination of exchange by markets. The Soviets succeeded in industrializing a relatively agrarian economy and for a time challenged Western countries in military might and space exploration. However, their economy was unable to generate more widespread technical dynamism, and it grew by raising input use, not by increasing productivity. While the large firms of market economies experience similar problems of collecting and transmitting information, motivating managers to reveal that information to their superiors, and inducing sub-units to pursue relevant goals with appropriate vigor, centrally planned systems suffer avoidable inefficiency because they impose a bureaucratic structure on an entire economy without letting bureaucratic and decentralized forms compete.

The portrayal of economic-system choice as one between all plan and all market is a false dichotomy. While few go as far as the Soviets did toward the elimination of markets, their economy was nonetheless a monetized one in which prices mediated the relationship between government, workers, and farmers, with some free and still more black markets existing on the margins of the official economy. Market economies, for their part, include not only managerial resource allocation in large corporations, but also important state roles. And capitalist nations vary in prevalence of state-owned enterprises (high in France, low in the United States and Sweden), extent of income redistribution (high in Sweden and Germany, lower in the U.S. and Japan), financing patterns (emphasis on stock markets in the U.S., on bank credit in Japan and Germany), and the practice of indicative planning (France) or industrial policy (Japan). Capitalist economies also include instances of workplace democracy in the forms of producer cooperatives, co-determination, and employee-owned firms.

Some socialist experiments have been more radical than the Soviet one, seeking more equality of income and less reliance on material incentives. But older planned economies sought to improve performance by emulating market decentralization and encouraging enterprises to pursue profits. The gradual transformation of what was once an ultra-left version of the Soviet model into a market economy in China after 1978 offers interesting contrasts to the more abrupt transitions that followed the collapse of Communist rule in Central and Eastern Europe in 1989.

Experience has done more than could a thousand volumes of theory to show the advantages market competition offers in meeting a society's economic needs. Whether more modest state planning (say, industrial policy) can improve upon the unfettered market, how far redistribution can go before unacceptably dampening incentives for work and investment, and whether more extensive employee participation in management and ownership will improve economic outcomes are among the important questions still actively debated, and upon which light can be shed by an economic-systems approach. Some of these questions will also be revisited from slightly different standpoints in the chapters that remain.

REFERENCES

Bardhan, Pranab, and John Roemer, eds., 1993, *Market Socialism: The Current Debate*. New York: Oxford University Press.

Barkai, Haim, 1977, *Growth Patterns of the Kibbutz Economy*. New York: North-Holland.

Barr, Nicholas, 1987, *The Economics of the Welfare State*. Stanford: Stanford University Press.

Blinder, Alan, ed., 1990, *Paying for Productivity: A Look at the Evidence*. Washington, D.C.: The Brookings Institution.

Bonin, John, Derek Jones, and Louis Putterman, 1993, "Theoretical and Empirical Research on Producers' Cooperatives: Will Ever the Twain Meet?" *Journal of Economic Literature* 31:1290–1320.

Cheng, Chu-yuan, 1982, *China's Economic Development: Growth and Structural Change*. Boulder, Colo.: Westview.

Cohen, Stephen, 1977, *Modern Capitalist Planning: The French Model*. Berkeley: University of California Press.

Durant, Will and Ariel, 1968, *The Lessons of History*. New York: Simon and Schuster.

Galbraith, John Kenneth, 1978, *The New Industrial State*, 3d ed. Boston: Houghton Mifflin.

Gregory, Paul, and Robert Stuart, 1998, *Russian and Soviet Economic Performance and Structure*, 6th ed. Reading, Mass.: Addison-Wesley.

Gregory, Paul, and Robert Stuart, 1999, *Comparative Economic Systems*, 6th ed. Boston: Houghton Mifflin.

Heilbroner, Robert, 1999, *The Worldly Philosophers: The Lives, Times, and Ideas of the Great Economic Thinkers*, 7th ed. New York: Touchstone.

Johnson, Chalmers, 1982, *MITI and the Japanese Miracle: The Growth of Industrial Policy, 1925–1975*. Stanford: Stanford University Press.

Kornai, Janos, 1992, *The Socialist System: The Political Economy of Communism*. Princeton: Princeton University Press.

Mill, John Stuart, 1929 [1848], *Principles of Political Economy with Some of Their Applications to Social Philosophy*, ed. Sir W. J. Ashley. London: Longmans, Green.

Moene, Karl, and Michael Wallerstein, 1993, "What's Wrong with Social Democracy," pp. 219–35 in Pranab Bardhan and John Roemer, eds., *Market Socialism: The Current Debate*. New York: Oxford University Press.

Putterman, Louis, 1993, *Continuity and Change in China's Rural Development: Collective and Reform Eras in Perspective*. New York: Oxford University Press.

Rothbard, Murray, 1973, *For a New Liberty*. New York: Macmillan.

Zimbalist, Andrew, Howard Sherman, and Stuart Brown, 1989, *Comparing Economic Systems: A Political-Economic Approach*. San Diego: Harcourt Brace Jovanovich.

SUGGESTIONS FOR FURTHER READING

Angresano, James, 1996, *Comparative Economics*, 2d ed. Upper Saddle River, N.J.: Prentice Hall.

Atkinson, Anthony, 1993, *Alternatives to Capitalism: The Economics of Partnership*. New York: St. Martin's.

Berliner, Joseph, 1999, *The Economics of the Good Society*. Malden, Mass.: Blackwell.

Bornstein, Morris, 1994, *Comparative Economics: Models and Cases*, 7th ed. Burr Ridge, Ill.: Richard D. Irwin.

Bradley, Keith, and Alan Gelb, 1983, *Cooperation at Work: The Mondragon Experience*. London: Heinemann.

Clague, Christopher, ed., 1997, *Institutions and Economic Development: Growth and Governance in Less-Developed and Post-Socialist Countries*. Baltimore: Johns Hopkins University Press.

Coase, Ronald, 1937, "The Nature of the Firm," *Economica* 4:386–405, reprinted in Louis Putterman and Randall Kroszner, eds., *The Economic Nature of the Firm: A Reader*, 2d ed. New York: Cambridge University Press, 1996.

Elster, Jon, and Karl Moene, 1989, *Alternatives to Capitalism*. Cambridge: Cambridge University Press.

Friedman, Milton, 1982, *Capitalism and Freedom*. Chicago: University of Chicago Press.

Friedman, Milton, and Rose Friedman, 1981, *Free to Choose: A Personal Statement*. New York: Avon.

Hayek, Friedrich A. von, 1948, "The Use of Knowledge in Society," *American Economic Review* 35:519–30, reprinted in abridged form in Louis Putterman and Randall Kroszner, eds., *The Economic Nature of the Firm: A Reader*, 2d ed. New York: Cambridge University Press, 1996.

Hayek, Friedrich A. von, 1960, *The Constitution of Liberty*. Chicago: University of Chicago Press.

Kuttner, Robert, 1997, *Everything for Sale: The Virtues and Limits of Markets*. New York: Knopf.

Nove, Alec, 1969, *An Economic History of the U.S.S.R.* London: Allen Lane.

Nove, Alec, 1983, *The Economics of Feasible Socialism*. London: George Allen & Unwin.

Putterman, Louis, 1990, *Division of Labor and Welfare: An Introduction to Economic Systems*. Oxford: Oxford University Press.

Riskin, Carl, 1987, *China's Political Economy: The Quest for Development Since 1949*. New York: Oxford University Press.

Roemer, John, 1994, *A Future for Socialism*. Cambridge: Harvard University Press.

Schumpeter, Joseph, 1950, *Capitalism, Socialism, and Democracy*, 3d ed. New York: Harper.

Stiglitz, Joseph, 1994, *Whither Socialism?* Cambridge: MIT Press.

Tucker, Robert, 1978, *The Marx-Engels Reader*, 2d ed. New York: Norton.

Vanek, Jaroslav, ed., 1975, *Self-Management: Economic Liberation of Man*. Harmondsworth, England: Penguin.

Williamson, Oliver, 1985, *The Economic Institutions of Capitalism: Firms, Markets, Relational Contracting*. New York: Free Press.

World Bank, 1996, *World Development Report: From Plan to Market*. New York: Oxford University Press.

THE LESS
DEVELOPED
WORLD
AND ITS
PROSPECTS

In the 13,000 years since the end of the last Ice Age, some parts of the world developed literate industrial societies with metal tools, other parts developed only nonliterate farming societies, and still others retained societies of hunter-gatherers with stone tools. Those historical inequalities have cast long shadows on the modern world, because the literate societies with metal tools have conquered or exterminated the other societies.
—Jared Diamond,
    Guns, Germs, and Steel

The experience of the past fifty years has demonstrated that development is possible, but not inevitable. While a few countries have succeeded in rapid economic growth, narrowing the gap between themselves and the more advanced countries, and bringing millions of their citizens out of poverty, many more countries have actually seen that gap grow and poverty increase. . . . Strategies of the past, even when they have been assiduously followed, have not guaranteed success. Furthermore, many of the most successful countries (representing the largest part of growth within the low income countries) have not actually followed the "recommended" strategies, but have carved out paths of their own.
—Joseph Stiglitz,
    chief economist of the World Bank

Sunrise over a barren landscape in central Tanzania, east Africa. It's a warm, dry day, a week after the end of the rainy season. Four women are making their way on bare feet over brown earth here and there covered with patches of wispy grasses and weeds. Each carries a large load of firewood on her head. They began their trek in the blackness before dawn in order to reach the forest four miles from their village and return home to cook a breakfast of cassava root and cooking bananas. Two of the women have sleeping infants strapped to their backs. It will be a long day in which they will feed scraps to the chickens and goats they are raising in the yards next to their thatch-covered mud-and-wattle houses, see school-aged children off to the village school, put in several hours of work on their plots of maize, walk again for drinking water, and prepare dinners of gruel and beans. The only break in this routine will be to attend the funeral party of a fellow villager who died last week after a short bout with AIDS, from which death comes quickly here as there is no affordable treatment. One of the women will help to supply this party with home-brewed millet beer, earning a little money from the family of the deceased. All will enjoy the opportunity to do a little drinking and gossiping.

The standard of living in their village has changed little on balance in recent years. On the upside, more children are receiving an education, more houses are being built with baked mud bricks instead of mud and wattle, and there has been a rise in awareness of sanitation and health issues, leading to the digging of improved latrines, the regular boiling of cooking water, and a consequent decline in infant and child mortality rates. More goods are available in the kiosk in the next village and in the market of the nearest town, now that the government has lifted price controls and constraints on imports. But prices on the few goods that they buy, basic things like matches, soap, and tea, have increased several fold. The government-sponsored farm cooperative that used to supply subsidized fertilizer and purchase villagers' surplus crops has ceased operations, and no one in the village can now afford fertilizer, although it is increasingly needed because the natural fertility of the soil is declining. Also on the downside are the increasing scarcity of firewood and hence the longer distances that must be walked to procure it, the low prices that private traders who reach the village offer for crops, and the AIDS epidemic.

One struggles to identify signs of modern economic development in the scene above. They are present if one looks hard enough: in the tins, jerrycans, and gunny sacks that the villagers use to collect water and store grain; in the battery-powered radio that will play music during the afternoon funeral party. They are present more generally as well, in the spread of ideas on health and sanitation, and in the influence of national policy changes. But the nearest paved road passes more than a hundred kilometers from this village, the nearest farmer rich enough to own a tractor lives fifteen kilometers away. Compare this with the following scene, where rich and poor rub elbows in a partly modern, partly ancient city, as happens frequently elsewhere in the developing world.

The scene in this case is Connaught Place in the heart of Delhi, India. An important commercial area with land prices among the highest in the developing world, the area's profile has undergone a radical change since the beginning of the liberalization efforts undertaken by the government. The piazzas are now lined with shops selling famous American and Western brand-name products. Advertisements by Levi's, Sony, General Motors, Compaq, and MacDonald's occupy the billboards. The nouveau-riche talk on their cell phones as they mill around or wait in line to get a table at the newly opened Pizza Hut or TGI Friday. And as they wait, they are accosted by an unending stream of street hawkers peddling goods, shoeshine boys, teenage mothers carrying starving babies, and limbless beggars.

In Delhi and other Indian cities, despite the increasing prosperity for some, the inescapable fact of poverty continues to show its face everywhere. On major streets, it is normal to find camel carts and BMWs waiting side by side for a red light to turn green. In southern Delhi, the rich live in their almost palatial mansions, surrounded by high walls atop which shards of glass are fixed in cement, with private security guards also standing by. The fear of robberies and thefts by pavement dwellers who live just next to the mansions is no doubt an important motivation for such elaborate protective measures. These "posh areas with rows of splendid buildings, spacious roads and glittering lights [coexist] with hovels and bustees [slums] with little or no sanitation and minimal amenities of living. . . . [There,] the narrow lanes . . . are half given over to open drains whose moldering contents are then carried past every door-step. . . . In the grimmest of these hovels, a fully grown man can neither stand nor lie at full length but families of five or six can be commonly found jammed together on the damp earth floors. Only in the best [of them] are there solid walls between one of these domiciles . . . and the next. Normally there are just a few boards, a strip of corrugated iron on a curtain fashioned from old gunny sack. Having seen such [slums], you discard the snap judgment that the pavement-dwellers must be [the] worst-off people in the world."[1]

1. The slum quotations are from Ray, 1986, pp. 101, 103, and include a quotation by Ray of a description of the slums of an Indian city by Joseph Lelyveld.

In Chapter 1, we saw that the evolution of the industrial market econo-mies as we find them today in the United States and Canada, Western Europe, Japan, and a few other nations was a process that began in earnest in the eighteenth century, that took place at different paces in different countries, and that has still not been completed in much of the world. Today, then, as throughout history, the bulk of the world's people still live under conditions far different from those that now characterize the in-dustrialized nations. Many live in shelters lacking the running water, electricity, and labor-saving amenities that are taken for granted in the industrialized countries. (Such shelters offer little protection from natu-ral disaster, so pictures of them turn up now and then in our newspapers or on our TV screens, demolished by earthquake, hurricane, or flood.) They survive on diets dominated by staple foods like rice, corn, cassava, or yams. They go without the conveniences of refrigeration, prepared foods, supermarkets, and microwave ovens. They support themselves by physical labor, producing or earning only enough to command basic nec-essities. Many endure chronically poor health, with a substantial number of their children failing to reach adulthood and with those who do often aging rapidly. Only a minority receive more than a few years of education, and family responsibilities and work begin at early ages.

In one sense, it is the state of economic development and prosperity, not that of underdevelopment and poverty, that is the new story of our times. Still, modern underdevelopment too is distinctive, because for the first time it occurs in a world in which very rich countries exist alongside very poor ones, with all kinds of ramifications for both. For much of the world, slipping behind technologically in the centuries leading up to about A.D. 1500 turned out to mean condemnation to generations of colo-nial rule. Even when the age of colonization ended in the mid–twentieth century, the legacy of underdevelopment continued to translate into posi-tions of inferior status in a world in which economic and other policies were most heavily influenced by the rich countries and by organizations and markets dominated by them. Poverty for many has become all the more severe due to overcrowding, depleting of woodlands, lack of clean water and other natural resources, and the need for cash to obtain man-ufactured goods and other things increasingly viewed as necessities, in-cluding medicine and school uniforms. The tragedy of poverty may be multiplied, at least subjectively, when the shack sits in the shadow of high-rise towers, or when the wealth of the world's "haves" is easily observable on movie screens or television sets. Is poverty not avoidable, now that the productive technologies that permit high living standards in the North are in principle available to all?

A recent study estimates that in 1870, the ratio of average incomes in the world's richest and poorest countries was around 8.7 to 1. By 1960, the gap had widened to 38.5 to 1, and by 1990, it stood at 45.2 to 1.[2] In this chapter we will ask why, instead of improving quickly once exposed to modern knowledge and world markets, the economic conditions of many in the developing world have improved only slowly, or have sometimes even worsened. Why has this been the case in spite of the fact that economic theory predicts that capital will have its highest return where it is most scarce, and that it will flow to where its return is highest (implying a torrent of investment funds heading to the poor countries of the South)? Why is it so despite enormous improvements in the availability of health care and education throughout the world? Will the economic development that has occurred in more prosperous nations soon be repeated elsewhere, as has happened already in a few countries including Korea and Taiwan? Or will these prove to be rare exceptions? Could competition from more and more nations with massive combined populations make high standards of living unsustainable in parts of the world that are *already* economically developed? Will world industrialization prove impossible because of environmental and resource constraints?

GROWTH AND DEVELOPMENT

The term "modern economic growth" describes the process by which an economy dominated by agricultural activities carried on with low levels of capital per laborer is transformed into one in which industry and other non-farm activities produce the bulk of society's output using high levels of capital per worker. Implicit in this definition of growth are two additional facts. First, along with the changes in economic structure, output per capita and thus average incomes increase significantly over their previous levels. Second, as growth occurs, the proportion of output that is produced for consumption by the producer goes down while the share produced for consumption by others, or for the production of other

2. These numbers are ratios of the average income of a citizen of the richest country to the average income of a citizen of the poorest country, from Pritchett, 1997.

goods, goes up. This second phenomenon can be summarized by the term "commercialization." Along with it comes an increasing monetization of economic life — that is, the increasing use of money.

Economic growth means an improvement in average productivity and income, not just an increase in gross output, which might result from population growth only. But even though we restrict use of the term "growth" to instances in which average incomes rise, growth does not automatically imply an improvement in *everyone's* standard of living or quality of life. Economists sometimes reserve the term "economic development" for the kind of growth that translates into widespread improvements in well-being, growth in which a large majority of a country's people achieve gains in their material standard of living and in accompanying dimensions like health and literacy. Growth can occur *without* development if it increases the incomes of a small group without benefiting the large majority of a country's people.

Even when growth does translate into development, there may exist undesirable side effects, such as negative impacts on the cohesiveness of families and communities, disaffection with the nature of the available work, or a faster pace of life with less time for leisure. Our plan of attack in this chapter, however, will be to keep questions of quality of life separate from those of income, health, and skill improvement. Thus, the terms "economic growth" and "development" will be used, sometimes interchangeably, without implying a value judgment as to the overall change in human well-being. A generally favorable view of development may be justified in part because at very low standards of living it is almost always welcomed by those who experience it, whatever the complications it brings with it. Questions about the costs and benefits of the modern economic way of life are worth raising, but they will be deferred for discussion in Chapter 6.

A FEW STATISTICS

To get a sense of the dimensions of underdevelopment in large regions of the world today, it is helpful to look at a few statistics. There are a variety of useful indicators of underdevelopment and poverty, and even if no one of them is adequate to the task by itself, together they help us to appreciate what development and underdevelopment mean.

Gross national product measures the total value of production by a country's residents plus net receipts from nonresident sources. Divided by the total number of citizens, it gives a first crude indicator of the average income and hence standard of living. In 2000, the International Bank for Reconstruction and Development, better known as the World Bank, classified 63 countries with per capita GNP below $760 as low-income economies. With a combined population of 3.515 billion, these countries accounted for about 58.6 percent of world population and enjoyed an average per capita GNP of only $520. This income level was only 2 percent of the $25,510 on average enjoyed by people living in the 31 high-income countries with a combined population of 885 million people, comprising 14.8 percent of world population.

The conversion of income figures into dollars at official rates of exchange may cause some distortion, so an alternative indicator of gross domestic product (GDP) per capita at what is called Purchasing Power Parity (PPP) is sometimes used. GDP differs from GNP in that it includes the value of production by nonresidents but excludes net transfers from abroad. By giving more weight to goods that are locally consumed and produced, the PPP measure tends to reduce the apparent relative income gap between poor and rich countries. But even it shows a huge gap between the low-income economies, which averaged $2,130 of income per capita in PPP terms, and the high-income countries, which averaged $23,440.

The World Bank classification provides for two other groups of countries, labeled lower-middle income and upper-middle income. In 1998, the lower-middle-income countries with combined populations of 908 million people, or 15.1 percent of world population, had an average GNP per capita of $1,710, or an average GDP in PPP terms of $4,080. In the same year, the 38 upper-middle-income countries with combined populations of 588 million people, or 9.8 percent of world population, had an average GNP per capita of $4,860, or an average GDP in PPP terms of $7,830.[3]

A good measure of the degree of modernity of a contemporary economy is the share of the population that works in agriculture. In the high-

3. The population shares of the four groups of countries listed add up to less than 100 percent due to the existence of some countries not listed because they are very small or do not belong to the international institutional system that includes the World Bank.

INDICATORS OF ECONOMIC DEVELOPMENT LEVELS

	Low-income countries	Lower-middle-income countries	Upper-middle-income countries	High-income countries
Share of world population (%)	58.6	15.1	9.8	14.8
Per capita GNP ($)	520	1,710	4,860	25,510
Per capita GDP ($), in PPP terms	2,130	4,080	7,830	23,440
Labor force in agriculture (%)	65	57	26	5
Secondary-school enrollment (%)				
Female	49	57	—	92
Male	62	64	—	94
Life expectancy (years)	63	67	69	77
Persons per doctor	1,000	500	667	357

Source: World Bank, *World Development Report,* various years, and *World Development Indicators,* 1998

income economies, this share averaged only 5 percent in 1997, while in the low-income economies it was 65 percent. The lower- and upper-middle-income economies lay between these extremes with averages of 57 percent and 26 percent, respectively, of their working-age populations in agriculture.

Health and education levels also distinguish rich and poor countries. Although average years of schooling have been rising rapidly in all groups of countries, only 49 percent of females and 62 percent of males of the relevant age group were enrolled in secondary school in the low-income countries in 1995, versus 92 percent and 94 percent respectively in the high-income countries. Lower-middle-income countries averaged 57 percent of females and 64 percent of males of the relevant age group in secondary school.[4] The gap with respect to higher education is much larger: only 4 percent of students of the relevant age range were enrolled in higher education in the low-income countries in 1990, versus 52 percent in the high-income countries. An average of 45 percent of adult females and 24 percent of adult males were illiterate in the low-income

4. The corresponding numbers for the upper-middle-income countries were unavailable.

countries in 1995, versus 22 percent and 14 percent respectively in the middle-income countries as a whole, and less than 1 percent for both males and females in the high-income countries.

The most widely used indicators of health outcomes are life expectancy at birth and the proportion of infants who die in their first year (known as the infant mortality rate). The World Bank lists 17 low-income countries with a combined population of about 216 million people in which life expectancy was less than 50 years (the average among these is 45 years) in 1996. For the poor countries as a whole, life expectancy as of 1996 averaged 63 years, compared with 77 years for the high-income countries. For every 1,000 children born in the low-income countries, 88 do not reach their first birthday, and 131 their fifth birthday. In the high-income countries, the corresponding figures are 6 and 7 per thousand. In low-income countries, an average of 6.8 women are expected to die in childbirth for every 1,000 births, compared with 0.06 deaths per 1,000 in the high-income countries.

Poor health outcomes are associated with poor sanitation, poor access to safe drinking water, chronically poor nutrition, and limited availability of health services. Whereas in high-income countries there was one doctor for every 357 people in the 1990s, in low-income countries as a group there were almost three times that many people per doctor (1,000 people). Likewise, while the high-income countries had a hospital bed for every 128 persons, the poor countries had one hospital bed per 680 persons. Things could be much worse in specific cases. For instance, there were almost 24,000 persons per doctor in Angola and 20,000 in Nepal. The latter country had only one hospital bed per 4,115 people. Such comparisons understate the gap by failing to indicate differences in levels of training and availability of medicines and equipment.

All of these numbers represent averages for various countries. But most poor countries have some better-off individuals who have relatively high incomes, good access to health care, and so forth. This good news is also bad news, for it implies that some people in these countries are even poorer than the country averages suggest! For instance, the World Bank estimates that at least 1.1 billion people in the world, including half or more of the populations of some very poor countries but also significant numbers in some less poor ones, were surviving on less than one dollar a day at the end of the 1990s.[5] Tens of millions of children were severely

5. From *World Development Report, 1998–99*, tables 1 and 4.

malnourished, including 66 percent of children under five years of age in India and 40 percent of children five and under in Indonesia and Pakistan.[6] Access to safe drinking water is lacking for 72 percent of the population in Papua New Guinea, 57 percent in Zambia, 52 percent in Nepal, and 36 percent in Argentina, to give a few examples.[7]

Alas, these are only numbers, and they do little to convey the depth of daily hardship and all too frequent tragedy that most in the developed world, and even the better-off in some developing countries, can scarcely imagine. They fail to evoke the tens of millions who make homes out of old boxes and tin sheets in shantytowns in Latin America and Asia where sewage runs in open ditches. The millions upon millions of African women and girls who spend their days walking miles in bare feet to collect firewood and water, carrying these back to their villages atop their heads, often with babies strapped to their backs. The laborers in Bangladesh working long hours under a hot sun to earn a few coins with which to purchase medicine for a sick child. The families cramped into inadequately ventilated dwellings spending sweltering nights without benefit of a fan, much less an air conditioner, in countless tropical villages and cities. The tens of millions of cases of avoidable blindness caused by infection and malnutrition. The children of seven or eight working ten-hour days making carpets and matches in factories in India. The death of a child under five in any one of the roughly thirty-two thousand families in the developing world that will experience this loss on the day you read this.[8]

THE QUEST FOR DEVELOPMENT AND THE WORLD AFTER THE SECOND WORLD WAR

Like the modern phenomenon of underdevelopment in a highly interconnected world shared by rich nations and poor, the modern literature on economic development is relatively recent in its origins. Most of this writing dates from after the Second World War. By this time, as we've seen, Western Europe and its offshoots in North America and elsewhere had reached high levels of per capita income and productivity, although it had taken the war to spur their recovery from a lingering depression. Also

6. Ibid., Table 2.
7. Ibid., Table 7.
8. Based on the estimate that 11.6 million children under five died in developing countries in 1995. See Murray and Lopez, eds., 1996.

by this time, the economic modernization of the first industrial economies had been partially emulated in central, eastern, and southern Europe, in a sector of the South African economy, and in a few places in
Latin America. Japan was the only non-Western country to have significantly industrialized, bringing some of its acquired know-how to colonies
in northeast China, Korea, and Taiwan. England and other colonial powers had built railroads and port facilities in colonial possessions in India,
sub-Saharan Africa, Southeast Asia, and elsewhere, but labor-intensive
domestic manufacturing and handicrafts were often unable to compete
with imports in these countries.

Meanwhile, Russia and lands ruled by it had come under the control of
a totalitarian Communist Party in 1917, and under that control it had
experienced a considerable buildup of basic industry between 1928 and
1940. This strengthened Soviet Union had managed to check the eastward expansion of Nazi Germany, and after the war was able to dominate the countries of Eastern and Central Europe. The "First World" of
Western industrial states, marked by private property and markets in
their economic systems and democratic electoral mechanisms in their
political systems, faced the "Second World" of Communist states behind
its "Iron Curtain." The remainder of the world, consisting mostly of the
less industrialized regions of Asia, Africa, and Latin America, some of
them just now achieving or yet to achieve independence from European
colonial rule, became known collectively as the "Third World."

In that world, West and East competed for political influence and
economic access. With portions of the region, like Vietnam and China,
falling to the control of their own homegrown Communists, and with
Communist insurgencies springing up widely in Asia and Latin America,
it appeared critical to the West that the non-Communist Third World be
helped to experience the fruits of capitalism and economic development,
lest it too join the Communist camp. Meanwhile, Asian and later Latin
American and African countries under Communist or Marxist governments also strove to foster economic growth, to show the superiority of
their model. Thus was born the modern quest for economic development
in Asia, Latin America, and Africa. And it was in this setting that that
quest would be played out for the next four decades.

The view from the Third World itself was complex. Governments,
which laid down policies to promote development and articulated them
in ideology and rhetoric, were not necessarily representative of their

populations. In parts of Latin America, for instance, a long history of domination of indigenous and mixed-race peoples by peoples of mainly European descent lived on into the era of statehood that began in the nineteenth century. The landscape here varied from cosmopolitan areas like Buenos Aires and Santiago, which had taken some strides toward industrialization and resembled southern Europe in culture and demography, to semifeudal and agrarian regions, such as the coffee, sugarcane, and banana zones of Central America and Brazil.

Africa's first generation of post-independence leaders hailed from a tiny elite educated first in the continent's mission schools and subsequently in England, France, or elsewhere in Europe. Many of its second-generation leaders hailed from militaries trained only recently by the colonial powers. From the northern edge of the Sahara to South Africa, the continent had very little industry, and what modern commercial activity existed in its cities was often dominated by Lebanese, Arab, and Indian populations. Roads, railroads, and ports were sparse, were sited mainly to facilitate the exporting of minerals and plantation crops, and would prove difficult to maintain, much less expand, using indigenous capabilities and resources. While vast numbers of people in the hinterlands lived by subsistence-oriented agriculture and animal rearing, Africa's cash economy was to be a creature of the mines, export crops, and projects funded by foreign donors for decades to come.

Asia had its own stories. Japan, already considerably industrialized before the war, experienced a burst of modernizing growth in the next few decades surpassing any previously experienced in the world. South Korea and Taiwan, recently freed from Japanese colonization, would follow not far behind. These three countries began the postwar period with land reforms and massive investments in education allowing more of their populations to participate in the modernization process. They were led by strong governments with close ties to domestic businesses and Western militaries, and they faced limited political competition and weak labor movements.

East Asia was one story. Other parts of the continent held others. The Indian subcontinent, for example, was emerging from over a century of British rule with a growing, literate middle class, a free press, political democracy, and significant commercial and industrial sectors, but also with its vast majority still rural, and with hundreds of millions of rural and urban poor in extreme deprivation. Massive populations, poverty, and

varied economies, including ones dominated by export agriculture, plantations, and nascent industries, also marked much of Southeast Asia,
whose countries, however, were without India's democratic dimension.
Other pictures can be painted for western Asia, as for North Africa and
numerous Pacific nations as yet unmentioned. China will be discussed
below.

In poor countries, economic and political links to richer protectors or
benefactors often played a decisive role in shaping policy. Both for Third
World countries still linked to the First World camp and for those allying
themselves with Communism, the link to one camp or another was often
maintained as much for the assistance it gave elites in maintaining domestic political control as for the assistance it gave the country more broadly
in its struggle for economic development. It can be argued that many
Third World elites were more interested in enhancing their own positions of power and privilege than in seeking the general economic development of their societies.

Nonetheless, most Third World leaders desired that their countries
catch up economically with the industrialized West. What path would
lead most surely to this result? The answer to that question could not
have been entirely clear in the immediate aftermath of the war. Recall that
the United States, Britain, and many other Western countries had experienced severe economic slowdowns marked by massive unemployment
and widespread business failures in the decade before the war. By contrast, the Soviet Union had achieved rapid progress in industrialization
during the same period using the very different approach of state ownership of industry and state control of the economy. Add to this the natural
resentment against the West due to colonialism, and the apparent link
between capitalism and colonialism, and it is easy to understand why
some Third World elites gave the Soviet approach a second look. Other
countries, to be sure, had staunchly anti-Communist governments, and a
Soviet-type strategy was hardly under consideration in many of these,
whether because of the strong influence of the Catholic Church, the
entrenchment of local business interests, or close economic relations with
a former colonial power.

But even where state control along Soviet lines was ruled out, the idea
that a leading role in economic modernization had to be played by government was widely subscribed to. True, England had industrialized with
lip service to the philosophy of laissez-faire. All later developers, however,

including Germany, the United States, Russia, and Japan, had engaged in significant protection of their domestic industries. In virtually every case of successful growth, there had been strong government involvement in banking, infrastructure projects, and sometimes even the ownership of key industries. Free trade and a hands-off government seemed to be the favored policies of countries that were already rich and industrialized — the policies they wished upon those they would be glad to continue to dominate! Other countries, whose economies consisted mainly of peasant agriculture and a few export-oriented plantations and mines, could never really develop under such policies, because anyone foolish enough to try to satisfy local demand for manufactured goods by setting up production in the home economy would be unable to compete with imports from the already industrialized countries.

IMPORT SUBSTITUTION AND
ITS PITFALLS

Economists refer to the family of approaches to development adopted in most of the non-Communist Third World in the early postwar decades as "import substitution industrialization" (ISI). The aim of ISI was to industrialize by encouraging the production at home of manufactured goods that had been imported from the developed world in the past. The mechanism by which this would be done was limiting imports either by setting restrictions on the quantities that could be imported (quotas) or by levying special taxes on their importation (tariffs). Similar policies had been followed in the nineteenth century in countries like Germany and the United States, on the theory that a period of protection was necessary before an "infant industry" could mature and be competitive with imports from world industrial leaders. Despite the strong tradition of free-trade advocacy that characterizes their discipline, even some economists had argued that there was indeed a rationale for such protection, and that the policy worked successfully in some times and places.

One reason that strategists of development looked for alternatives to free trade is that many developing economies were highly dependent on exports of primary commodities, that is, of agricultural or mineral products whose production depended mainly on natural resources and unskilled labor. According to the theory of comparative advantage, a cornerstone of mainstream economics, if the ratio of the cost of producing automobiles to the cost of producing cocoa is higher in Ghana and lower in Britain, then both Ghana and Britain can benefit (each country can enjoy both more cocoa and more cars) by letting the former specialize in cocoa production, the latter in autos, and each trade with the other the product it produces relatively cheaply (see also the discussion in Chapter 1). In practice, however, modern economic development has always gone hand in hand with industrialization, so it is not clear that an economy can achieve modern growth by producing only cocoa and similar products. Moreover, primary product prices have tended to decline over time relative to those of manufactured goods, so that it takes more and more cocoa, rubber, coffee, tea, bananas, tin, or copper to buy an automobile, a truck, or a piece of heavy equipment. When an index of the prices of nonfuel primary commodities is divided by an index of the unit value of manufactured goods constructed so that their ratio is 100 in 1960, this ratio is found to have fallen from 131 in 1900, and it continues falling to reach 67 in 1986.[9] With more and more primary exports required to purchase each unit of manufactured goods, many policymakers believed that free trade per se could not be the way forward.

Although some economists believe that the temporary protection of industries from imports can sometimes be justified, at least two provisos must be met before the policy can hope to succeed. First, protection must be no greater than needed to foster domestic production, and it must be temporary, so that there is pressure on the infant firms to mature in technological and marketing sophistication, rather than indefinitely enjoying a comfortable protected life as inefficient, high-cost producers. Second, protection should be targeted at appropriate sectors and should not become part of a larger set of price-distorting policies that ultimately discourage capital formation, job creation, and a sustainable balance between imports and exports.

Postwar ISI in the developing world tended to fail these tests. First, the firms benefiting from import protection tended to become big players in the economy and therefore they often obtained the political clout with which they could safeguard the protection that assured them high profitability, instead of facing pressure to catch up with world production costs and standards as the prospect of lower tariffs and higher quotas

9. Based on the data in a review of this issue by Grilli and Yang, 1988.

came closer. The temporary nature required for successful infant industry protection was thus severely compromised.

Second, countries pursuing infant industry protection under ISI tended to pile on other policies that compromised the overall health of their economies. One of these was an overvalued exchange rate. As we have seen, specialization and exchange has been a driving force of rising productivity throughout modern economic history. When people face different relative costs of providing themselves with different wants, all can benefit from specializing in the production of the items each produces at comparatively lower cost and trading with one another. The only real difference between exchange in a local economy and trade across national borders is that the latter is usually between agents who use different currencies. But the imposition of a currency exchange barrier can make a big difference to the trading process. Unless the cross-border trade is a bartering of good for good — which is possible only when each party has exactly what the other party wants — the attractiveness of international trade to those involved depends on the terms at which one currency exchanges for the other.

In countries pursuing ISI, currency exchange was overseen by governments, and prescribed foreign exchange rates were set by them. Over time, domestic currencies tended to become "overvalued" in terms of convertible foreign currencies like the U.S. dollar. This meant that the peso, the rupee, and so on could be officially exchanged for more dollars than it would have fetched in a free market. The impact was that at the prescribed exchange rates imports were attractively cheap to local consumers while exports were unattractively expensive from foreign buyers' points of view. Since local consumers demanded lots of imports while foreign buyers demanded fewer exports or insisted on prices too low to encourage export production, a balance between foreign currency earned and foreign currency demanded could not be maintained.

Why would a government that was trying to discourage imports want its imports to be cheap? The answer is that overvaluation was not generally intended, but was rather an unintended consequence of various forces. First, to maintain balance between supply and demand for currency, exchange rates would have had to be periodically adjusted because widespread deficit spending in developing countries generated inflation, causing domestic prices to rise more rapidly than did prices in hard-currency industrial countries like the United States, the United

Kingdom, and Germany. The required adjustments amounted to devaluations — that is, increases in the price of foreign exchange. But these devaluations were resisted because, while helpful to protecting the product markets of targeted domestic industries, they made other imported goods more expensive; this included machinery, oil, and other inputs needed for import substitute industries and infrastructure projects, as well as some consumer goods lacking good domestic substitutes or highly valued by local elites. Misplaced economic nationalism and ambivalence about the promotion of the traditional, primary product exports also played their parts. When resisting suggestions from multilateral lending institutions that their currencies should be devalued, leaders often appealed to the popular belief that a decline in the relative value of their currency was an affront to national pride.

As a result of currency overvaluation, imports became relatively inexpensive, so even greater protection was required for the intended beneficiaries of ISI. But overvalued exchange rates had other serious effects. Since countries with overvalued exchange rates could not earn enough foreign currency to pay for the imports their people wanted, foreign currency had to be rationed in one way or another, a common method being to allow only licensed individuals and companies to import goods. With imports in short supply, domestic prices were bid up, and those with access to import licenses could earn windfall profits. Having contacts with the right officials thus became one of the best ways to get rich, crowding out the incentive to find new markets or cheaper ways to produce one's product. The lavishing of effort on licenses to earn windfalls, an activity economists dubbed "rent seeking," represented a massive waste of potential entrepreneurial talents.

In addition to the excessive incentive to import, the disincentive to export, and the incentive to engage in rent seeking, still other economic distortions were endemic in countries following the ISI strategy. One of these was an artificial cheapening of the cost of capital and a consequent disincentive to capital formation. ISI tended to be associated with a pattern that economists call "shallow finance," where interest rates are constrained by legal ceilings, discouraging people from making use of the financial intermediation services of banks and related institutions. Although low-cost borrowing would benefit the companies obtaining loans, there would be more demand for capital than could be met by the available supply, and its allocation would be governed more by political considerations and personal connections than by competition based on pro-spective rates of return. Meanwhile, private wealth tended to flow into bank accounts and other assets abroad, which could earn higher returns, thus further starving the economy of capital.

Some developing countries also promulgated regulations on for-mal employment, for instance employment taxes, which discouraged the creation of jobs in the modern sector. Artificially cheap capital and ex-pensive labor gave exactly the wrong signals to companies, which should have been saving on capital and favoring labor-intensive production methods. With agricultural earnings also depressed by low export prices and other "urban biased" policies,[10] and with population often growing rapidly, a massive flow of job seekers came into the cities. Frustrated in their search for modern-sector employment, most of them wound up in low-productivity self-employment and other operations too small to be monitored by government — the so-called informal sector.

ISI did spur the growth of industry in some countries that followed it, but it eventually came to be seen as a dead end. Consider a country that produces mainly agricultural products, construction materials, housing, and nontradable services (services like haircuts, meal preparation, or con-struction, which must be provided on the spot). Suppose that this country imports the bulk of its manufactured goods. Because the country has traditionally imported things like cloth, flashlights, and appliances, it has needed neither to manufacture *nor* to import the machinery and raw materials for making such goods. So when the country begins a campaign to substitute domestic production for imported manufactures, what it is trying to produce at home are mainly manufactured consumer goods. To the extent that it succeeds in this campaign, its economy will be meeting some of its need for these goods at home, but it will now find itself needing goods that it never required before, namely the materials and machinery that are needed to produce these consumer goods. The coun-try has not then lessened its dependence on imports, but has just switched from being an importer of consumer goods to being an importer of the equipment and materials with which to produce them. If high tariffs are levied on the targeted consumer goods, if the exchange rate is overvalued, and if tariffs are kept low on the equipment imports needed to build up the domestic industry, then there is a likelihood that equipment will

10. See Lipton, 1977.

appear misleadingly cheap. The developing economy will therefore copy the capital-intensive production methods used in developed countries where capital is less scarce, whereas it should try to conserve on capital and use more of its abundant resources, especially labor. At the same time, the foreign currency with which to buy the equipment becomes less and less available as export earnings fall off or fail to grow rapidly enough.

The final and in some ways fatal problem of ISI was foreign debt. We have seen that the inability to earn as much foreign exchange through exports as a country wants to spend on imports can lead to import restrictions that lead to a variety of problems. However, there is another short-run way that a country can cover its needs for foreign currency out of export earnings: it can buy goods on credit or with borrowed funds. Most practitioners of ISI ran up foreign debts to cover the shortfall between export earnings and import demand, a process that seemed justified as a way of paying for capital goods imports that would eventually pay for themselves. But in the 1970s, the availability of funds from Western banks awash with deposits from newly wealthy petroleum exporters enticed governments into borrowing to finance not only potentially self-funding investments but also consumption and deficit spending. Borrowing needs were further exacerbated by the flight of domestic capital abroad due to the "shallow finance" policies mentioned above. Outstanding debt owed to commercial banks by developing countries grew from $20 billion in 1970 to $335 billion in 1983.

The growth of foreign debt did not cause problems initially, as the borrowers were able to repay their loans by borrowing more money. But the cost of borrowing shot up when interest rates rose as a result of the tight money policies that rich countries adopted to put the brakes on their own rising inflation rates in the early 1980s. The same high energy prices that had contributed to industrial economies' inflation had also further increased the foreign exchange requirements of the many oil-importing developing countries, even as their exporting was made difficult by weak economies in the North. In Latin America, the stock of long-term debt reached 25 percent of GNP in 1980 and over 50 percent of GNP in the mid-1980s. Payments to service the debt ate up nearly half of all export earnings at the height of that decade's debt crisis.

The crisis came to a head in 1982 when Mexico declared a moratorium on the payment of interest on its foreign debt. Western governments and banks, the International Monetary Fund (IMF), and the governments of more than twenty separate less developed countries (LDCs) negotiated debt rescheduling packages affecting a total of over \$300 billion of debt repayments. Although a portion of the debt was written off as uncollectable, the banks lost far less in the crisis than did the people of the LDCs. From a net inflow of almost \$36 billion in 1981, the net flow of capital turned negative, reaching an outflow of \$35 billion going from poor to rich countries in 1987. Positive economic growth in the 1970s gave way to widespread economic contraction in the 1980s. Between 1980 and 1990, real per capita GDP dropped by 6 percent in Brazil, 7 percent in Mexico, 16 percent in Venezuela, and 20 percent in Argentina.[11]

Management of the debt crisis by developing-country governments typically entailed agreement with the IMF and World Bank on packages of policy reforms referred to as stabilization or structural adjustment programs. These reforms included devaluation of national currencies toward market-clearing exchange rates, sharp reductions in government spending, reduction of subsidies and tariff barriers, and removal of price controls. Government expenditures on social services were curtailed, and, in conjunction with declines in GDP and outflows of capital, poverty rose in many countries. For Latin America as a whole, the share of the population living in poverty is estimated to have risen from 45 percent to 53 percent in rural areas and from 17 percent to 22 percent in urban areas.[12] Poverty also increased in African countries experiencing negative economic growth in the late 1980s. At least one in-depth study of the incidence of structural adjustment programs in Africa, however, concludes that the reduction of exchange-rate overvaluation and of government expenditures necessitated by the economic crisis hit higher-income groups harder than it did the poor, partly because better-placed citizens had been capturing the economic rents from controlled markets.[13]

By the early 1980s, the intellectual underpinning of the ISI approach was beginning to be widely questioned, as the superior economic performances of the more outward-looking economies of East Asia began to attract the attention of both developing and developed worlds. Some Latin American economies, including Mexico and Brazil, were already increas-

11. Morley, 1995, p. 8.

12. Ibid., p. 44. For another discussion of economic reform and income distribution in Latin America, see Berry, ed., 1998.

13. See Sahn, Dorosh, and Younger, 1997.

ing their emphasis on exports when the debt crisis struck. Their reorienta-
tion was too slow and too late to ward off that crisis, which was in any case
partly due to the exogenous forces of oil price increases and to inflation
and recession in the North. Nevertheless, the crisis accelerated a trend
toward questioning the old policies. That trend was further strengthened
by a surge in the popularity of pro-market ideas in the Western economics
profession in the 1980s, and by the enormously greater leverage acquired
by First World and multilateral banks due to the less developed countries'
dire needs for financial help. By the late 1980s, the virtues of market-based
exchange rates, lower tariffs, higher domestic interest rates, and greater
fiscal balance were increasingly proclaimed in the South as well as in the
North. Although vestiges of ISI-type policies could still be seen in the
1990s, their blatant and energetic pursuit had clearly ended.

SOME CAPITALIST VARIANTS

Before turning to the new policies that came into vogue in the 1980s, we
will pause for a slightly less aggregated look at some of the countries of
the developing world, in this section looking at non-socialist countries, in
the next at socialist ones. The import substitution model has been used to
describe the development strategies of most countries of the non-socialist
developing world, but it was most directly developed to explain the policies of certain middle-income economies, especially in Latin America. It
is instructive to look at some examples from other regions.

One set of examples includes the nations of sub-Saharan Africa, the
boundaries of whose multiethnic societies were established little more
than a century ago with the continent's carving up by European powers,
especially France and Britain. Despite ethnic fragmentation, a dearth of
experienced and educated manpower, largely illiterate populations, and
poor transport and communications infrastructures, these countries were
viewed as highly promising candidates for economic growth upon gain-
ing independence in the 1960s. The balance between resources and population appeared more favorable than in Asia, and inequalities, racial
divides, and class conflicts were more muted than in Latin America. The
expectations were unfortunately mistaken.

As a group, the economies of sub-Saharan Africa recorded far worse
economic outcomes from 1966 to 1996 than did those of other regions.

Thus, while GDP per capita grew at an average rate of 1.9 percent per year in Asia and 1.4 percent per year in Latin America in this period, the comparable rate for the sub-Saharan African countries (excluding South Africa) was 0.6 percent. The longer trend can be decomposed into the early independence decade of the 1960s, which saw encouraging economic growth (2.72 percent per year from 1966–72), the era of oil shocks and deepening economic gloom from 1973 to 1985 (growth of 1.6 percent per year), and an era of reform and restructuring from 1986–96 that saw some countries reestablish positive growth (an average of 1.95 percent per year in the eight fastest-growing countries) but an overall negative regional average growth rate of –0.64 percent. In 1966, Africans had annual per capita incomes of about $550, versus $1,592 for Latin Americans and $3,003 for Asians. By 1996, the gap had widened as African incomes were still only $690, versus $2,184 for Latin Americans and $3,309 for Asians (all figures in constant U.S. dollars of 1987).[14]

The disappointing performance of so many African economies may in part have been due to problems similar to those of other inward-oriented LDCs. Exchange rates were overvalued, traditional exports especially of agricultural products thus stagnated or declined, and debt rapidly accumulated. Interest rates tended to be capped, discouraging capital formation while encouraging inappropriate pursuit of capital-intensive projects. The oil shocks of the 1970s exacerbated balance-of-payments problems for all but the few oil exporters, and those countries did a poor job of investing their oil revenues in economic diversification, instead allowing other sectors to atrophy. Declining terms of trade for primary products hit Africa's non-oil primary exporters hard.

But some factors distinguished Africa. Unlike Latin America, capital inflows were largely from government or multilateral agency to government, frequently on advantageous terms or in outright grants. Yet the weakness of Africa's economies and governments, and the size of these flows relative to national output, allowed much economic decision making to be aid driven. Indeed, the modern, monetized sector was often a kind of enclave composed of government, its foreign benefactors, and a

14. In the foregoing paragraph, regional averages are calculated weighting individual countries by their respective populations. Asia is defined as all countries in geographic Asia except Japan, Turkey, and Israel. Africa is defined as Africa south of the Sahara excluding South Africa.

smattering of firms, many owned by foreigners or nonindigenous minorities. Agriculture as a whole suffered from the setting of low prices by government purchasing monopolies, which, with their high implicit tax rates, compounded by exchange rate overvaluation, discouraged the exports of cocoa, coffee, and other crops that had been pillars of many of the region's economies and foundations for their rural "middle classes" in the late colonial era. Social expenditure had a pronounced urban bias, and the construction and upkeep of crucial transportation infrastructure was often neglected. Political problems compounded economic ones, with more than half the continent's countries affected by at least one coup in the early post-independence period. In the 1990s alone, seven countries accounting for 12 percent of the region's population suffered from civil wars with devastating economic as well as humanitarian consequences.

Many African countries arrived at the mid-1980s with punishing debt burdens, with the ratio of debt service to exports averaging 23.6 percent, and with six countries having ratios of over 40 percent. Because sub-Saharan Africa's economies were so poor, their combined external debt accounted for only 9 percent of that of the developing world as a whole. This, and their relative unimportance to the developed world's trade and foreign investment, meant that the continent's debt received little attention in the context of the overall debt crisis. Some of the debt was forgiven, and almost all was renegotiated, with most countries bowing to pressures to devalue their currencies and reduce government expenditure. Even so, the average ratio of debt to GNP in sub-Saharan Africa was still a high 42 percent in 1996, compared with 36 percent for Latin America and 27 percent for Asia.

Another interesting and important case is India, whose 984 million people as of 1998 fell only a little short of the combined populations of sub-Saharan Africa (559 million) and Latin America (490 million), accounting in its own right for some 20 percent of the developing world's people. After achieving independence in 1947 following 173 years of British rule and commencing the new era with a traumatic partition from Pakistan, this country established one of the few successful democratic regimes in the developing world, especially low-income economies. Although it started the period with a per capita income below the sub-Saharan African average, the country had larger educated and urban populations, better established traditions of commerce and manufacturing, zones of fertile farmland with intensive irrigated agricultural practices, and a better transport and communications infrastructure. Adopting a nationalist and anti-imperialist economic posture, it established some state-owned industry and heavily protected its manufacturing from competing imports. Like many African countries, its prices were not favorable to farming. Unlike those countries, though, there was much agricultural progress thanks to the new seed and fertilizer packages of the so-called Green Revolution. Also unlike those countries, however, there was a significant intensification of rural inequality, with vast numbers of landless peasants living in desperate poverty. Compared with Latin America, protectionism ran deeper in India but so did economic isolation, including a near total absence of reliance on foreign debt. Like other developing regions, the country began market-oriented restructuring in the 1980s, achieving some improvement in its economic fortunes. Per capita GDP grew at an average rate of 1.6 percent per year in the 1950s, '60s, and '70s, but the rate of growth rose to 3.5 percent per year between 1980 and 1996.

One last group to be mentioned here, and readily distinguished from the others, comprises the Middle Eastern countries that have attained considerable prosperity thanks to their oil revenues. By the end of the 1990s two of these, Kuwait and the United Arab Emirates, were included among the World Bank's high-income economies, with incomes that put them just behind the United Kingdom. Another two, Oman and Saudi Arabia, were ranked among the upper-middle-income economies, ahead of Malaysia and Brazil but somewhat behind Argentina and Greece. These economies obviously differed from other LDCs in that oil price increases were for them a positive rather than a negative shock. Indeed, dependence on oil revenues was such that per capita income actually fluctuated sharply across years, with negative growth rates being recorded during periods when oil prices declined. Overall, their problem was not debt but how to invest surplus funds and spread the benefits of oil revenues through a variety of public measures. Compared with the larger developing countries like India, Indonesia, or Pakistan, these countries are small, with three of the four having populations under three million, and the largest, Saudi Arabia, having nineteen million people in 1995. Their experience raised the interesting question of whether a windfall income that in large part preceded the modernization of human capital and infrastructure could be converted into a sustainable modern economy. The outlook may be favorable in those cases where the oil-to-population ratio is highest. How much oil revenues can contribute to the development of the region as a whole is a more difficult question whose answer remains to be seen.

THIRD WORLD SOCIALISM

As mentioned earlier, a number of Third World countries came under Communist or Marxist rule during the early postwar decades. And as would be expected, their economic paths were rather different from those of non-Communist LDCs. For instance, unlike countries pursuing ISI, Communist countries like China and Vietnam attempted to become self-sufficient in the production of both consumer goods and producer goods (including machinery). Indeed, like the Soviet Union before them, these countries were noteworthy for an emphasis on heavy industry that quickly made the output shares of sectors like machine building and steel exceed those of even the most industrialized economies. Also unlike countries pursuing ISI, they did not rely on altering market signals to producers, such as by raising tariffs to make domestic production of a good more profitable. Instead, producers were part of the government apparatus, and direct governmental control over the allocation of resources dictated which industries would expand at what rates. This meant that the direction of resources away from patterns of market advantage was accompanied by different kinds of costs — excessive materials use and poor incentives, for instance, but not rent seeking by businesses, lower capital formation, or capital flight.

Indeed, whereas some inward-oriented economies discouraged domestic saving by capping interest rates, countries with planned economies like China achieved high rates of saving despite almost total suppression of capital markets, because planners had the power to set the share of investment in national product. By manipulating wages and farm prices, they kept disposable incomes and hence consumption at the corresponding target levels. Finally, unlike countries pursuing ISI, foreign exchange considerations were relatively unimportant to them, because they followed the Soviet Union in treating trade as a purely subsidiary matter, and in arranging it largely through treaties with Communist allies, rather than by commercial means. In the 1950s, '60s, and '70s, China and countries with similar economies did not run up large debts to other countries, nor did they suffer mounting imbalances between imports and exports.

China, which by itself contained more than half the Communist world's population and nearly half of the population of the LDCs, was successful in following the Soviet Union's lead with respect to the rapid development of its heavy industry and the transformation of its economy to be both more industrialized and more self-sufficient. With adequate domestic energy supplies, and energy consumption still low, it was not much affected by the world oil price shocks. Also like the Soviet Union, however, the country found itself unable to modernize its production methods beyond rather basic levels — indeed, the Chinese in the 1970s were using large amounts of Soviet-designed equipment that had been based on that used in Western countries as early as the 1930s! By focusing attention on basic education and health care, and by distributing its modest supply of foodstuffs relatively equally, the country achieved respectable gains in literacy and dramatic increases in life expectancy. In 1978, life expectancy in China was sixty-five years (up from thirty-two in 1949), compared with only fifty-one in India and fifty-two in Indonesia.

The country's emphasis on heavy industry meant that material living standards remained quite basic, however, whereas neighboring countries like South Korea and Taiwan were beginning to enjoy the new consumer opulence of the West. From the 1950s through the late '70s, China also experienced periods of political turmoil as leftist advocates of a pure communism battled pragmatists and orthodox Stalinists putting a premium on economic construction. When China and Vietnam opened their borders to greater trade with the West and exposed their populations to the consumer culture of their neighbors in the early 1980s, the demand to emulate such countries made the call for economic reforms irreversible.[15]

Most smaller countries that attempted to emulate the Soviet model were far less successful than China. Without large domestic reserves of raw materials and energy, and lacking China's depth of experience with the operation of a large and powerful state, they could not well proceed

15. In fact, the momentum for reform probably began as much within the Communist leaderships as among the ordinary people. China's reformers, in particular, skillfully used mass exposure to outside consumer culture as a way to cripple the political hand of opponents who wanted to maintain Communist orthodoxy.

down the Soviet and Chinese path of heavy industrialization. Thus, Cuba remained dependent on sugar exports and Soviet assistance until the collapse of the Soviet Union in 1991, although, like China, it accomplished much in education and health compared with comparably developed neighbors. In 1991, for instance, life expectancy was seventy-six years in Cuba, and only 6 to 7 percent of adults were illiterate, whereas in other lower-middle-income countries the corresponding average figures were sixty-seven years and 26 percent.[16] African socialist economies like those of Mozambique, Angola, and Ethiopia, producing little or no agricultural surplus and having governments with limited experience in hands-on economic management, registered still worse results. Attempts at eclectic forms of socialism in regimes not directly linked to Soviet Communism, such as the short-lived socialist regimes in Chile, Peru, and Jamaica, or a longer-lived socialist government in Tanzania, also suffered from economic mismanagement or political destabilization. Owing to its greater comprehensiveness, the across-the-board industrialization strategy of the Soviet Union may have had short-run advantages over ISI in a large, well-endowed economy with a strong government, but those advantages stubbornly eluded smaller and more poorly endowed imitators.

THE NEWLY INDUSTRIALIZING COUNTRIES AND THE WINDS OF CHANGE

In the 1960s and '70s, when the Soviet model was still respectable in some quarters and ISI was being pursued in much of the Third World, it was common to hear the view that the developing countries were locked into a subordinate position in a world division of labor from which the only possible escape was government-led structural change. Thus, the "dependencia" school of thought on development, which was popular among Latin American intellectuals and in modified versions also among their African counterparts, argued that local elites with strong cultural and political links to the dominant classes in the "metropolitan countries" (the United States, those of Europe) caused them to pursue policies that were consistent with their own narrow interests rather than promote the eco-

16. World Bank, *World Development Report, 1993*, tables 1 and 1a.

nomic development of their nations. Even if genuinely nationalistic figures came into power, it was argued, they could not much improve the positions of their countries' economies in view of the domination of world
markets for raw materials by gigantic metropolitan corporations, and
control over international monetary and financial institutions by Western
banks and governments. The only hope for the less developed countries
lay in "de-linking" from the international capitalist system and pursuing a
policy of self-reliant development and state-led structural change — or,
others argued, of alignment with a friendly Communist power.[17]

Whereas such views were still common in the late 1970s, by the middle
of the 1980s an economic, political, and intellectual sea change had occurred. Even as much of Latin America and Africa faced stark economic
crises, development pessimists found themselves on the defensive in the
face of the dramatic successes of a few high-growth economies. Japan had
not only rebuilt its war-damaged industries but had risen to challenge
U.S. companies in such fields as automobiles and consumer electronics.
While Japan itself had long since ceased to be counted as a "developing
economy," the more striking news was that two regions once occupied by
it (Taiwan and South Korea), and two small former (Singapore) or current (Hong Kong) British colonies, were now following in its footsteps.
And by the late 1980s, neighboring countries, especially Thailand, Malaysia, and Indonesia, as well as the coastal provinces of a now-reforming
China, which border on the same region, showed signs of joining in this
unprecedented spurt of industrialization. Some Latin American countries
that took early steps to emulate them — Chile, for instance, and later
Mexico — also showed signs of improved industrial growth. The rise of
East Asia did more than shake the confidence of American industrialists
and speed the end of Communism in the eastern bloc and its rapid meta-
morphosis in China and Vietnam. It also altered perceptions about what
is possible and desirable with respect to economic growth in developing
countries quite generally.

The annual growth rate of per capita output in Great Britain between
1820 and 1870 had been about 1.2 percent, that of the United States from
1870 to 1913 about 1.8 percent, and that of the Soviet Union about 5
percent a year at its peak in the 1930s. Japan's successful industrialization

17. Readings in the "dependencia" school and related views are found in Wilber,
ed., 1984.

drive between 1870 and 1913 produced an average growth rate of 1.4 percent per year. Following slower average growth of 0.9 percent during the intervening period, which included two world wars, Japan had resumed the process of economic modernization, achieving an unprecedented rate of growth in output per capita of roughly 8 percent per year between 1950 and 1973.[18] By the mid-1960s, Japan was regarded as the only non-Western country to have successfully joined the industrialized world. What was to be the "next generation" of fast-growing Asian economies — South Korea, Taiwan, Hong Kong, and Singapore — were still regarded as middle-income developing countries, not distinguished from others such as Mexico or the Philippines.

Between 1965 and 1988, however, these countries grew rapidly, with GNP per capita rising at annual rates above 6 percent in every case, above 7 percent in two.[19] By the mid-1990s, the members of this "gang of four," or "four tigers," could be treated as high-income economies, with average per capita incomes reaching about 65 percent that of Britain and 45 percent that of the United States.[20] And there were signs of growth spreading to a next tier of newly industrialized countries, or NICs, neighbors of Japan and the tigers whose somewhat lower wages made them attractive recipients of investment funds flowing out of the maturing tiger economies. Thailand, Malaysia, and Indonesia, the economies of which each grew in per capita terms at about 4 percent a year from 1965 to 1985, accelerated to growth rates of 8.4 percent, 5.7 percent, and 6.0 percent, respectively, during 1985–95. China's economy, which adopted market-oriented reforms at the end of the 1970s, grew at 8.3 percent in the latter period, during which several of its coastal provinces with combined populations dwarfing those of the tigers achieved considerably higher rates of growth still.

Conservative Western governments, multilateral development banks, and the economists who advised them initially offered a simple diagnosis of the causes of East Asian success. What pursuers of ISI had done, they held, was to "get prices wrong" — that is, to cause the prices facing their

18. All figures from Maddison, 1991, p. 49, except that for the Soviet Union, which is from Nove, 1972.

19. Gillis et al., 1992, p. 470.

20. Based on World Bank figures on GNP per capita in 1995, which do not include data for Taiwan. Hong Kong's and Singapore's per capita GNP actually exceeded Britain's in that year.

producers to fail to reflect underlying scarcities, leading to gross resource misallocation and thus severe economic inefficiency. Foreign exchange was made too cheap, for instance, causing imported machines, food, and tractors to appear inexpensive, and thus discouraging adoption of more labor-intensive technologies in industry and agriculture. Cheap food imports and low returns from exports, due to exchange rate overvaluation, discouraged agricultural development. Ceilings on interest rates artificially depressed the cost of capital, further encouraging capital-intensity and discouraging saving. In some cases, wages in the so-called formal sectors of the economy (those covered by minimum-wage laws and payroll taxes) were artificially high due to laws, to union-government collusion, or to the lingering influence of colonial, international civil service, and multinational corporation wage scales. This also discouraged the use of more labor-intensive production methods. The fast-growing Asian economies, it was argued, had come closer to "getting prices right," especially with respect to exchange rates, but also from the standpoint of wages (unions were suppressed until the 1980s by these countries' authoritarian regimes). Their growth was a direct result of this fact and of the resulting high rates of savings and investment. Public investment in education might also get some share of the credit.

Although few disputed that some prices may have been "less distorted" in the East Asian economies, some observers offered explanations of their successes that put the emphasis on very different factors. One strand of alternative explanation noted the role played by exports of manufactured goods. From 1965 to 1988, for instance, the total value of exports grew by 23 percent a year in South Korea and 17.3 percent a year in Taiwan.[21] Such exports, it was said, may have been encouraged not only by more realistic exchange rates but also by explicit government inducements, such as access to credits from government financial institutions for those succeeding at export expansion. Such export subsidies are at one level just as much a departure from laissez-faire as are tariffs on imports. Yet they had at least two major advantages over tariffs, it was argued.

First, import protection gives domestic producers privileged access to a sometimes small domestic market, where it faces at most the competition of other domestic producers and may well be able to sell substandard products at internationally uncompetitive prices. Export promotion, by

21. Gillis et al., 1992.

contrast, pushes producers into external markets that are often vast compared with those available domestically, and in which they must compete with foreign producers in both cost and quality, encouraging improvement in both areas. Second, whereas tariffs bring governments revenues and quantitative import restrictions put officials in a good position to earn bribes or favors for their awarding of licenses, export subsidies do not bring direct benefits to the governments offering them, and indeed they help to drain government treasuries. This means there will be built-in political pressures to control or gradually eliminate such subsidies, whereas the reverse may hold with tariffs and quotas. While the distortions associated with ISI may become worse with time, those associated with export promotion tend to be self-correcting, according to this argument.

Even this second explanation of the success of the export-oriented East Asian economies is basically consistent with the spirit of neoclassical economics, the spirit that the "getting prices right" slogan embodied so well. But some observers offered a less orthodox analysis. Far from confirming the basic wisdom of laissez-faire, they argued, East Asia's successes were in actuality supportive of the part of the "dependencia" argument that had contended that industrialization could not occur in developing countries without strong government intervention. East Asia, including Japan, did not eschew protection of domestic industry, they pointed out. Indeed, its governments continued to face charges of protectionism at the end of the twentieth century. Where the East Asian success stories differed from pursuers of ISI, the revised view argued, was in simultaneously pursuing both protection of domestic industry from imports and promotion of hitherto nontraditional exports, with sequential targeting of markets for more and more sophisticated types of manufactured goods (for example, first promote textiles, then break into basic machines, then autos and electronics). These policies were hardly of a laissez-faire bent, although they did include setting foreign exchange rates closer to market-clearing levels so as not to be biased against exporters. At least some types of credit were kept artificially cheap, and the government played a major role in its allocation, such as with rewards for good export performance. Also, governments not only tolerated but even encouraged interfirm cooperation and the emergence of cartels and oligopolies, most notably in the case of Japan's *keiretsu* and South Korea's *chaebols*. Keeping wage growth in line by resisting worker demands in the political arena and containing militant unions was also a proactive policy of a strong, pro-business state.

If governments intervened not less but just differently in the export-oriented economies, as these observers argued, the natural question to ask is: why were their interventions helpful where others had been harmful to industrial progress? One possibility is that the East Asian governments bet on a better economic strategy than did their counterparts in most of Latin America or South Asia due to accidents of history and culture. Perhaps Latin American wariness of the "colossus to the North" and Indian anti-colonialism and admiration of the Soviet Union had led to too much export or market pessimism, whereas Japan's neighbors and the British outposts of Hong Kong and Singapore saw the world through more self-confident and optimistic glasses for reasons of geography, culture, or history. Perhaps the example of Japan convinced its neighbors that mimicking Western industrial growth by means of a private enterprise system and supportive government policies was a real possibility, whereas that example was too remote or implausible for countries in other regions.

Some economists coined the phrase "market friendly" to refer to the interventions favored by the successful exporters. There was plenty of government intervention, they argued, but these governments used the yardstick of success in the marketplace, not a preconceived set of goals, to determine which firms would be rewarded. Others argued that the ingredients of success were not just market-friendly policies but a state that was strong enough to be developmental in its orientation, withstanding the temptations of petty corruption in favor of the longer-term successes flowing from faster economic development. According to these arguments, a strong government is not only not an obstacle to economic growth under current circumstances; it is in fact a necessary condition for such growth.

HOW HISTORY MIGHT MATTER

While arguments about development strategy focus mainly on economic policies, an obvious question that comes to mind when trying to explain why some countries and regions have grown faster than others in the past fifty years is what roles culture and geography play. The so-called Confucian culture, with its emphasis on duty and family relationships and its respect for knowledge, looks like a plausible explanatory variable in view of its prevalence in Japan, Korea, and the ethnically Chinese areas of Taiwan, Hong Kong, and Singapore. In support of a cultural explanation, moreover, one could argue that the Philippines, once both richer and widely viewed as more promising than, say, Korea, grew far more slowly than the latter did partly because it did not share that culture and instead shared Latin and Roman Catholic influences with countries in faraway Central and South America.

Such arguments are suspect, however. It has not been many years, after all, since Asian cultures had themselves been unfavorably compared with northern European ones as fatalistic and overly collectivist, and thus unpromising for development. Before "Confucian culture" was deemed promising for growth, Japan was said to lack the critical "Protestant ethic." It can be misleading, moreover, to view culture as something fixed and linked to an ethnic or linguistic group, rather than a response to social conditions and environment that both supports and changes along with them. In our example, Philippine similarities to Central America, with its plantation crops, landholding patterns, and wealth distribution, and the contrast with East Asia's land reforms and more equal distribution of wealth, may be a better focus of attention than is culture per se.

A more promising alternative to explanations based on culture is suggested by the fact that the historical differences between countries that happened to be less developed as of around 1950 or 1960 are so great that the whole concept of a Third World can be questioned. The only common feature linking its members is that they were not industrialized as of the Second World War. Their levels of economic development and their social structures differed enormously. Guatemala and Colombia, for instance, have been characterized by highly unequal distributions of wealth and political influence in part as an outgrowth of their histories of European conquest and immigration and of marginalization of indigenous populations. Korea, on the other hand, has been marked by more social and economic equality, partly due to ethnic homogeneity and a heritage of small-scale, intensive farming. The country was briefly colonized by Japan, but it never saw vast tracts of land handed over to foreign settlers pushing aside the prior inhabitants. Studies show that equality and growth have been positively correlated in the postwar period, with likely reasons including the greater spread of education and its benefits, reduced rates of population growth, and greater political stability in countries with more equal distributions of income.[22]

22. See Perotti, 1996.

A long-term historical framework may help explain many of those differences among countries and regions that underlie differences in rates of modern growth. We might usefully think of the world on the eve of the European expansion discussed in Chapter 1 as being characterized by economies at rather different levels of development. One way of classifying those economies is to array them along a continuum ranging from the smallest scale and least socially stratified (hunters and gatherers in small band-like societies, such as those then found in Australia) to the largest scale and most stratified and complex (imperial China and Japan), with others (sub-Saharan Africa, central Asia, Central America) occupying various positions in between. Closely associated with the complexity and state-scale dimensions were population densities and intensities of cultivation systems. The more complex, densely populated, socially differentiated, and intensive in production methods was the economy, one might hypothesize, the more similar to a modern industrial one (for instance, in the complexity of its organizations, experience with hierarchical systems of administration, acclimation to trading, and separation between work and leisure), and thus the greater the ease with which the society might make the transition to modernity.

Northern Europe's relative freedom of commerce and ideas may have helped it to make this transition earliest, but other European countries and parts of Asia where large states and commerce had long traditions have also found it fairly easy to make the transition at a not much later stage. In most (although not all) of sub-Saharan Africa, by contrast, there was neither a tradition of large statecraft and bureaucratic administration, nor one of intensive, specialized production systems, and long-distance trade had been dominated by nonindigenous minorities. Accordingly, the building of industrial societies may require a longer transition period, during the early stages of which capabilities in modern administration and commerce would slowly be built up. The importance of human capital helps to explain why European countries devastated by war could recover economically in less than a generation, while decades of efforts at development assistance in Africa have proven disappointing.

Although European expansion affected almost every region of the world after 1500, the Americas and Australia differed from most of the Old World, as we have seen, because indigenous populations were either small relative to land area, decimated by the diseases of European newcomers, or both. Where indigenous populations had been least dense, as in most of North America and Australia, the post-colonial countries that emerged were almost entirely European in population and culture, and hence could relatively quickly translate technology and organization into modern economic growth. Where production systems had been more intensive and populations more dense, indigenous people and colonizers lived side by side. Countries like Guatemala and Colombia, and to some degree also the Philippines, have inherited highly unequal distributions of wealth and power in large part as an outgrowth of their histories of European conquest and immigration, during which large amounts of land were acquired as plantations by people of European or mixed ancestry and indigenous populations were shunted off onto inferior land. This contrasts with Korea and Japan, where relative economic equality is related to ethnic homogeneity and to a heritage of small-scale, intensive farming, and long-standing state-level societies marked by high population densities and well-developed internal commerce. It was this pattern that was reinforced by U.S.-promoted land reforms.

The hypothesis that societies more similar to Europe's on the eve of its industrial revolution (in their degree of agricultural intensification, level of commercialization, and emergence of state-level political structures) will have been able to achieve modern economic growth more readily is supported by tests using the growth experiences of a large number of countries from all parts of the developing world. In these tests, early development is measured or proxied by early population density, the man-land ratio in agriculture, and the extent of the irrigation of cultivated land. The rates of economic growth of some sixty-nine countries in Asia, Africa, and Latin America over the years 1960 to 1995 turn out to be higher for those countries with denser populations, higher man-land ratios, and greater irrigation usage, when variations in initial income levels and other standard economic variables are statistically controlled for. Thus, the "economic culture" or "societal capital" of countries that were more "advanced" on the eve of industrialization could help to explain their earlier success in achieving modern economic growth.[23]

23. Initial tests, using a sample of forty-eight countries, growth rates for 1960–90, and data on population density in 1960, are presented in Putterman, 2000. These results have since been confirmed in unpublished research by Areendam Chanda and the author, using data on growth rates for 1960–95, population density in both 1960 and 1850, and samples of up to sixty-nine developing countries. The same result holds when developed countries are included in the analysis, substantially enlarging the size of the sample.

Such analyses are inevitably oversimplified, and more careful conclusions can be reached only by studying individual countries and their constituent regions, ethnic groups, and so forth. However, this sketch does suggest that the problems facing different societies attempting to industrialize are distinctive functions of their social and economic histories. Building up human capital may be the highest priority for Africa, and addressing deep socioeconomic fissures may be critical in parts of Latin America, whereas sustaining the advantages conferred by ethnic homogeneity and relative equality by allowing more and more people to share in the fruits of development may be key to further economic progress in countries like China. If this is so, one-size-fits-all government policies focusing on macroeconomic or external balances alone may well miss the mark.

THE RELEVANCE OF
ECONOMIC THEORY

Although the foregoing suggests that the experiences of different developing countries can be fully understood only with an adequate appreciation of relevant historical processes, it by no means implies that economic analysis has little to offer to an understanding of economic behaviors and their consequences, or to guiding policymakers, in developing countries today. Consider, for example, the neoclassical admonition to "get prices right." Although correcting harmful price distortions may be no panacea, and although there may be valid exceptions to the principle of laissez-faire, the insight that prices influenced by market forces offer powerful guides to resource allocation is one that can be ignored only at the peril of those concerned. There is overwhelming evidence, for instance, of the damage done to agriculture in many countries by policies that reduced the prices that farmers received for their crops. Lowered import prices have caused damaging substitution away from domestic inputs and toward technologies too intensive in the use of imported equipment. Interest caps have depressed savings. And so forth.

The study of landholding patterns and the potential benefits of land reform offers another interesting illustration of the insights that economic analysis offers. Examining the data from thousands of farmers in developing countries, agricultural and development economists discovered that small farms tended to produce more per unit of land than do larger ones. Sophisticated econometric methods helped sort out whether this was due to differences in the underlying quality of the land, to the fact that more inputs tended to be applied to each acre on smaller farms, or to other causes. As the general pattern of findings held up, other economists began theoretical explorations of why the smaller farms might be more productive, building abstract models in which individual decision makers determine their application of effort and other inputs to farmland according to rational utility maximizing criteria. One of the promising explanations that such models offered was that the family farmer might face a lower effective cost of labor because he does not need to monitor his own effort, whereas hired workers will seek opportunities to shirk on effort if not closely supervised, which adds to the farmer's cost. Some of this empirical and theoretical analysis lent support to programs of farmland redistribution. These programs possessed a political rationale, but economic analysis helped by shedding light on their potentially low or even negative cost in terms of output and efficiency. Other economic research has illuminated the conditions, including availability of input distribution channels and farm credit, under which land reforms could be most successful.

Yet another example of the value of economic analysis comes in the area of population growth. As we have seen, early population growth went hand in hand with the growth of the advanced agrarian societies that laid the groundwork for modern economies. The benefits that a dense population offers as a prod to specialization, commerce, and scale economies, however, are likely eventually to be offset by costs of congestion, environmental destruction, and oversupply of labor relative to other resources. Economists have made important contributions to the field of demography, helping to elucidate the conditions under which population growth should be deemed excessive and, more important, helping to explain the determinants of family size and thus to suggest ways of slowing population growth. Whereas Malthus, the seminal thinker in this area, had taken the pessimistic view that population will always continue growing until its pressure on resources drives people into starvation, we now realize the possibility of virtuous cycles, wherein rising incomes lead to falling, not rising, rates of population growth. The demographic transition that has been documented in every region of the world is marked by a pattern in which death rates first fall in advance of changes in birth rates, generating rapid population growth, but birth rates eventually slow until they approach the lowered death rate, leading population to stabilize.

Although the linkage of demographic change to improvements in living standards holds out the hope that population will cease its explosive growth once countries achieve economic development, there is still a problem, because economic development may be delayed or rendered impossible if in the meantime population grows too rapidly. Economists have shed light on how population growth retards development, for instance by making it too costly for the working-age population to invest sufficiently in the human capital of their offspring. More important, economic research is advancing our understanding of the determinants of fertility by building theoretical models of the "privately rational" choice of household size and schooling, and by testing those models on large family-level data sets, using sophisticated statistical techniques that help to discern the relevant chains of causality. By demonstrating, for example, that providing more schooling to girls in developing countries is one of the most cost-effective ways both of dampening population growth and of directly increasing those countries' stocks of human capital, such research offers immediate and vital information to policymakers.

GROWTH SO FAR:
TENTATIVE CONCLUSIONS, AND
QUESTION MARKS FOR THE FUTURE

Much somber ink has been spilled over the yawning gap between the modern world's "have" and "have-not" nations, and it could hardly be otherwise given the stark contrast between the comfortable life of so many in the North, the abominable poverty facing so many in the South, and the reduction of the globe to a "village" brought about by modern modes of transportation and communications. Few questions are as important on either a moral or a practical level as whether that gap can be closed, and how soon.

Since the *problems* of Third World development are what has been emphasized thus far in this chapter, it is important to recognize that the record of the past half century is far from entirely gloomy. As a group, countries classified as developing ones in 1960 achieved average annual growth of GDP per capita of 1.3 percent between that year and 1995. While this does not compare favorably enough with the corresponding 2.4 percent rate for the industrialized countries, it is worth keeping in mind that average per capita incomes for the poorer countries may have increased little if at all in the centuries preceding the twentieth, and that even slow growth was the rare exception when the industrial revolution began raising the incomes of the British by 1.2 percent a year in the middle of the nineteenth century. Sustained economic development is, in other words, a wholly modern phenomenon, and many LDCs seem to be successfully jumping on the bandwagon after lagging behind Western Europe and its offshoots for a century or two. Moreover, at least a few countries grew faster than the developed countries, some registering growth rates over 6 percent a year. At such rates, per capita output doubles every ten years, and the gap with advanced countries will not take very long to close.

Most other indicators of development show even more dramatic gains than does income. Average life expectancy at birth in the developing world rose from 50.5 years in 1960 to 63.5 years in 1996. In the same period, the average infant mortality rate declined from 123 to 55 per thousand. The average adult literacy rate rose from 46.7 percent to 69.9 percent. Gains were scored even in the poorest regions. In sub-Saharan Africa, for instance, life expectancy rose by ten years and adult literacy by 31 percentage points during this period, while infant mortality declined by 68 per thousand. These figures suggest that a general pessimism is probably ill founded, and that the possibilities for ultimate success may be good. This is especially the case if growth continues to be self-expanding: from the four tigers to the next-tier East Asian NICs, from coastal to inland China, from the rich Persian Gulf states to other Arab countries, from central to eastern Europe, and so on.

Too much optimism could of course also be misplaced. Even in successful East and Southeast Asia, the financial crisis at the end of the 1990s brought real pain to the poor. And for still poorer countries, the debt crisis that captured world attention in the early 1980s has never really ended. Such countries as Uganda and Mozambique, which adopted liberal economic policies and ended the downward slides of their economies in the 1990s, still appear unable to grow their way out of their debt obligations, and many voices — including those of leading economists — have called for more drastic write-offs of their debts. In 1996, the World Bank and the IMF launched an initiative for heavily indebted poor countries (HIPCs), which was endorsed by 180 governments around the world as a way to help poor, severely indebted countries reduce their debt burdens. The program was expanded in 1999, when the group of seven (G-7) industrialized countries promised $100 billion in debt cancellation. Some individual governments, including those of the United States and Britain, promised cancellation of 100 percent of the bilateral debt owed them by the world's poorest countries, on condition that the money is spent on basic human needs. But it remained unclear whether the domestic political hurdles could be cleared.[24]

Even with substantial debt forgiveness, one can readily imagine scenarios in which conditions improve greatly in much of Latin America and Southeast Asia, yet large pockets of poverty in sub-Saharan Africa, South Asia, and inland China remain intractable for years to come due to problems of disease and climate, high rates of population growth, high transportation costs, and inadequate skill formation. In the poorest regions of the world, tens of millions may well face a wait of two or more generations before their descendants have much hope of finding an escape from grinding poverty.

Some argue that the success of the fast-growing East Asian economies, on which so much growth optimism has rested, has been substantially based on exports to richer countries, especially the United States. The absorptive capacity of these markets cannot be unlimited, it is pointed out, so not everyone can follow East Asia's lead. Yet the huge coastal strip of China has done just that, as are other manufacturing centers from Mexico to Indonesia. The strong American economy of the late 1980s and 1990s has helped, but an issue for the future is when the successful tigers and Japan, which themselves achieved growth based on high savings and exports, will switch gears toward greater consumption, and thus begin to do their part in absorbing manufactured imports from less prosperous parts of the world.

A question for some in the rich nations is whether a further flood of imports from countries with low labor costs will undermine living standards at home, or, as a Harvard labor economist asked: "Are your wages set in Beijing?"[25] How can the United States or Germany or Sweden

24. Such groups as Jubilee 2000, an international campaign to forgive the debts of poor countries, called the announced cancellations inadequate. But at the same time, a World Bank economist warned: "Although debt relief is done in the name of the poor, the poor are worse off if debt relief creates incentives to delay reforms needed for growth." See Easterly, 1999.

25. Freeman, 1995.

maintain the high incomes of even their semiskilled working people, it is asked, when millions of workers in poor countries are willing and able to sew garments, assemble electronic goods, and do record keeping at less than a tenth of rich-country wages? Will the technological catch-up of the developing world really mean a leveling up to rich-country living standards, or does it instead threaten the workers of the currently rich countries with a leveling downward toward the standards of poorer ones? Do the stagnation of wages for unskilled and semiskilled workers, and the widening of income differences between the most skilled and other work-ers — trends observed in the rich countries since 1980 — signal the begin-ning of such a downward leveling process for all but a high-tech elite? And what will happen to the gains made by working people in the rich countries in terms of social insurance and other protections when their economies feel still more pressure to be internationally competitive?

Economists are divided on the extent to which low-cost imports ac-count for wage stagnation and the rising wage differentials by skill in developed countries. Few think it is the whole story, and many think other factors more important. The fact that the U.S. economy especially resumed strong growth in the 1990s, so that increasing inequality was not by and large associated with absolute declines in income for the less skilled, supports at least short-run optimism that there need be no large downward leveling of wages. The convergence of the European Union's economies toward roughly German-style social welfare guarantees, if not the somewhat more generous ones that had characterized Sweden, and the successes at the polls of pragmatic labor-oriented governments in Europe in the 1990s, despite "globalization," are also favorable signs that high living standards and pro-welfare policies can survive vigorous global competition.

The biggest question about long-run development must be that of ecological sustainability. Recent decades have been marked by a new-found agreement that *exploitation* of the natural environment must give way to *husbandry*, lest depletion and poisoning of the resources that have sustained mankind to this point close the door on a human future. If signals of danger like ozone thinning, receding of polar ice, and climatic instability are already at hand in a world of six billion people, of whom only 15 percent enjoy First World standards of living, consuming 53 percent of the world's energy and generating a similarly disproportionate share of its solid waste, what would be the consequence of extending prosperity to an entire world with billions more to be added before population levels off? The distressing projections of such a scenario convince some that it is imperative that growth *not* succeed.

It is no doubt true that major changes in technology would be needed before ten billion people could enjoy developed-country living standards on a sustainable basis. Indeed, it may prove impossible to maintain so much prosperity for so many, and a combination of smaller populations and checks on consumption may be needed if a decent standard of living is to be enjoyed by all nations. In the end, our judgments as to whether the necessary changes will be forthcoming turn on little more than our relative optimism or pessimism. Human beings, it can be pointed out, have been finding novel solutions to environmental problems ever since their ancestors evolved a bipedal lifestyle in response to the thinning of the tree cover in eastern Africa some seven million years ago. And they have been devising solutions to ecological problems of their own making at least since agriculture was developed in likely response to population pressures and overhunting. In a now famous story, optimism won out when environmentalist Paul Ehrlich had to pay up $576.07 on a wager with population economist Julian Simon because, rather than rising due to increasing scarcity, the prices of five metals (chromium, copper, nickel, tin, and tungsten) fell between September 29, 1980, and September 29, 1990. But we stake our future on a high-risk strategy by betting that "something will turn up; it always does."

The past few hundred years do bear out the fact that scientific knowledge has grown at an ever more rapid pace. There have already been small victories in the battle to clean up air and waterways and to save endangered animal species in the developed countries, and with increasing scientific and policy attention focused on environmental problems, the necessity faced by the North may well bear fruit in the form of solutions to environmental problems that will be available on a global scale. Restraining the South's development in the meantime is unlikely to prove wise. Perpetuation of poverty there could slow the buildup of some poisons, but it simultaneously increases pressure on other resources, most notably woodlands, which are disappearing at an ever more alarming rate. We cannot say whether an environmentally sustainable civilization in which the people of the currently poor nations can join those now rich in a comfortable standard of living is in fact attainable. But there seems no alternative other than to work to create one.

REFERENCES

Berry, Albert, ed., 1998, *Poverty, Economic Reform, and Income Distribution in Latin America*. Boulder, Colo.: Lynne Rienner.

Easterly, William, 1999, "How Did Highly Indebted Poor Countries Become Highly Indebted? Reviewing Two Decades of Debt Relief," World Bank Policy Research Working Paper, November.

Freeman, Richard, 1995, "Are Your Wages Set in Beijing?" *Journal of Economic Perspectives* 9:15–32.

Gillis, Malcolm, Dwight Perkins, Michael Roemer, and Donald Snodgrass, 1992, *Economics of Development*, 3d ed. New York: Norton.

Grilli, Enzo, and Maw Cheng Yang, 1988, "Primary Commodity Prices, Manufactured Goods Prices, and the Terms of Trade of Developing Countries: What the Long Run Shows," *World Bank Economic Review* 2 (1):1–47.

Maddison, Angus, 1991, *Dynamic Forces in Capitalist Development: A Long Run Comparative View*. New York: Oxford University Press.

Morley, Samuel, 1995, *Poverty and Inequality in Latin America: The Impact of Adjustment and Recovery in the 1980s*. Baltimore: Johns Hopkins University Press.

Murray, Christopher, and Alan Lopez, eds., 1996, *The Global Burden of Disease: A Comprehensive Assessment of Mortality and Disability from Diseases, Injuries, and Risk Factors in 1990 and Projected to 2020*. Cambridge, Mass.: Published by the Harvard School of Public Health on behalf of the World Health Organization and the World Bank.

Nove, Alec, 1972, *An Economic History of the U.S.S.R.*, rev. ed. New York: Penguin.

Perotti, Roberto, 1996, "Growth, Income Distribution, and Democracy: What the Data Say," *Journal of Economic Growth* 1:149–87.

Pritchett, Lant, 1997, "Divergence, Big Time," *Journal of Economic Perspectives* 11:3–17.

Putterman, Louis, 2000, "Can an Evolutionary Approach to Development Predict Post-War Economic Growth?" *Journal of Development Studies* 36:1–30.

Ray, Nisith, 1986, *Calcutta: The Profile of a City*. Calcutta: K. P. Bagchi.

Sahn, David, Paul Dorosh, and Stephen Younger, 1997, *Structural Adjustment Reconsidered: Economic Policy and Poverty in Africa*. Cambridge: Cambridge University Press.

Wilber, Charles K., ed., 1984, *The Political Economy of Development and Underdevelopment*, 3d ed. New York: Random House.

World Bank, various years, *World Development Report*. New York: Oxford University Press.

SUGGESTIONS FOR FURTHER READING

Amsden, Alice, 1989, *Asia's Next Giant: South Korea and Late Industrialization*. New York: Oxford University Press.

Barro, Robert, 1997, *Determinants of Economic Growth: A Cross-Country Empirical Study*. Cambridge: MIT Press.

Bhagwati, Jagdish, ed., 1987, *International Trade: Selected Readings*, 2d ed. Cambridge: MIT Press.

Collier, Paul, and Jan Willem Gunning, 1999, "Explaining African Economic Performance," *Journal of Economic Literature* 37:64–111.

Dasgupta, Partha, and Karl-Göran Mäler, eds., 1997, *The Environment and Emerging Development Issues*. New York: Oxford University Press,

Drèze, Jean, and Amartya Sen, 1991, *The Political Economy of Hunger*. Oxford: Clarendon.

Hayami, Yujiro, 1997, *Development Economics: From the Poverty to the Wealth of Nations*. New York: Oxford University Press.

Jones, Charles, 1998, *Introduction to Economic Growth*. New York: Norton.

Koo, Bon Ho, and Dwight Perkins, 1995, *Social Capability and Long-Term Economic Growth*. New York: St. Martin's.

Kuo, Shirley, Gustav Ranis, and John Fei, 1981, *The Taiwan Success Story: Rapid Growth with Improved Distribution in the Republic of China, 1952–1979*. Boulder, Colo.: Westview.

Lipton, Michael, 1977, *Why Poor People Stay Poor: A Study of Urban Bias in World Development*. London: Maurice Temple Smith.

Meier, Gerald, ed., 1995, *Leading Issues in Economic Development*, 6th ed. New York: Oxford University Press.

Perkins, Dwight, 1986, *China, Asia's Next Economic Giant?* Seattle: University of Washington Press.

Ranis, Gustav, and John Fei, 1997, *Growth and Development from an Evolutionary Perspective*. Oxford: Blackwell.

Reynolds, Lloyd, 1985, *Economic Growth in the Third World, 1850–1980*. New Haven: Yale University Press.

Smith, Stephen, 1997, *Case Studies in Economic Development*, 2d ed. Reading, Mass.: Addison-Wesley.

Stewart, Frances, ed., 1987, *Macro-Policies for Appropriate Technology in Developing Countries*. Boulder, Colo.: Westview.

Todaro, Michael, 1999, *Economic Development*, 7th ed. New York: Longman.

United Nations Development Program, annual (beginning 1990), *Human Development Report*. New York: Oxford University Press.

Wade, Robert, 1990, *Governing the Market: Economic Theory and the Role of Government in East Asian Industrialization*. Princeton: Princeton University Press.

World Bank, 1993, *The East Asian Miracle: Economic Growth and Public Policy*. New York: Oxford University Press.

5

ECONOMICS
AND
JUSTICE

And when you reap the harvest of your land, you
shall not wholly reap the corners of your field,
neither shall you gather the gleanings of your
harvest. And you shall not glean your vineyard,
neither shall you gather every grape of your
vineyard; you shall leave them for the poor and
stranger: I am the Lord your God.
   —Leviticus 19:9–10

Every man has property in his own person: this
nobody has any right to but himself. . . .
Whatsoever then he removes out of the state that
nature has provided, and left it in, he has mixed
his labor with, and joined to it something that is
his own, and thereby makes it his property. . . .
For this labor being the unquestionable property
of the laborer, no man but he can have a right to
what that is once joined to, at least where there is
enough and as good left in common for others.
   —John Locke,
    "Of Property"

This, then, is held to be the duty of the man of
Wealth: First, to set an example of modest,
unostentatious living, shunning display or
extravagance; to provide moderately for the
legitimate wants of those dependent upon him;
and after doing so to consider all surplus revenues
which come to him simply as trust funds, which
he is called upon to administer, and strictly bound
as a matter of duty to administer in the manner
which, in his judgment, is best calculated to
produce the most beneficial results for the
community. . . . Men who continue hoarding
great sums all their lives, the proper use of which

for public ends would work good to the
community, should be made to feel that the
community, in the form of the state, cannot thus
be deprived of its proper share. By taxing estates
heavily at death the state marks its
condemnation of the selfish millionaire's
unworthy life.
   —Andrew Carnegie, "Wealth"

Property is theft.
   —Pierre-Joseph Proudhon

Some people have lots of capital to rent, and some
people have very valuable labor to sell. Usually
we think of industrialists, doctors and lawyers in
this regard, but T.V. personalities, rock music
stars, and movie stars are better examples. And
some people have no capital to lend or rent, and
very little valuable labor to sell. Some people
have few talents, few skills, and maybe not even
much muscle power. There are haves, and there
are have nots. And the have nots might be have
nots through no fault of their own. They might
be disabled, afflicted by disease, or just very
unlucky. The free market mechanism will
produce a distribution of goods that gives Rolls-
Royces and homes in Palm Springs to the rock
stars. The distribution will give Fords and
suburban tract homes to most of us. But it will
give worn-out shoes and crowded tenements to
the have nots. And the result will very likely be
Pareto optimal.
   —Allan M. Feldman,
    Welfare Economics and
    Social Choice Theory

John Martin and Mary Johnson have spent their lives as near neighbors, although they don't know each other. Both were born on the same day in April 1964 in the same hospital in Cleveland, Ohio, and the two babies may have briefly occupied neighboring bassinets in the newborn unit of its maternity ward. They grew up in homes separated by only half a mile, though on opposite sides of the city line. Mary's family lived in the city, in a rowhouse on a quiet side street a short distance from a larger thoroughfare. John's family lived in a three-bedroom home in a small development off the same road, a quarter mile beyond the city line. John's dad was an engineer employed by a local manufacturing firm, his mom a schoolteacher. Mary's dad drove a city bus, her mom cleaned houses and worked part time in a school cafeteria. John attended suburban public schools where classes were typically smaller than in the city schools that Mary went to, and to which better teachers were lured by higher pay and more pleasant working conditions. John's high school had a 90 percent graduation rate, with 60 percent going on to college; Mary's high school graduated 55 percent and sent 25 percent to college.

John did well in school, went to a good private college, got into a top law school, and returned to Cleveland to take up an offer from a large private practice. Mary completed high school, started attending a community college, then dropped out after becoming pregnant and marrying. John became a partner in his firm and today earns $160,000 in a typical year. He is married, his wife also being a lawyer who has an individual practice. They live in a suburb some ten miles from the city, and have two small children attending an expensive private school. Mary lives with her two teenage children in a small city apartment, her husband having long since left them. She has worked in a variety of low-paying jobs. A pack-a-day cigarette smoker who is twenty-five pounds over her ideal weight and suffers from high blood pressure, she has recently taken a job working for a laundry service that cleans the towels from the health club to which John and his family belong. She carries no health insurance.

When John and Mary were in high school in the late 1970s, incomes such as those that John and his wife earn today were taxed by the U.S. government at a rate of around 40 percent. Changes in the tax rates in the early 1980s reduced this rate to 28 percent, and the modest restoration of tax progressivity in the 1990s left the rate at 33 percent, so John and his wife pay some $18,000 less in taxes each year than they might otherwise have. Along with their high incomes, this has helped them to accumulate over a million dollars, which is invested in a diverse portfolio of stocks, bonds, and mutual funds. Much of this money is sheltered from taxes because it is placed in retirement accounts. Their net worth has also been much boosted by the stock market boom that tripled share prices in the 1990s, and by the appreciation in the market value of their home, on which they took out a substantial mortgage with tax-deductible interest payments. John recently took an ownership position in an Internet start-up in which a friend from law school is a principal investor.

Mary has $1,200 in the bank, a credit card debt of $3,000, and pays monthly rent and heating bills that contribute nothing to her personal worth and generate no tax deductions. The economic growth of the 1990s has meant that work is easier for her to find, but market rents on apartments have risen sharply, too. She is on the waiting list to receive a subsidized housing voucher from the government, but it is reported that available units in the city are few and far between.

Are the differences of fortune that separate John and Mary fair? Might they have been avoided?

How an economy is organized and the related policies adopted by governments can have far-reaching effects, not only on the overall level of productivity and prosperity of a nation, but also on how such prosperity as there is will be distributed among its people. How wealth, income, and economic well-being more generally are distributed, and the degree to which these patterns of distribution satisfy basic conceptions of fairness or justice, will be the topics of this chapter. Do market processes, left to themselves, deliver fair outcomes? Can economic policy pursue prosperity, efficiency, and equity at the same time, or are there trade-offs between these goals? These are among the core questions to be considered here.

ECONOMICS AND ETHICAL QUESTIONS: THE EARLY HISTORY

Given the intimate relationship between economic variables and issues of distributive justice, fairness in business dealings, and so on, one might expect economists to devote a substantial amount of their attention to ethical problems. Partly owing to the way in which different academic fields divide these questions among themselves, however, ethical issues actually occupy a very small part of the usual economics curriculum or of economists' research agendas. How this came to be is an interesting story that goes somewhat beyond the outline of the history of economics sketched in Chapter 2.

In the eighteenth and nineteenth centuries, writers on political economy took a strong interest in issues of welfare and its distribution. Adam Smith believed that the well-being of every class of a nation's people tends to grow with the freedom of external and internal trade. Thomas Robert Malthus argued more pessimistically that poverty was an inescapable fact of life. Both John Stuart Mill and Karl Marx resisted Malthus's conclusion, but for somewhat different reasons. Mill argued that the working class could better its lot through education, and that the economy would gradually come to consist of mainly cooperatively owned firms. Marx argued that conflicts among classes were inherent in capitalism, but that these conflicts could be overcome by replacing the capitalist system with a socialist one.

With its emphasis on mathematical precision and its movement toward intellectual specialization — as reflected in the change of name from "political economy" to "economics" — neoclassical economics appears in some respects to have been determined from the outset to steer clear of the normative (that is, "ought") questions of income distribution and justice. Yet such questions were by no means ignored by early members of the now-dominant school of economists. According to neoclassical theory, the contributions of land, labor, and capital to output are in principle measurable, and in a competitive market system, each input owner receives for his factor's contribution exactly what its use adds to society's total output — the value of its "marginal product." The Austrian economist Eugen von Bohm-Bawerk argued that the existence of well-defined and in principle measurable contributions of land and capital to production proved the fallacy of Marx's theory that only labor produces value.[1] The American economist John Bates Clark asserted that no fairer distribution of income could be conceived than that which occurs under a competitive market system, where each factor of production receives back from the economy exactly what its presence adds to it (that is, the value of its marginal product).

The positions of Bohm-Bawerk and Clark are not particularly surprising, since they were inheritors of Adam Smith's doctrine that the best way to engender prosperity is usually to leave people to pursue their own interests in their own enterprising ways. What is more remarkable, perhaps, is that while they and others saw in neoclassical economics the ultimate defense of the private enterprise system, some practitioners saw in the school's theories the seeds of a theory of welfare that might be far less accepting of the economic inequalities associated with the unfettered operation of markets. Recall that classical economics found itself unable to connect prices with demand in any formal manner, and that neoclassical economics had resolved this problem by arguing that prices reflect a consumer's utility from the last, or marginal, unit of a good. Price varies

1. The theoretical notions of the marginal physical product of a factor input (that is, the extra output attributable to one more unit of the input), and of the value of that marginal product (the output multiplied by its price per unit), were initially developed in the late nineteenth century. In the twentieth century, the mathematical structure of production functions has been studied empirically, and marginal products of labor and land can now be estimated in practice, provided that some basic theoretical structure is assumed to hold. As we shall see, however, the fact that a marginal product can be estimated does not by itself resolve the controversy over what way of distributing income is either efficient or equitable.

with quantity, Jevons and the others argued, because the utility of a good depends upon the amount consumed. Indeed, even income itself displays declining marginal utility as the value of extra dollars becomes less to one who has more of them.

Now, in adopting the idea that consumers act so as to maximize their *utility*, the marginal economists were borrowing a term from the nineteenth-century moral and political philosopher Jeremy Bentham, who had argued that since individuals always strive to increase pleasure and to decrease pain, society itself (or the government acting as its agent) should act so as to maximize the net *sum* of pleasure or utility. Some economists, who were philosophical utilitarians, believed that people are similar enough that one can in principle compare their levels of utility, making it possible to sum up the utilities of individuals to derive the utility of society, and to meaningfully compare one person's utility losses with another person's utility gains. The job of the Benthamite economist who is concerned with welfare is then to discover what policies would lead to the maximum sum of utilities—what Bentham had called "the greatest happiness for the greatest number." And this is where the early theory of marginal utility, which declines with additions to consumption and income, had a radical implication. For if marginal utility declines with consumption and income, and if people have similar utility functions, then it follows that the total utility of society (the sum of their individual utilities) is at its maximum when their consumption levels are equal! Since the marginal utility of a unit consumed is low to a rich person and high to a poor person, transferring a dollar from rich to poor raises total utility, because the utility loss of the rich is smaller than the utility gain of the poor.

Few neoclassical economists were so extreme as to call for immediate and comprehensive redistribution of wealth on the basis of such reasoning. Remaining consistent with its classical antecedents, neoclassical economics suggested that social prosperity was served by private property and the free pursuit of wealth in a setting of unfettered markets, in which inequalities had to be countenanced as spurs to enterprise and thrift. But some believers in utilitarian welfare theory did see it as pointing to the desirability of searching for feasible social reforms—such as free public education, the provision of assistance to the infirm, or even progressive taxation—that might facilitate an approach to more nearly equal utilities or incomes.

DISTRIBUTION THEORY AND PARETO

At the end of the nineteenth century, the thinking of economists regarding welfare and distribution underwent a dramatic transformation as a result of the work of an Italian economist, Vilfredo Pareto. Pareto undertook to formalize the idea of economic efficiency, including the efficiency of the distribution of incomes, goods, or utilities. He concluded that an economy could be said to be efficient if it could not produce more of any good without sacrificing some units of another good, and if it could not alter either the set of goods produced or the way in which those goods were distributed so as to make someone better off without making anyone else worse off. These conditions continue to be accepted today as defining efficiency, and the name of their originator became probably the most oft-used in economics, as the term "Pareto optimality" came to be used as a synonym for efficiency.

Now, Pareto realized that several differing outcomes that involve different ways of distributing goods among a set of individuals will often simultaneously meet his criterion. For instance, a hypothetical two-person economy might be efficient when person 1 earns $900 and person 2 earns $100, and it might also be efficient when person 1 earns $100 and person 2 earns $900, as well as when persons 1 and 2 each earn $500. All these different ways of distributing $1,000 would be efficient as long as it is the case that moving away from the distribution in question could only raise the welfare of one of the two persons at the expense of that of the other person.[2] If that is so, argued Pareto, then it is impossible to state objectively which of the three alternative distributions is best. All of them are equally efficient, and economics can offer no further guidance on the matter.

Clearly, Pareto's conclusions differed dramatically from those of the Benthamite utilitarians. In the example just given, the latter would have found the distribution of $500 to each person to be unambiguously better than the other two alternatives, since the utility gain of an individual rising from a $100 to a $500 income clearly exceeds the utility loss of a

2. That is, the distribution of $900 to person 1 and $100 to person 2 is Pareto optimal if there is no way to increase person 2's income to more than $100, thereby increasing his utility, without reducing the income and utility of person 1.

person falling from a $900 to a $500 income, given the law of declining marginal utility. Indeed, utilitarians might even find it preferable that persons 1 and 2 have an equal split of $900 (that is, $450 each) rather than share a total of $1,000 in so *unequal* a ratio as 9 to 1.

Why do the conclusions of Pareto and the utilitarians differ? The reason is that while the utilitarians assumed utility to be in principle measurable and comparable among persons, Pareto denied the possibility of objective comparisons of utility. Thus, while he accepted the assumption that each person gets a little less utility from the one thousandth dollar that she earns than she got from the nine hundred and ninety-ninth dollar, Pareto believed that there is no basis for concluding that two different persons get the same marginal utility from their thousandth dollar, nor is there even an objective way of knowing whether person 1 gets more utility from his five hundredth dollar than person 2 gets from her thousandth dollar. Indeed, whether a beggar in Calcutta would experience a greater increase in welfare from an additional dollar than would Bill Gates, reputedly the world's richest man, has no scientific answer if interpersonal comparisons of utility cannot be made.

Pareto remained interested in aspects of the distribution of welfare that lay beyond the boundaries of his discussion of efficiency, but he believed that these also lay outside the proper scope of the science of economics. He therefore switched to studying them in what he considered to be the field of "sociology."[3] When economists adopted Pareto's approach to the economics of welfare, they paid no attention to his work in this sister field. Economics adopted the view that utility cannot be measured in natural units or compared across individuals, and that an economy is accordingly efficient if it meets the conditions detailed by Pareto. No more, it was agreed, could be said scientifically about the desirability of a distribution of income or goods. The field of economics that deals with normative questions, called welfare economics, focused on the effects of policy changes on an economy's efficiency, leaving questions of equity to be debated by philosophers. It showed, for instance, that competition is unambiguously "better" than monopoly, because competition is associated with efficient production levels but monopoly is not.[4]

3. See Tarascio, 1969.

4. Neoclassical microeconomics predicts that a monopolist will produce and sell that quantity of its product at which the addition to revenue from the last unit added

The new, or Paretian, welfare economics, however, had little or nothing to say about how quite different distributions that were equally efficient could be compared. In effect, the boundaries of economic science were redrawn so that questions of justice were shipped off to neighboring disciplines, because it seemed impossible for economists to make scientific headway with them.

The Benthamite utilitarian approach to social welfare was not the only one to be jettisoned by most economists as they developed modern welfare economics. The conservative marginalist position of Bohm-Bawerk and Clark also came in for heavy criticism and was eventually dropped by neoclassical economists. Recall that Clark had argued that since in perfect competition each factor earns the value of its marginal product, and since this is what the factor's use adds to society's total output, therefore no fairer way of distributing income could be conceived. The main problem with that position is that while the connection it draws between contributions, marginal products, and rewards may seem attractive, it says nothing about why a particular *person* should claim the marginal-product-based reward of a specific *thing*, for instance a plot of land. Perhaps each factor of production has earned *its* marginal product, but are we, then, to shove the money accruing from a plot of land into its soil, or to slide the monetary value of a machine's marginal product between its gears? We return to this question of property rights later in the chapter.

By contrast with the ethical interpretation of the marginal productivity theory of distribution, and with the radical version of Bentham's utilitarianism, the post-Paretian approach of treating the equity of distribution as falling outside the boundaries of economics can be viewed as a socially and ethically neutral one. Yet by declaring concerns about equity to be outside the scope of their discipline and focusing attention on efficiency, a property that is virtually inherent in competitive markets, economists might be said to have been subtly deflecting criticism from the prevailing insti-

---

equals the additional cost of producing that unit. For a monopolist, however, the addition to revenue is less than the price paid by the consumer, assuming that selling another unit requires lowering the price to all consumers. Had the monopolist produced units beyond the number that maximizes its profits, it would have raised society's well-being, because the cost of the extra units is less than what they are worth to some buyer. Firms operating in perfect competition, by contrast, automatically satisfy the optimality condition as they maximize their profits: the cost of producing the last unit is just equal to what the last consumer is willing to pay.

tutions of private property and exchange. Whether its focus on efficiency effectively separates economics from those ethical domains in which value judgments are unavoidable is the question to which we turn next.

EFFICIENCY AND EQUITY:
THE IMPOSSIBILITY OF "NONNORMATIVE JUDGMENT"

As we have just seen, the "marginal revolution," with its concepts of marginal utility and marginal product, carried both a potentially radical distributive implication and a corresponding conservative one. However, both of these interpretations were discarded by most economists with the adoption of Pareto's approach. Economists saw that approach as a more scientific one because it avoided thorny problems of measuring and observing utility, and of the comparison of utility across individuals. They saw economics as a science striving for descriptive and predictive accuracy, an enterprise thus positive and nonjudgmental in nature.[5] Since judging whether one of several alternative distributions is more or less equitable is an unavoidably normative activity, it must lie beyond the boundaries of economics, in this view. There is no scientific way of saying whether one person's judgment of what is fair or unfair is any better or worse than the different judgment of another, according to positive economics.

Although the shift to Pareto's conception of efficiency and of the boundary between economics and other fields has been defended as a move toward a more scientific economics, this does not rule out some subtle influence from ideology. Perhaps Pareto's approach was embraced by some economists as much because of its consistency with their private philosophical dispositions as because of its scientific superiority. After all, the philosophy that has dominated the mainstream of economics since the days of Adam Smith is one that favors freedom of choice and a "hands off" approach by government. Saying that one distribution of income is better than another could invite government intervention, so economists could have been expected to welcome an innovation such as Pareto's. Also, proposing that one judgment about distribution may be better than another might seem unacceptably "paternalistic" to the philosophical

---

5. "Positive" as used here is essentially the complement of "normative." Positive statements and inquiries concern what *is*, normative ones what *ought to be*.

liberal, who believes that each person should be free to hold her own opinion, and that the state has no place intervening, even on behalf of an opinion that is popular with many or most. Some radical economists, however, argued that the mainstream of economics adopted approaches more consonant with the interests of the dominant socioeconomic class for the same reasons that the political economists of Marx's time eagerly served the wealthy and powerful as "ideologues for hire."

Whatever the motivation behind treating equity as a normative concept lying beyond the boundaries of economics, it is worth pointing out the potential inconsistency of doing this while keeping efficiency within the economic circle. After all, the idea that efficiency is desirable is no less normative than is the idea that we should seek equity. The difference between efficiency and equity in this regard, it is sometimes argued, is that only efficiency can be defined in an unambiguous and rigorous fashion, but equity is not even definable without value judgment. Moreover, because everyone agrees that efficiency is desirable, the equation of the efficient with the good in a field that eschews value judgments is at most a very minor infraction of the quest to be scientific. Where problems are likely to arise, though, is at the point at which choices must be made between, or different degrees of importance must be assigned to, efficiency and other goals.

Just about everyone can agree on the desirability of efficiency, once it is clearly explained to them. Unless we are misanthropic or equate salvation with suffering, why would we not favor having more goods or making somebody better off if no "bads" are created in the process and if nobody is rendered worse off? Yet even the efficiency concept must be used carefully if one wishes to avoid stepping beyond the bounds of science. Suppose, for instance, that everyone agrees that to make someone better off without harming anyone else is plainly desirable, as economists usually assume. Problems nonetheless arise when one encounters trade-offs between this first desirable objective and another objective held desirable by some but not others — in other words, an objective that more obviously entails a value judgment, such as the goal of fairness.[6]

To give an example, suppose it is possible to achieve what some people view as a substantial increase in equity or fairness at a small cost in effi-

6. Note, by the way, that even the statement "making someone better off is good" entails a value judgment. The distinction here is only that this judgment is so widely held as to make debate unnecessary for most purposes.

ciency. Using the example above, say, suppose that the feasible distributions between persons 1 and 2 are (listing first the income of person 1, then that of person 2): ($900, $100), ($100, $900), and ($450, $450). In this example, moving away from either of the unequal divisions toward an equal one causes the available total to fall from $1,000 to $900, due, say, to some costs of administering the redistribution scheme, or to a reduction in incentives to produce or invest resulting from the associated taxes and transfers. Suppose that the amounts of goods produced and consumed vary proportionately with income levels, so that an economy with incomes ($450, $450) produces and consumes somewhat less of all goods than one with incomes ($900, $100) or ($100, $900). Then according to the efficiency criterion, the egalitarian economy, with incomes ($450, $450), is strictly inferior to both of the inegalitarian economies, because less of some and no more of any goods are produced and consumed in it. Also, from a distributional efficiency standpoint, no unambiguous improvement is available whether one begins at ($900, $100), ($100, $900), or ($450, $450), since whatever change makes person 1 better off has to make person 2 worse off, and vice versa.

Yet even though the case can be made that overall efficiency is higher at one of the two unequal distributions, since more is being produced, many people might still prefer the inefficient third outcome for reasons of equity. Here is where the trade-off between efficiency and another goal — in this case equity — appears. A careless defender of efficiency could slip into saying that the people who favored the egalitarian outcome were ignoring the only objective economic criterion, or that they showed an inability to think in an economic fashion, or that the egalitarian outcome is objectively inferior to the inegalitarian ones, or that it requires no value judgment to conclude that the egalitarian outcome was undesirable (since everyone agrees that efficiency is good). But all such statements plainly would be in error. To give heed to one value while ignoring others may be your preference, but it needn't be mine! It is itself a value judgment, no matter how uncontroversial the first value might be.

CONCEPTIONS OF JUSTICE

One of the reasons why questions of fairness are more controversial than those of efficiency is that different people hold different views of what fairness entails. Although we can easily agree on a definition of "equality" (a descriptive term), we do not necessarily agree on what we mean by "equity" (a normative one). One conception, to be sure, is that the *fair* division of income, property, or goods *is* the equal one (equality equals equity). When some contribute more than others to generating what is to be divided, however, many people would consider an equal division to be less just than one somehow proportionate to those contributions. The matter is further complicated by issues of ability or endowment. If you contributed more than I did only because I own fewer resources or am infirm, some would hold that we may then be entitled to equal shares after all. If I own fewer resources because I have always been lazier, on the other hand, that may reverse their judgment. For others, what has been produced by us separately, each with his or her own resources, is not even to be included in the "what is to be divided" referred to just above; only products of directly joint or collective effort are up for grabs in the justice game, and what we produce on our own is our own and no one else's business.

The popular conceptions of justice just considered tend to take equality as a neutral starting point and then take into account, to varying degrees, considerations of contribution, effort, and ability. Still another common consideration is that of need. If we both have the same capacity to generate income but you require an expensive medical treatment while I do not, some would feel it just that you receive this treatment or that you be given the income with which to pay for it, if necessary. But opinions may vary, depending, for instance, on the cost of the treatment, the deprivation I would have to suffer to help you pay for it, and so on.

Although the idea that it is morally desirable that people's needs be met is fairly widely shared — indeed, this may be the essence of the spirit of charity embraced by the world's major religions — few people believe that earnings should be completely independent of a person's actions and choices. Even if traditional religions give their blessing to notions of charity, they have rarely attempted to overturn the idea of property or of individual entitlement to the fruits of hard work. Even egalitarians can believe that individuals should take responsibility for their actions, thus urging that equality of opportunities, not of outcomes, is what should be sought. If John and Jane are given the same opportunities but Jane achieves a higher standard of living due to her greater efforts, this would appear just, from such a standpoint. This suggests a different formulation of the matter, according to which it is not equality of outcomes, but rather equality of opportunities, that we are after.[7] The possibility that Jane's greater efforts derive from a better upbringing, of which John was deprived — due, for instance, to his socioeconomic background or that of his parents — may complicate things, but it does nothing to rule out the principle of equal opportunity, which might have to be pursued through efforts to reduce or to offset unequal advantages of background.

THE DESIRABLE VERSUS THE FEASIBLE

It is often suggested that what is morally desirable, where matters of distribution are concerned, may differ from what is in practice feasible. For instance, suppose that two individuals work equally hard but one is substantially more productive than the other due to the possession of superior skills. To the extent that the differences in the skills of the two derive from different innate talents, it might be felt that the more productive one should receive no more material compensation than does the less productive, since no one deserves credit for an accident of birth. However, creating a useful skill may require a *combination* of genetic potential, an appropriate environment, and effort on the part of the worker.

Now, several problems of feasibility arise here. First, while purely ethical considerations may make some feel that only that part of the difference in productivity that is attributable to the worker's *effort* should be rewarded, it may well be impossible to determine the relative contributions of the three forces — genes, environment, and effort. Thus, to separate out for reward only the share of the extra productivity that is due to additional effort may be a practical impossibility. Suppose, secondly, that it is felt to be unfair that the worker be rewarded for the luck of a better environment. Here, there arises another problem, namely that much of the superiority or inferiority of environment may result from parental decisions that might themselves be influenced by whether or not the parents expect the child to receive extra rewards for exhibiting certain behaviors (being industrious, having good language skills, and so on). Thus, if society *could* withhold rewards for skill differentials based on superior environments or upbringing, it might prove unwise for it to do so, for the withdrawal of rewards could cause a damaging decline in the

7. See Roemer, 1998.

effort parents make to provide advantageous environments to children, with detriment to the whole society.[8] Finally, one can imagine a moral argument for not rewarding materially even productivity differences due to one's own effort — for instance, the propensity to exert effort might be viewed as itself genetically and environmentally derived, and social status or more desirable job assignments might be seen as sufficient rewards in themselves. However, a moral argument against rewarding effort would run up against the practical consideration that if effort is not materially rewarded, and if praise and status proved an inadequate incentive, the needed effort might not be forthcoming.

Here, of course, the discussion of feasibility hinges importantly on our assumptions about human nature. If human beings do not require material rewards to induce them to supply socially beneficial efforts, or if it is feasible to alter their psychological makeups so that this is the case, then the problems just mentioned may not have to arise. But we need not take an extreme position regarding the selfishness or materialistic orientation of the typical individual to believe that these problems will arise to some degree in almost any human society. The problem of human nature is discussed further in the next chapter.

Another dimension that interacts with our problem is that of liberty. Faced with the concern that individuals and their parents might withhold socially useful effort without adequate compensation, a possible response might be to propose denying them the right to do so — that is, mandating that the efforts be made, and if necessary enforcing the mandate by one or another form of coercion. If freedom is desirable, though, this route may have to be foreclosed. In practice, moreover, the quality of effort that is elicited by coercion could differ importantly from that which follows from self-interest or other motivations. Creative, energetic, problem-solving effort may be virtually impossible to coerce. The mandatory approach also runs up against problems of information: not knowing your true potential, others will find it very difficult to enforce a demand that you develop it to its fullest. You may prefer to hide your potential and reduce your effort, if there is not enough in it for you.

8. Recall that according to economic theory the productivity of an individual is determined not only by her own contributions but also by the levels of other inputs with which she works. In technical terms, the marginal product of an input is positively influenced by the levels of other useful inputs. Thus, many others, not only the bearers themselves, stand to gain from having their society contain more skilled individuals, just as they do from its having a larger stock of useful capital goods.

For the time being, we assume a degree of self-interest and conclude that when people are free to choose their actions and society lacks perfect information about their genetic capabilities, some material rewards will be necessary to elicit socially desirable work effort, desired investments in training, and the provision of the conditions under which skills can best be developed. Lacking the ability to discriminate between differences in contribution attributable to innate ability and those due to training and incentive-responsive elements of the environment, society may have to accept the use of motivational systems that reward all three elements — genes, environment, and effort — even if this strikes many members as a regrettable compromise.

CONTRIBUTIONS OTHER THAN LABOR

We earlier encountered the argument that paying each factor of production according to its marginal product was the fairest possible approach, and the counter-argument that applying this view to *things* is a non sequitur. We return now to the latter issue. We can begin by noting that rewarding contributions of labor and rewarding contributions of other resources raise somewhat different moral and practical issues. Modern societies view labor as *inalienable* from the individual. As discussed above, we would not want to be coerced into providing our labor services, nor might we provide them as effectively if we were operating under compulsion. Skills, once learned, cannot be redistributed among individuals. The government can't confiscate the abilities of a brilliant surgeon and transfer them to a deserving cab driver, nor can it transfer from Bill Gates to the surgeon the ability to guide product development for Microsoft. If material rewards are needed to elicit effort and investments in learning, payments that reflect labor contributions are unavoidable. This has probably contributed to the fact that such payments are also widely viewed as just.

Inputs like land and machines are different. The statement that "I deserve to be rewarded for contributing my land to a certain project" may be viewed differently from the corresponding statement about "my labor," for the possessive pronoun "my" appears in the former case to have a more questionable basis. When I contribute my labor, I must do so in person. I cannot be elsewhere attending to other things. If the work is demanding, it is I who bear its physical and psychic costs. If the work goes badly, I may be injured and lose some future enjoyment of life. When I contribute my land, in contrast, my presence is not required. Although the land gives up some of its fertility in the process, this is not a direct cost to my person. Unlike my right to my labor, my right to my land seems more in need of justification. How did I acquire the land? If I acquired it justly, my right to its fruits will be respected, but if I acquired it unjustly, they may not be. But what would constitute just acquisition?

That rights to returns from labor and property are different is brought home by the fact that almost every popular justification of property rights rests on foundations of labor rights. John Locke, who is widely viewed as the father of the liberal theory of property, argued that a person is entitled to the property created by "mixing his labor" with the resources of nature, provided that similar resources remain available for others to mix their labor with. This attempt to put property rights on an equal footing with rights to the fruits of labor thus in fact illustrates the primacy of the latter rights: the more one's property is viewed as resulting from one's own hard work—that is, *labor*—the fewer the moral challenges that are likely to be raised. Even debates over inheritance usually turn indirectly on labor. People may question the fairness of my being a millionaire simply because my grandparents left part of their fortune to me. A defense of inheritance that has more moral appeal to many, however, is that my grandparents worked hard for their fortune, and thus they justly earned the right to use it as they wished, including giving it to me. Again, labor—that of my grandparents—underlies moral legitimacy here.

If the principle of inheritance is accepted, however, it may bring other moral dilemmas in its train. The least legitimate sources of property rights, most would agree, are the gain of property through theft or by virtue of pure status, say in a caste or feudal class system. However, if we accept that I am entitled to the bequest of my grandparents, who were hardworking, will it be fair to deny *you* the bequest of *your grandparents*, who were of high-born class or caste, or were thieves, or clients of a political despot? Is it fair to treat you differently from me because your grandparents were different?

Would it be fair to deny you a share of an inheritance similarly obtained by your great-grandparents, or your great-great-grandparents, especially when it could be argued that your grandparents and parents had husbanded this fortune honorably, however it may have been obtained by their forebears?

An important point not touched on thus far is that once property rights are established through labor or by some other justification, changes in property brought about by voluntary choices and decisions are typically viewed as legitimate. For instance, suppose that your grandparents gave you land and mine gave me money, and suppose that we accept that both of these inheritances are morally legitimate. Now, suppose that you and I swap your land for my money. There appears to be no reason, at least initially, to question my right to the fruits of that land. Questions arise where luck enters the picture, however. Suppose, for instance, that I swapped Mexican pesos for your piece of California land, following which the peso lost 50 percent of its value and my land gained 50 percent in a real estate boom. A month or two later, I am three times richer than you, though our grandparents had given us inheritances that had equal market values. To the extent that I benefited from sheer luck, my moral right to greater wealth might be questioned by some. But here feasibility enters again: if we can't separate luck from foresight, we probably have to permit people to keep the gains from such trading lest the incentive to shift resources into better uses be destroyed.

Once a property right is in force, many of the same practical considerations relevant to labor and distribution become relevant here as well. For instance, some may question whether it is moral that I should earn interest or profits from the investment of the money that I inherited, an act that may require next to no effort on my part. But if I am to be left free to invest or not to invest the money, and if I prefer to earn a return on the money, then it may be necessary to allow me to pocket the resulting interest or profit. If not, there is no reason to expect the funds to be steered into their most socially beneficial use — which, in the theory of competitive markets, is that use with the highest financial return. Similarly, people might not save (withhold from consumption) a sufficient amount to meet society's investment needs without an attractive return to their funds. While in theory the return to my land may be what economists call a "pure economic rent,"[9] because there is no cost to society of bringing the land into being, in practice I may not bother making my land available or leasing it to the user with the most promising project unless I am motivated by adequate compensation.

9. In economics, a "rent" is the return to a factor of production above and beyond the cost of bringing it into use or what it could earn elsewhere.

THEORIES OF JUSTICE

Many theories of justice have been proposed by philosophers. Locke's theory that a person is entitled to the property created by "mixing his labor" with the resources of nature has been mentioned above. Some critics suggest that Locke's ideas cannot justify property in an age of resource scarcity — there is little left in a natural state with which to mix one's labor today, and what is left cannot be treated as a free good without inviting environmental disaster. However, modern libertarians such as Robert Nozick join with Locke in arguing that the fairness of a distribution should be judged solely on the basis of the *procedures* by which it was obtained. Nozick finds the basic institutions of a free market and private property to be comfortably validated on procedure-based ethical grounds.

The opposite end of the ideological spectrum from the libertarianism of Locke and Nozick has long been occupied by Marxism. Although Marx asserted that the claim that labor is the source of value is a positive one, not the expression of a value judgment, his labor theory has often been interpreted in ethical terms. The unstated implication of Marx's theory, it seems to some, is that laborers are entitled to the full product of their labor, and that capitalists who appropriate some of that product are little better than thieves. Marx himself rejected the idea of a general ethical theory, arguing that concepts of justice are simply social artifacts (part of the social "superstructure") reflecting a given epoch's "mode of production." The morality of a capitalist society, for instance, serves the interests of the capitalists, while the morality of feudalism served that of the nobility. Under a socialist system, Marx suggested, each person would receive that part of the social product that is proportionate to the amount of labor she had put in. Such a distribution would not immediately make many people better off, he warned, since a portion of output would still have to be devoted to investment and government services. Furthermore, socialist distribution would not be egalitarian, since some households would have more labor capability per member than would others. Marx suggested that under a more advanced communist system, which would develop only after the epoch of socialism, individuals would receive in proportion to their needs, with the motivation for work coming from some combination of its intrinsic satisfaction and identification with societal interests.

We have also discussed above the implications of another influential social philosophy, that of utilitarianism, which identifies the ideal social objective as being the maximization of the sum total of individuals' utility levels. When combined with the notion that each person's level of utility is a declining function of his or her level of consumption, this philosophy suggests a preference for more equal distributions.[10] This approach contrasts with Marx's in that it entails an apparently universal conception of justice, and it contrasts with Nozick's in that it focuses on end results rather than procedures. Although utilitarianism in this form has a built-in bias in favor of equality, it does not necessarily call for complete equality, among other reasons because it may take into consideration the question of incentives. If individuals differ in their abilities and in their propensities to supply effort in response to varying rewards, the sum of utilities may be higher when a certain amount of inequality is permitted than when it is not.

One final approach that merits mention in even such a brief review as this one is the influential moral philosophy of John Rawls. Rawls's approach puts as much emphasis on procedure as on outcomes, and it challenges the idea that utilitarianism is the natural friend of the weak. Rawls proposes that the just distribution is that which results from just rules, and that the latter are rules to which each member of society would agree "from behind a veil of ignorance" — that is, in an imaginary state in which she considers herself equally likely to be in any of the various economic positions of the society. According to Rawls, adopting the viewpoint of this "original position" will lead each individual to favor a set of rules that permits inequalities only when they will tend to benefit the person who is least well off. Private property rights and the market may be just, although they lead to great inequalities, but only if the least well off person is better off under these institutions than under an alternative set of arrangements. If not, the alternative arrangements are better.[11] The as-

10. The depiction of society's utility as a sum of the utilities of its members, while inconsistent with the dominant Paretian approach, is nonetheless used in some discussions of welfare, following the "social welfare function" conception of economists Abram Bergson and Paul Samuelson.

11. This discussion is of course far too brief to give the full flavor of Rawls's argument. In particular, it should be noted that Rawls is concerned not only with economic outcomes but also with liberty, and that he speaks of "primary goods" rather than incomes or utilities. It might also be noted that the utilitarian position

sent to a particular set of rules or procedures is viewed as a social contract, which has force in the actual conduct of affairs in the just society.

One place where Rawls's approach clashes with that of the utilitarians is that while utilitarianism generally favors equality, it does not always favor the poor. Rawlsians point out that the utilitarian assumption of the ability to compare pains and pleasures across individuals, and their objective of maximizing total utility, opens the door to changes that make some worse off as long as others gain relatively more. Thus, if a certain class (which might even be the poor) must suffer to make others (say, the middle and upper classes) prosperous, it seems that this can be justified on utilitarian grounds, so long as the gains of the beneficiaries are large enough. It cannot be justified on Rawlsian grounds, however, unless the beneficiaries are the least well off. The Rawlsian approach is in this sense consistent with a focus not only on the relative equality of an income distribution but on the alleviation of poverty in particular.

TAXATION AND REDISTRIBUTION

In modern market economies, respect for legally earned income and property, while embraced as both moral and useful, is limited by at least one major consideration. As discussed in the previous chapter and in standard textbooks, some goods, called "public goods," are typically provided by an entity — the government — that has the power to collect payments without having to reach an individual agreement with each of those who pay. The conventional explanation for this is that if all individuals were permitted to select their own voluntary contribution to the provision of these goods, selfish individuals would contribute too little, hoping to "free ride" on the contributions of others. Before long, there might be few such gullible others upon whom to free ride, and the goods in question would simply not be provided (or would be provided in grossly inadequate quantities). Therefore, people consent to constitutions under which provision and contribution levels approved through some stipu-

---

itself has been presented as one of rational rule selection from behind a veil of ignorance. The difference in conclusions appears to stem from the utilitarian individual choosing as if unconcerned about risk, whereas the Rawlsian individual chooses as if maximally risk-averse. On the utilitarian approach, see Harsanyi, 1982. For Rawls's approach, see Rawls, 1971.

lated process have the force of law.[12] Public goods, in sum, are financed through the mandatory contributions that we call taxes.

Although the problem of collecting funds for the provision of public goods can be conceptually separated from the question of the distribution of income, the two are closely related. People's preferences for public goods are not readily apparent, and they have at least one reason to conceal them: if tax assessments are linked to how much of the good each person says he desires, then an individual has an incentive to "free ride" at the point of revealing his preference, just as he does to shirk on contributing to pay for the goods. People differ in incomes and wealth, however, and their differing levels of income and wealth may be easier to detect than are their differing desires for public goods. While it is difficult if not impossible to link taxes to preferences for or benefits from the services provided, it *is* feasible to link tax assessments to incomes.

But just how ought incomes and taxes to be related? Suppose that all benefit equally from the public goods to be provided. Equal contributions for equal benefits can be offered as one plausible principle. But the fact that the poor person will be paying a larger *proportion* of her income than the rich strikes many as unfair. Taxation should reflect the ability to pay, they would say. This opens the door to proposals that the tax burden be proportionate to income, in which case the rich pay more in absolute terms, although not in relative ones, than do the poor.

The proportionality of taxes to incomes is not accepted by everyone. Some oppose it as unfair to those with higher incomes. Others, however, argue that it does not go far enough, for it may be said that those with high incomes can cover their tax burden by a fairly small reduction in savings, while those with very low incomes may be able to do so only by reducing consumption of basic goods. These critics of proportionality propose an alternative principle, that of progressive taxation. Let the rich pay *more* than a proportionate share, to the point at which rich and poor

12. Of course, many economists suggest that tax compliance is still largely voluntary, because the probability of discovery of cheating and the associated penalties are in many cases too small to explain observed compliance levels. "Tax morale," brought about by consent to a constitution, belief in the democratic process, or socialization into certain "civic virtues," may be at least as important as outright coercion in determining what taxes are paid. The difference between paying taxes and paying for a good you choose to purchase from a private vendor should nonetheless be apparent.

make a more equal *sacrifice*. If it takes a sacrifice of 40 percent of income at $200,000 a year to equal the "pain" imposed by a 10 percent tax at $30,000, then the percentage paid ought to rise with income in this more than proportionate fashion.

How the burden of paying for public goods is apportioned among people of different incomes will affect the way that post-tax income is redistributed. Only a proportionate tax leaves a household's share of the total post-tax income in the overall population the same as was its share of pre-tax income. A progressive tax raises the income share of the poor relative to the rich, reducing most measures of inequality. A regressive tax, including equal absolute tax payments, increases inequality.

From this recognition of the effect upon income distribution of different ways of assessing contributions to the provision of a public good, it is only a short step to the discussion of outright *redistribution* through the tax mechanism. Paying unequal taxes for *equal* services may already be viewed as redistributive. But further possibilities arise if there is also the option of providing *unequal* services — for instance, the poor might not only pay a smaller share of the taxes, but might also receive a larger share of the benefits. Nor need the benefits be limited to purely public goods: the state can redistribute tax proceeds in money form, or in the form of goods and services tradable in the marketplace. Perhaps the rich household should pay 40 percent of its income while the poor one not only pays nothing, but in addition receives a transfer boosting its income by 10 or 20 percent. Once taxation and government services are institutionalized, they may be used to carry out whatever program of altering income or wealth distribution the politically decisive group happens to agree upon.

Clearly the rules of the political game become central here. Taxes played redistributive roles over long epochs of history. Although initially they tended to transfer wealth upward from the laboring to the ruling classes of empires and feudal domains, they were also at times used to buy support from the masses, as with the bread subsidies for the population of ancient Rome. In a democratic polity, there may be still more tendency to redistribute downward: if the majority of people have less than average wealth and if that majority decides on taxes and transfers, it may vote to collect property from the wealthy and to redistribute it to itself.[13] Actual

13. In practice, countries exhibit distributions of income that are skewed in the sense that there are many more households whose income is below the mean,

patterns of transfers are more complex than this, with some redistribution to middle and upper classes as well (sometimes disguised as tax breaks or subsidies to particular industries).

How much redistribution will there be? This depends on a great many factors, including the notions of justice common in a population, the real and perceived costs of redistribution, and the nature of political coalitions and the balance of forces among them. In industrial countries like the United States, the wealthiest 1 percent of households typically own about a third of total wealth, so the poorest 60, 80, or even 90 percent of the population could benefit from redistributing assets to themselves, unless there were hidden costs.[14] One possible cost is that the expectation of periodic redistributions will reduce incentives to save and invest, lowering potential incomes for all. Redistribution might also take property away from those especially talented in managing it, reducing its benefits to the economy. Finally, people who are not now wealthy may see a chance that they or their descendants will become wealthy in the future, and this may lead them to desist from voting for confiscatory taxes, which would in that case affect them some time in the future.

Redistribution may also remain mild, despite the apparent interest of the majority, for reasons related to the political process. Although the poorest 51 percent might be attracted to a party that favors redistribution, if some 2 percent of them are induced to switch sides by the promise of a special and better deal, their coalition may collapse.[15] The wealthy may also escape confiscatory taxation because they have greater than average political clout and the ability to hire lawyers to write loopholes

---

derived by dividing total income by total number of households, than those whose income is above the mean. This is because, although there are fewer and fewer households at higher and higher income levels, a few households with very high incomes will exert as much influence on the mean as a large number of households with more modest incomes.

14. The exact measure of the wealth share of the top brackets of wealth holders is sensitive to what is included. Wolff, 1994, gives a figure of 36 percent for the share of *marketable wealth* held by the top 1 percent of households in the United States in 1989; this definition of wealth excludes the expected value of future Social Security payments.

15. The branch of economics that deals with collective decision making shows that, unless the set of admissible redistribution formulas were strictly limited, there would be no stable coalition for any one plan, for reasons of the type that the example begins to illustrate.

into tax codes and to take advantage of them.[16] An inefficient government may permit much that the electorate would redistribute to end up in the pockets of corrupt officials and contractors, lowering the public's appetite for redistribution. Finally, a moral consensus about what property people are fairly entitled to may lead many to oppose even a redistribution from which they would privately benefit. For instance, the existing distribution might be deemed just if people feel that it meets standards such as those advanced by Nozick, or Rawls. They might thus oppose redistribution, although it would put more in their pockets. Whether this represents higher values or mere gullibility is debated, of course. The majority comes to have whatever moral ideas are fostered by the beneficiaries of the status quo, alleged Marx, thus not even realizing what their "true" interests are.

While wealth and bequest taxes exist in many countries, their impact on the distribution of wealth, and their contributions to overall tax revenue, are typically not great. Even in Sweden, with the world's most progressive tax system for many decades, the top 1 percent of wealth-holders owned around 20 percent of marketable assets in the mid- to late 1980s, and wealth and bequest taxes contributed less than 1 percent of total tax revenues.[17] Inequality of income, which is far less pronounced than that of property, appears the target of choice for progressive taxation, which often does have substantial effects. Thus, in the United States in the early 1990s, personal income taxes accounted for 40 percent of federal tax revenue, almost four times the share of corporate income taxes and forty times that of estate and gift taxes.[18] While the bottom 20 percent of households by income, with a pre-tax share of 3.8 percent of household personal income, faced a slightly negative effective income tax rate, and while the middle 20 percent of households, with a pre-tax share of 14.5

16. Even without using extraordinary means, the wealthy have more influence simply because they vote more regularly, perhaps because of their higher education or greater ability to afford the costs involved. In the U.S. presidential election of 1972, only 46 percent of eligible voters with incomes below $2,000 went to the polls, whereas 86 percent of voters with incomes over $25,000 did so. See Wolfinger and Rosenstone, 1980.

17. Wolff, 1994, and Organization for Economic Cooperation and Development tax data.

18. Unlike some other industrialized countries, the United States has no tax on wealth holding per se. The data used here and in the remainder of this paragraph are taken from Mishel and Bernstein, 1994.

percent of income, faced an effective income tax rate of 6.2 percent, the top 20 percent, with 51 percent of pre-tax incomes, faced an average effective income tax rate of 16.2 percent of their labor earnings (the rate facing the top 1 percent was about 25 percent). Such tax patterns suggest either a social consensus favoring progressivity in taxation, or that models of selfish voting are correct in predicting redistributive preferences at least in the case of income taxes.

Tax systems, of course, include a great variety of revenue sources, and actual taxes in most countries range from ones progressive in their distributive impacts to others that tend to be regressive (that is, to place a greater burden on the poor than on the rich). Lawrence Mishel and Jared Bernstein (1994), for instance, classify as progressive three types of taxes accounting for about 52 percent of federal but only 22 percent of state revenue in the United States: personal income tax, corporate income tax, and estate and gift taxes. Excise, customs, and sales taxes, which tend to be regressive in incidence because they tax consumption (which takes a larger chunk of the incomes of the poor than of the rich), accounted for about 6 percent of federal and 39 percent of state revenues in 1993, according to their calculations. Contributions for social insurance programs, accounting for 41 percent of federal and 27 percent of state revenues, were also judged by those authors to be regressive. Why U.S. federal taxes were more progressive than state taxes is an interesting political and economic question for which there is no obvious answer.

It does appear to be consistent with models of redistribution that the broadening of eligibility for participation in the political process, which occurred in all the industrial democracies in this century, was followed by large increases in government taxation and transfers. Government expenditure rose from an average of 12 percent of GDP in 1913 to 28 percent in 1939, 37 percent in 1973, and 46 percent in 1987 in a sample of industrialized countries. In a more inclusive set of industrialized countries, transfers and subsidies to households rose from 26 percent of government expenditure, during 1955–57, to 34 percent during 1974–76, or from 7.5 percent to 13.9 percent of GDP.[19] Such increases largely ended in the 1980s. The share of social spending in the U.S. federal budget, for

19. Government expenditure data are from Maddison, 1991, and include France, Germany, Japan, the Netherlands, the United Kingdom, and the United States. Transfer and subsidy data are for these and other countries belonging to the Organization for Economic Cooperation and Development, as cited by Glyn et al., 1990.

instance, which had gone from 2 percent to 10.9 percent between 1950 and 1980, saw no further increase in that decade.[20] Nevertheless, in the 1980s and '90s, the distribution of disposable income in the industrial democracies was noticeably more equal than the distribution of earnings before taxes and transfers. By 1972, the income share of the poorest 40 percent of households in Sweden was 22 percent of the income of all households combined after taxes and transfers, but only 7.3 percent of combined income before taxes and transfers.[21] While Sweden was an early leader in this respect, the average increase in the share of income accruing to the poorest 50 percent of households due to taxes and transfers was over 18 percentage points in the industrial democracies as a group in the mid-1980s to early 1990s.[22] Growth of taxation and government spending was widely seen as calling for restraint or reversal, by this time, because it was deemed harmful to economic growth and incentives, or was perceived to benefit too much the undeserving.

Just how harmful redistribution has been to economic growth remains a topic of considerable controversy. Some economic studies of the cost of taxation and redistribution suggest that the fiscal approach to egalitarianism can carry a large price tag. Yet the record shows that the period during which the welfare state was growing most rapidly — 1950–73 — was also the period of the most rapid growth of real GDP, GDP per capita, and productivity per man-hour in sixteen nations belonging to the Organization for Economic Cooperation and Development, suggesting that "under favorable institutional circumstances egalitarian outcomes are not incompatible with the growth of productivity and other valued macroeconomic outcomes."[23] And one economist who is frequently critical of welfare state excesses admits: "It may . . . be argued that welfare state policies have helped make the western economic system . . . more acceptable to the general public. In this way [they] may have contributed to a degree of social harmony that is an important prerequisite for a rea-

20. Based on Office of Management and Budget data presented by Penner, 1994. Categories included as social spending are education, training, employment, social services, health, Medicare, income security, and Social Security.

21. See Sawyer, 1976.

22. Milanovic, 1999, based on data from the Luxembourg Income Survey conducted in the mid-1980s to mid-1990s in seventeen industrial market economies.

23. Quoted from Bowles and Gintis, 1999, with reference to the data in Maddison, 1991.

sonably smoothly functioning, and hence efficient, economic system."[24] This consideration may explain why some recent studies of the effects of government spending programs do not confirm the expectation that transfers are harmful to economic growth. Studies of large cross-sections of countries also show that those with more equal distributions of income have enjoyed higher rates of economic growth during much of the post–World War II era.[25]

DISTRIBUTION ACROSS GENERATIONS

So far, this chapter has considered matters of justice and distribution from an essentially static point of view. We have focused, that is, on distribution among the members of the population that is alive today. But another dimension of the distribution question that deserves some mention is the intertemporal question of distribution between different generations. What is a fair distribution of income between generations? What in fact determines this distribution?

Questions of intergenerational distribution assume considerable importance in the economics of growth and development. Consider, for example, a very poor country in which average annual income is now only $200. If, say, only 6 percent of the nation's product goes into capital formation, supported by a 6 percent rate of savings, the country may be able only to replace depreciating capital goods and to provide equipment for the new entrants to its labor force, permitting per capita income to be sustained at the $200 level in future years. Should savings and capital formation decline to, say, 3 percent of income, current consumption could rise, but income in the future would be even less than $200. Should saving and capital formation instead rise to, say, 10 percent of income, current consumption would fall, but per capita income could begin to rise. Consuming 4 percent less for a whole generation (beginning with an $8 decline in consumption this year) might allow average income to rise to, say, $400 in the next generation, to $1,000 a generation later, and so forth, until the country may attain a high standard of living. But is it fair to

24. Lindbeck, 1994, p. 3.
25. Persson and Tabellini, 1994, and Perotti, 1996, are among the studies showing a positive relationship between equality and growth but the absence of a negative relationship between transfers and growth.

demand sacrifices of the very poor generation living today to help a future generation that might, with such sacrifices, be relatively rich?

This kind of question arose most obviously in planned economies like the Soviet Union. Leaders in those countries could determine national saving and investment levels by fixing wages and farm prices and by setting targets for consumer and producer good production. Sacrifices were imposed on the first generation or two under those systems for the supposed benefit of future generations, as well as to bolster the nation and the prestige of its ideology. More recently, China has imposed heavy costs on its next generation by deciding that families should have only one child. Perhaps the next generation is best off this way, because a smaller population may be able to have a higher standard of living in an otherwise overpopulated country. But the policy also means that fewer working-age people will have to support more retired parents when they come of age.

Now, it might appear that the question need *not* be addressed by policymakers in market economies, so that its interest will soon be a matter of historical curiosity only. After all, the levels of savings and investment in a market economy are determined in a decentralized fashion. A household decides how much to save based on its projected future income and consumption needs, on the availability of relevant types of insurance, and on its desire to bequeath wealth to its heirs. Firms make investment decisions based on the cost of capital (including funds channeled from individual savers by financial intermediaries like banks and insurance companies), and on the projected returns to investment. The intergenerational distributive choices of individual households and the savings and growth rate of a national economy result from the aggregation of such decisions, without overall policy determination.

Intergenerational trade-offs do, however, present themselves to policymakers in market economies. Many developing countries, despite the use of markets and private enterprises, have sought to raise national investment rates to levels consistent with high growth targets, using a large variety of tools including government spending on infrastructure, and borrowing from foreign sources. Even in a developed economy, the tax treatment accorded to investment and savings (for instance, depreciation allowances, capital gains taxes, deductions for interest payments) influence choices between current and future consumption. Whether the taxes paid by a smaller working-age population can support the Social

Security program for a large population of "baby boom" retirees has become a hot political issue in the United States. The size of the national debt has likewise been depicted as an economic "ball and chain" to be bequeathed to the grandchildren of the currently living generation. Intergenerational trade-offs also arise when discussing environmental policy.

One aspect that makes intergenerational choices interesting is that, when long enough time frames are considered, not all of the individuals concerned can voice an opinion or attempt to influence decisions in their favor. The future generation is not yet born, so how is it to have a voice in current deliberations? Also, while some current redistribution is probably motivated by the desire to avoid social strains that might result in crime or even violence, the current generation needn't worry that its great-grandchildren will rise up against it!

Socialists have argued that bringing decisions on national growth and investment targets into the political arena is a step in the direction of giving the future generation a voice. Although not present in any literal sense, that is, at least their interests are being given formal consideration. Indeed, it has been argued that some households would support a higher national savings rate provided that they can be assured that others will make equal sacrifices. The only way to achieve such guarantees may be through the political process.

Unfortunately, there is no guarantee that politics will favor the future any more than do markets, nor is there a consensus that future generations are disadvantaged by the intergenerational choices made in a decentralized economy. A case can be made that they are not, at least in the industrial economies, where continuing economic growth and technological change may well assure that posterity is far richer than those living today. The real guarantor of the future, it might be argued, is the genetic imperative to see one's offspring survive and prosper: this may be the ultimate behavioral underpinning of the whole range of investments that people make in their children and grandchildren.[26] The case for a relatively decentralized approach comes in for more questions, though, when

26. The decision on present versus future consumption is not made by a strictly selfish "Homo economicus," according to this argument, but rather by a "selfish gene" that considers its future bearers just as worthy of resources as are its present ones. See Dawkins, 1989, and Bergstrom, 1996 (cited in Chapter 1).

we ask whether our progeny, for all of their gadgets and comforts, will inherit a livable, as opposed to an irreparably poisoned, planet — an issue to be revisited in our final chapter.

ALTERNATIVE WAYS OF REDUCING INEQUALITY

Let us now return to our primary concern, which is with distribution among the members of a given generation. The welfare state as it has been known in the industrialized economies in recent decades is one way of altering the income distribution resulting from the operation of the market. Others have also been proposed. One of these suggestions is called the "basic income grant."[27] Each citizen would receive a fixed, unconditional income grant, and the minimum wage and employer contributions to Social Security would be reduced. Thus, the grant could be viewed as an employment subsidy given to the worker rather than to the employer, and would be available even during spells of unemployment (or if the worker chooses to remain unemployed). As the grant would be unconditional but not sufficient by itself to provide more than basic necessities, it would arguably increase the supply of low-wage labor, while the demand for such labor would increase due to the fall in the minimum wage and other employer contributions. Proponents argue that the labor market would become more flexible, not only for the above reasons, but because part-time work (and hence job sharing) might increase, as it became more affordable. Workers might also use the grant to sustain them during periods of retraining or sabbatical. One obstacle to the adoption of such an approach is ideological: the idea that people are entitled to an income whether or not they choose to work does not square well with conventional social norms, which view income as a reward for work. Indeed, the proposal has the familiar earmarks of what American politicians derisively refer to as an "entitlement program," so proof that it would not increase overall government spending would be crucial to its adoption and maintenance.

Some other proposals focus on the relative equalization of capital holdings and earnings. Neoclassical economics includes a core theorem called

---

27. See Van Parijs, 1992.

the Second Fundamental Theorem of Welfare Economics, which says that any desired end distribution of goods or income can be achieved as the equilibrium of a competitive market economy given an appropriate distribution of endowments or purchasing power.[28] What this means is that any end state of incomes in which one might be interested can in principle be reached as the end result of the operation of competitive labor and other factor markets, without redistribution of incomes through the fiscal system, provided that ownership of capital and land were first distributed among individuals in the right fashion. To see that Joe and Jane end up with high incomes and Dan and Diane with low ones, just have Joe and Jane start out with sufficiently more assets than Dan and Diane do; do the reverse to achieve the opposite pattern of inequality; and to achieve approximate equality between them, give them roughly equal initial assets. If Dan and Diane will still be advantaged because they have skills that are in demand in the labor market — note that skills cannot readily be taken from one individual and given to another — just give Joe and Jane a sufficiently larger share of the financial or physical assets. And if you want, alter the future distribution of human assets by offering better job training and educational access to the formerly disadvantaged.

Why is redistribution of wealth not favored over redistribution of income, given that redistributing income is believed by many to harm work incentives? One reason is that transferring wealth would also have incentive effects. Of course, if wealth were redistributed once and only once, to establish the desired new pattern, and if this one-time redistribution were not anticipated before it occurred, it would not affect anyone's decisions regarding saving and investment. But the operation of the market tends to breed new inequalities over time, because of differences in households' demographic structures, propensities to save, labor market skills, and luck. For this reason, maintaining a relatively equal distribution of income would probably require periodic redistributions of wealth, which would be anticipated, and which could therefore deter saving. There are also a number of practical and moral obstacles to large-scale redistribution of wealth. Under existing institutions, personal wealth is

28. The theorem is seen by some as a vindication of John Stuart Mill's view (see Chapter 2) that economics can and should make a conceptual separation between production and distribution: society can use capitalism in the sphere of production but need not consider itself subject to immutable and impersonal laws governing the distribution of income.

much more difficult to monitor than is income, so evasion is easier. There is probably broad resistance to tampering with the accumulations from past effort and frugality, which have moral legitimacy with most segments of the populations of developed countries. It may be more acceptable to tax incomes before they have been claimed, thus working incrementally. Altering the asset distribution by changing the distribution of skills may also be more palatable than outright wealth transfers, due to its more incremental nature. Compared with income transfers, changing the distribution of human capital may have longer-lasting effects, too. This kind of change can be pursued by improving the access to education of the disadvantaged, and by countering early childhood deficits through preschool and other programs.

Although outright confiscation and redistribution of financial wealth is almost universally shunned, a few economists have suggested that rough equality in the distribution of financial assets could be achieved by having the government issue each citizen, upon reaching adulthood, a number of coupons redeemable for company stock shares. The coupons would earn the holder dividends, which can be more or less depending on company performance. Citizens would be motivated to invest their coupons in the companies judged to have the best prospects, and companies would be motivated to compete for the coupons by the fact that they would receive a payment out of a tax-financed national capital fund for each coupon placed with them. Citizens would have unequal earnings, reflecting differences in the skill (and luck) with which they placed their coupons. These earnings differences would motivate citizens to place their coupons carefully among prospective investments, and as a result the market in which coupons are traded for shares would, like a conventional stock market, serve as a barometer of how people evaluate each company's performance, and thus as one possible indicator upon which to base decisions on hiring, promoting, and compensating managers. But inequality of capital earnings would be small compared with that in existing capitalism, since the number of coupons each person could hold would be the same, coupons themselves could not be traded among individuals, and an individual's coupons would revert to the treasury upon her death.[29]

29. The coupon proposal is developed in Roemer, 1994. Possible deficiencies of the coupon stock market relative to the familiar one are that an absence of large stockholders would reduce the disciplinary check placed on managers by the threat of a shareholder-led ouster of management, and that small investors might not have

Worker cooperatives have sometimes been viewed as a means of combining the promise of economic justice with the dynamism and efficiency of markets and the profit motive. John Stuart Mill, for instance, whose views on the subject were mentioned in Chapter 3, referred to the cooperative system as "the nearest approach to social justice, and the most beneficial ordering of industrial affairs for the universal good, which it is possible at present to foresee."[30] Mill, living before the advent of universal education and suffrage, believed that educated workers would prefer to be self-employed members of cooperatives rather than subordinates working for the profit of an employer. He felt that this system would be advantageous not only from the standpoint of economic equality but also from that of productivity, due to the superior motivation with which it would afford workers.

Mill's productivity prediction has been confirmed by numerous studies. Yet his expectations regarding the demands of educated and politically emancipated workers have not been borne out. Perhaps aversion to bearing the full risks of enterprise plays a role here. The approach to worker participation in management by the legislative route of mandating co-determination, seen in several European countries including Germany, might be viewed, from this standpoint, as having arisen to play the role of a less risky substitute for Mill's cooperatives.[31] In any case, workers' participation in the ownership and control of their firms is recommended by

---

enough time or incentive to actively follow their companies' performances. Some of these difficulties could be remedied by allowing coupon holders to invest through intermediary mutual funds, which would pool large numbers of coupons and could thus exercise more clout in the market, while having an incentive to employ full-time investment analysts so as to rack up a good record and attract more coupons. Banks that help finance companies through loans could also play a greater role in monitoring company managers, as they do in economies like Japan's.

30. Mill, 1929, p. 792.

31. As mentioned in Chapter 3, Germany's co-determination laws require that employees elect half the members of the company boards of large firms. Full ownership of their own firms might require workers to bear substantially more risk than they do as employees earning mostly guaranteed wages. While worker-owners could go to outside financiers for additional financing, the cost of credit rises with the proportion of the firm's capital that is borrowed and unsecured by physical assets transferrable to the lender. This financial penalty to firms that cannot also attract financing by outside (nonemployee) owners is mitigated to the extent that all firms in an economy share a degree of worker control, as they do when co-determination is made mandatory.

many as an important element of a more egalitarian, market-based economic system due to its capacity to motivate workers with reduced supervisory costs. It may also contribute to workers' pride and self-esteem and, thus, to great equality of *social* rewards. Worker ownership of firms does not guarantee income equality, however, because it brings no guarantee of full employment in an economy as a whole, nor does it assure that workers in firms with differing capital-labor ratios, market advantages, and so on will earn equal profits. More egalitarian economic outcomes may thus require complementary policies to facilitate competition, financing, retraining, and firm creation.

When considering alternatives such as those just mentioned, it is worth remarking that the now conventional framework of progressive taxation and transfers (the welfare state) may also be susceptible to creative innovations. While such discussion is for the time being speculative in nature, the future may well see dramatic improvements over existing methods, which could in part derive from improved selection of targets of taxation, from better checks on bureaucratic waste, and from more intelligent delimitation of eligibility criteria. Cross-disciplinary approaches that take into account the causes of welfare dependency, the determinants of morale and professionalism in government bureaucracies, the causes of tax fraud, and so forth might prove helpful in this regard.

TRADE-OFF, OR EXPANDABLE FRONTIER?

So far our discussion has tended to assume that gains in equity will have to be purchased at a cost of losses in efficiency. It thus presumes what economist Arthur Okun memorably dubbed "the big trade-off" between those two goals.[32] The example of participatory firms, however, suggests that there are ways to promote both equity and efficiency simultaneously. In that example, firms in which workers share in ownership and risks generate stronger work incentives and thus more productivity and earnings, while simultaneously increasing the proportion of profits going to labor providers rather than financiers. Both financiers and workers increase their earnings, and society has more goods to consume. Other examples of this type are also worth mentioning.

32. Okun, 1975.

One of these is education. Because credit systems are imperfect and poor families are often unable to finance their children's education, the absence of public funding or assistance means that children from wealthier households will tend to get more education, all else being equal. But the potential to acquire the skills imparted by education is not necessarily correlated with wealth. Thus, the overall benefit to society from a given level of resources spent on education will be somewhat less when education is distributed based on wealth than when it is distributed based on potential. Selectively redistributing income to overcome the barriers to education for those with great promise but little wealth is a way of redistributing income that may make for both more equal economic outcomes *and* higher national productivity.

A third illustration is the distribution of productive assets like land and capital. These assets are likely to be most productive when put in the hands of people who are most knowledgeable about their specific features and who have the most skill in using them. Yet, the individuals filling that description are sometimes not in a position to purchase them. Take, for instance, a farmer who works a particular plot of land and is thus most capable of managing it productively. That farmer will get the most out of this land if his income falls or rises depending on its productivity, as would be the case if he were to own it. If he is too poor for such ownership and is instead hired by an absentee landowner who pays him a fixed wage, or even some portion of the harvest, he has less incentive to put in maximum effort. Helping the farmer to buy the land not only improves the distribution of wealth; it also increases total output, in this case. The same may apply to the ownership of tools or a small business, which may be facilitated, for instance, by favorable treatment of small business loans.

DISTRIBUTION OF NONPECUNIARY GOODS

Most discussions of economic justice focus, as this chapter has done, on the distribution of income and wealth. But there are several reasons why a discussion of these factors alone is incomplete. First, as we have noted already, the justice of a given distribution cannot be ascertained, according to most people's moral principles, without knowing something about the individual contributions of effort that are associated with it. Equality of incomes or of wealth may be accepted as a rough proxy for overall equality of well-being, but most people would agree that this is only a rough approximation to what really interests us.

One reason why effort levels may be pertinent to assessing the justice of an economy is that, if both leisure and income are desirable, two people can be equally well off when one enjoys less income than the other but has more leisure. However, this is not always the case. An unemployed individual may prefer to be employed because she values the income she could thus obtain more than the leisure she would forgo. But she may also want to be employed for other reasons. It is widely recognized that work is a source of self-respect, identity, social contact, and emotional support. An able-bodied person unable to find work may experience a loss of well-being that goes beyond the loss of income entailed.

More broadly, it is the nature of the job, as much as the effort and time involved, that is relevant to assessing its contribution to well-being. Some jobs may come with rewards in the form of pleasant surroundings, amiable companions, challenges and the satisfactions of meeting them, or social status; other jobs may offer only some of these benefits; and still other jobs may entail little of any of them. Other roles that do not entail pay, such as the role of a homemaker and care provider within a household, or that of a volunteer in a hospital or tutoring program, must also be assessed along similar lines. Insofar as well-being is a function of satisfaction with one's occupation, on the one hand, and of income on the other, a more complete assessment of economic justice should take all of these factors into account.

Unfortunately, the case can be made that the distribution of well-being in modern economies is typically even more unequal than is that of incomes, because the people who earn more money, such as physicians, business executives, and athletes, often also have more sources of satisfaction in their work, more social status and respect, and so forth, while those who earn less, such as workers in certain services, often also have less satisfying work and lower status. One should avoid drawing overly sweeping conclusions, of course, since high income is also associated in many instances with high stress, long hours, and even social isolation from or tensions with subordinates. Lower income, on the other hand, can be associated with great satisfactions, for instance in some nursing or teaching jobs. It isn't rare to find a person who seems as cheerful as can be interacting with people while emptying wastebaskets or making sandwiches, and another who is always tense and irritable doing work that requires a high degree of concentration. The freedom to choose one's occupation should in principle help people to sort themselves across jobs according to their personal preferences with respect to the earnings potential, sociability, and demandingness of different lines of work—though crucial decisions must sometimes be taken before one knows one's preferences very well.

These brief remarks serve to highlight the complexity of undertaking a more comprehensive assessment of economic justice. Although corners must be cut if we are to make judgments in finite time, the general point still stands: a complete discussion of economic fairness needs to look at more than the distribution of incomes alone.

CONCLUSION

In public discussions of the economy, questions of equity or fairness rarely trail far behind those of growth and efficiency. It may therefore seem surprising that much economics teaching treats the fairness issue as falling outside the scope of the discipline. Striving as they do to approach their subject matter scientifically, economists feel more comfortable discussing efficiency, which they can define unambiguously and which no one seems opposed to, than equity, which has many contending definitions, each of which at least some group objects to. The fact that efficiency is relatively uncontroversial does not, however, justify its treatment as a preferred or somehow ethically neutral objective. Some feelings about fairness, such as its relation to contributions and needs, are widely shared, moreover. Both the appropriateness and the necessity of linking reward to effort is widely agreed to, for example, as is the desirability of some equality, and of helping those unable to do so to meet their needs.

While ethical concerns are never far from the picture, the economics of income and wealth distribution is susceptible to positive analysis too. Redistribution of income and wealth, for example, can be analyzed using a model in which people vote on the progressivity of taxation. With such a model in hand, we can ask why the industrial democracies, in which wealth is quite unequally distributed, do not engage in more radical redistribution of property, which on a naive view would appear to be in the interest of the average voter. The impacts of incentive considerations, of coalition structure, and of moral beliefs are all likely to figure in the answer. The industrial democracies do alter distributive outcomes using progressive taxation and expenditures, and alternatives like the basic income grant, "coupon socialism," and worker ownership have also been proposed.

When we look at contending views of justice, we notice that pure principles tend to run up against problems of feasibility. For instance, we may wish to reward only the productivity resulting from an individual's hard work, but it may be difficult to know what part of her output results from her own efforts versus the luck of the draw with respect to genes and upbringing. What is feasible, with respect to income distribution, is also unavoidably constrained if people are at least partly self-interested and if they are to be free in determining their own effort levels. While there are sometimes trade-offs between provision of incentives and equality, however, equity and efficiency are by no means always in conflict. Nor is there evidence that society can accord weight to equity concerns only at massive and unacceptable costs to economic efficiency. On the contrary, societies that have enjoyed the greatest prosperity have also engaged in the highest levels of redistribution, and economic growth has proceeded more favorably in societies with relatively equal distributions of resources than in those where wealth is concentrated in a few hands.

REFERENCES

Bowles, Samuel, and Herbert Gintis, 1999, "Efficient Redistribution: New Rules for Markets, States, and Communities," *Politics and Society* 24:307–42.

Dawkins, Richard, 1989, *The Selfish Gene*, new ed. Oxford: Oxford University Press.

Feldman, Allan, 1980, *Welfare Economics and Social Choice Theory*. Boston: Kluwer-Nijhoff.

Glyn, Andrew, Alan Hughes, Alain Lipietz, and Ajit Singh, 1990, "The Rise and Fall of the Golden Age," pp. 39–125 in Stephen Marglin and Juliet Schor, eds., *The Golden Age of Capitalism: Reinterpreting the Postwar Experience*. Oxford: Clarendon.

Harsanyi, John, 1982, "Morality and the Theory of Rational Behavior," in Amartya Sen and Bernard Williams, eds., *Utilitarianism and Beyond*. New York: Cambridge University Press.

Maddison, Angus, 1991, *Dynamic Forces in Capitalist Development: A Long-Run Comparative View*. Oxford: Oxford University Press.

Milanovic, Branko, 1999, "Do More Unequal Countries Redistribute More? Does the Median Voter Hypothesis Hold?" unpublished paper, World Bank.

Mill, John Stuart, 1929 [1848], *Principles of Political Economy with Some of Their Applications to Social Philosophy*, ed. Sir W. J. Ashley. London: Longmans, Green.

Mishel, Lawrence, and Jared Bernstein, 1994, *The State of Working America, 1994–1995*. Armonk, N.Y.: M. E. Sharpe.

Nozick, Robert, 1977, *Anarchy, State, and Utopia*. New York: Basic.

Okun, Arthur M., 1975, *Equality and Efficiency: The Big Trade-Off*. Washington D.C.: The Brookings Institution.

Penner, Rudolph, 1994, "Federal Budget," in D. Greenwald, ed., *McGraw-Hill Encyclopedia of Economics*. New York: McGraw-Hill.

Perotti, Roberto, 1996, "Growth, Income Distribution, and Democracy: What the Data Say," *Journal of Economic Growth* 1:149–87.

Persson, Torsten, and Guido Tabellini, 1994, "Is Inequality Harmful for Growth?" *American Economic Review* 84:600–621.

Rawls, John, 1971, *A Theory of Justice*. Cambridge: Harvard University Press.

Roemer, John, 1994, "A Future for Socialism," *Politics and Society* 22:451–78.

Roemer, John, 1998, *Equality of Opportunity*. Cambridge: Harvard University Press.

Rothbard, Murray, 1973, *For a New Liberty*. New York: Macmillan.

Sawyer, Malcolm, 1976, "Income Distribution in OECD Countries," OECD Occasional Studies. Paris: OECD.

Tarascio, Vincent, 1969, "Paretian Welfare Theory: Some Neglected Aspects," *Journal of Political Economy* 77:1–20.

Van Parijs, Philippe, ed., 1992, *Arguing for Basic Income*. London: Verso.

Wolff, Edward, 1994, "International Wealth Inequality in the 1980s," paper presented at the annual meetings of the American Economic Association, Boston.

Wolfinger, Raymond, and Steven Rosenstone, 1980, *Who Votes?* New Haven: Yale University Press.

SUGGESTIONS FOR FURTHER READING

Atkinson, Anthony, 1980, *Wealth, Income, and Inequality*, 2d ed. Oxford: Oxford University Press.

Atkinson, Anthony, 1983, *The Economics of Inequality*. Oxford: Clarendon.

Combee, Jerry, and Edgar Norton, 1991, *Economic Justice in Perspective: A Book of Readings*. Englewood Cliffs, N.J.: Prentice Hall.

Meade, James, 1965, *Efficiency, Equality, and the Ownership of Property*. Cambridge: Harvard University Press.

Roemer, John, 1988, *Free to Lose: An Introduction to Marxist Economic Philosophy*. Cambridge: Harvard University Press.

Sen, Amartya, 1997, *On Economic Inequality* (enlarged ed. with an annex "On Economic Inequality After a Quarter Century" by James Foster and Amartya Sen). New York: Oxford University Press.

Wolff, Edward, ed., 1987, *International Comparisons of the Distribution of Household Wealth*. New York: Oxford University Press.

Wolff, Edward, 1996, *Top Heavy: The Increasing Inequality of Wealth in America and What Can Be Done About It*. New York: New Press.

THE
ECONOMY
AND
QUALITY
OF LIFE

Some persons are led to believe that making money is the object of household management, and the whole idea of their lives is that they ought either to increase their money without limit, or at any rate not to lose it. The origin of this disposition in men is that they are intent upon living only, and not upon living well; and, as their desires are unlimited, they also desire that the means of gratifying them should be without limit.
—*Aristotle*, Politics

I know not why it should be a matter of congratulation that persons who are already richer than any one needs to be, should have doubled their means of consuming things which give little or no pleasure except as representative of wealth.
—*John Stuart Mill*,
Principles of Political Economy

The most important challenge for the twenty-first century is to bridge the paradox between the harsh business reality and human and social values.
—*Klaus Schwab,*
president of the World Economic Forum

Turn the whole wide world into a TV show
So it's just the same game wherever you go
You never meet a soul that you don't already know
One big advertisement for the status quo
As if these celebrities were your close friends
As if you knew how the story ends
As if you weren't sitting in a room alone
And there was somebody real at the other end of the phone
—*James Taylor,* "Slap Leather"

"Much of the world's water is stored in glaciers and the great polar ice sheets. But these frozen reservoirs are melting rapidly, and the water they release could cause a catastrophic rise in sea levels. Within the next 50 years or so, the last of the rivers of ice that gave Glacier National Park in Montana its name will run dry. In 1850 the area was home to more than 150 glaciers; today there are fewer than 50. More inland glaciers are melting away in Europe and around the world. Last year, researchers from the National Snow and Ice Data Center (NSIDC) at the University of Colorado in Boulder reported that the largest glacier on Africa's Mount Kenya had lost 92 percent of its mass and that the glaciers in the Russian Caucasus Mountains had shriveled to half their former size the past century. Glaciologists monitor these mid-latitude glaciers, such as those in Glacier National Park, as a barometer of global climate change. And there is no question that the world—whether as part of a natural cycle, from the result of human activity, or both—is becoming a warmer place. The impact of this global meltdown is more than aesthetic—the water released ends up in the oceans, raising sea levels and having potentially devastating economic and social impacts.

"But the mountain glaciers contain only 6 percent of the world's ice. More worrisome to researchers are the vast ice sheets of Antarctica and Greenland, which hold about 90 percent of the world's fresh water. If just 10 percent of the water locked in these frozen reservoirs is added to the oceans, geologists predict that sea levels will rise by more than 20 feet, drowning low-lying islands and inundating continental coasts. So far, these ice sheets have seemed to be stable and firmly anchored to islands and the nearby coasts, but new data indicate that they, too, are crumbling in the face of the thermal onslaught. Over the past 50 years, the Antarctic has warmed by about 4.5 degrees Celsius. In a 1978 article J. H. Mercer of Ohio State University predicted that if the south polar regions were warmed five degrees Celsius, the floating ice shelves surrounding the West Antarctic ice sheet would quickly disintegrate, flooding coastlines around the world in the process. [In] October [1998], Mercer's once controversial idea gained credibility when scientists at the National Oceanic and Atmospheric Administration's National Ice Center revealed satellite data showing a massive iceberg 92 miles long by 30 miles wide, with an area of 2,751 square miles [well over twice the size of the state of Rhode Island], breaking free from the Ronne Ice Shelf in Antarctica."[1]

1. Alan Hall, "Going, Going—Gone?" *Scientific American* Web site April 26, 1999.

Every now and then, the purchases we've been putting off mount up, and the right weekend arrives for the members of my family to get into our car and drive to our favorite shopping mall. After driving for about twenty minutes, we exit a four-lane highway and head for an expanse of department and specialty stores surrounded on four sides by vast stretches of parking lots. Anchoring the mall are three large department stores that sell men's, women's, and children's clothing, watches, electronic products, furniture, perfumes, shoes, and much more. Connecting these larger stores is a huge enclosure lined with two tiers of smaller shops. Some of these shops specialize in greeting cards and stationery, others in fancy gift items, others in sporting equipment and shoes, others in CDs and tapes, others in children's toys. There are bank teller machines, restaurants, and a "food court" where I can buy Indian curry from one vendor while my daughter has a hot dog from a second, my son a slice of pizza from a third, and my wife some Japanese food. The mall is large and attractive, with quarried stone floors and entryways, fountains, glass elevators, several sets of escalators that my kids liked riding on when they were younger, and open product displays including at least one shiny new automobile. People dressed in casual, stylish clothing, many of them in family groups, some couples, some groups of teenagers, and some lone shoppers, stroll by us on all sides. Beyond the mall lie more stores, banks, medical buildings, and office parks.

From the look of things, a vast amount of purchasing power passes through our mall every day. Certainly it must do so on a Saturday! People are buying everything from fine tableware to exercise equipment to electronic knick-knacks to hundred-dollar pairs of sneakers, sweaters, and designer neckties. The Egyptian pharoah Cheops for whom the great pyramid at Gizeh was built, the Chinese emperor Qin Shi-Huang who had vast armies of terra-cotta soldiers made for his burial site, the Inca emperor Atahuallpa who, carried on a litter by eighty attendants and accompanied by an army of forty thousand soldiers, came to meet the Spanish conquistador Francisco Pizarro in 1532, Sir Isaac Newton, or a person plucked from any of a dozen poor countries that I could reach within a day's flight from my local international airport—any and all of them would be amazed could they see this display of wealth at the local mall that my family takes for granted. Some of my contemporaries, by contrast, are bored by the mall and avoid trips there by logging on to the

Internet with their personal computers and ordering what they want on-line, with delivery by mail or parcel service a few days later.

Our brick-and-mortar mall and the equally well stocked marketplaces we find on-line certainly suggest to me that, from the standpoint of material goods, and at least for those with a well-paying job, the combination of modern capitalism and modern science has been a dream-fulfilling cornucopia, a goose that lays golden eggs! Still, I have to wonder at times whether all of this translates into a high standard of living in some deeper sense, into a high quality of life. Does this material abundance in any sense purchase happiness? Does it invite opportunities for personal growth and fulfillment? Does it in any way improve the quality of our social interactions, or raise the level of our moral discourse? And what if it is dooming our descendants to suffer the consequences of environmental catastrophe? The answers to these questions are less self-evident than is the fact that this goose we have gotten for ourselves is one that we are loath to part with.

One could ask, perhaps, what questions about the quality of life have to do with economics or the economy. Isn't economics really about the production and distribution of goods and services, about the generation of wealth, and about rational decision making? And must we really ask more of an economy than that it bring us material prosperity? Isn't it up to people, once they have the requisite physical goods, to show the wisdom to live a good life upon that material platform, without blaming any shortcomings on their economy?

One could plausibly answer those last questions in the affirmative and be done with the matter as a student of economics. But one aim of this book has been to look a bit further, at questions that are often forgotten because they fall between the stools of the disciplines. One could argue, moreover, that how we organize our lives for economic purposes — to make a living and to provide ourselves with the things we want or need — is the most important single factor driving nearly all of our life choices. Economic considerations help to determine where we live, the layout of our cities, suburbs, and towns, how long we go to school for, what we study, whether or not we remain in the place we grew up in, close to family and friends, how likely we are to get to know our neighbors. What we expect with regard to having interesting and satisfying work, to being able to live in accordance with our moral values, and more are all deeply influenced by the economic dimensions of our lives and the lives of those we know. If all this is true, then it may not be enough to judge economic arrangements only by how full the shopping malls are (or what is available on-line). The economy should be judged, as well, on the basis of its innumerable consequences for the quality of our lives. And from this standpoint, it is worth asking not only, as we did in Chapter 4, whether a prosperous economy can be maintained and generalized to the world as a whole, or as in Chapter 5, whether prosperity can be distributed fairly. There are also compelling reasons to ask to what degree a prosperous economy can be made compatible with a good life, and how this can be done. If economics is to have something to say about which arrangements or outcomes are more or less *socially optimal*, then it is obliged to join with philosophers, psychologists, sociologists, and others in thinking about such issues.

THE SAGA OF DR. DOE

The doctrinaire economist and the dyed-in-the-wool humanist may have a difficult time communicating with each other. The economist hears the questions just raised and says, "I don't see what all of the fuss is about. If we can simply attain perfect competition, then the economy will produce the goods and even provide the jobs that people want. If you don't like what it is that people happen to want, don't blame the economy for that." But the humanist sees a red flag. "Perfect competition," she asks; "how good is *that*? Is the human ideal really one of every person for his or herself, each one *competing* against the other?"

Deadlock. Talking past each other. But the encounter between economics, narrowly construed, and human concerns of a broader sort doesn't have to go this way. To illustrate this, consider Professor Darin Doe, a newly minted junior faculty member at a large American university. Our story begins with Dr. Doe quietly sitting in his office preparing for his lecture on indifference curves. Suddenly, a small group of Ec 101 students descends upon him. Ec 101 is one of the most heavily enrolled courses at Doe's university, a "must take" for each prospective economics or business major, but sampled also by students representing a wide variety of interests. The course is about to enter its third week, and lately an eclectic group of budding English, philosophy, sociology, environmental studies, anthropology, psychology, and political science majors, who make up about 15 percent of Doe's class, have been comparing their reactions to it. Some are thinking of dropping the course, saying it confirms their expectation that economists have nothing to say about the issues that concern them. Others argue that it is important not to dismiss the economic approach too quickly. But after scanning the remaining chapters of their textbook, they too feel a bit uncertain. After one heated discussion, this second group decides to go talk to Professor Doe. When, if at all, they want to know, will the course be getting around to some of the things that *really* matter to them?

"How's that?" responds a confused Professor Doe.

"Well, sure, supply and demand are important," one of the students explains, "but they barely scratch the surface of the ways in which the economy affects our lives. There are bigger issues out there, like vanishing leisure time, runaway consumerism, global warming, job insecurity, and the influence of money on politics. Doesn't economics have anything to say about these things?"

"Those certainly *are* big issues," says Professor Doe, setting the textbook down on his desk. "But I'm not sure that I can say very much about them, when there are declining marginal utility and diminishing returns and substitution effects and more still to come in our course. Besides, there's probably no scientific consensus about some of the things that you mention, and I can't talk about them with any expertise. But I'd be happy to discuss them with you outside of class time. Why don't you let me finish preparing for this afternoon's lecture right now, and if you'd like, we can all meet here again sometime tomorrow or next week."

A time is agreed upon, and the students leave the professor to his textbook. Outside in the hall, they meet briefly to prepare for their discussion, coming up with a list of topics, and dividing them among themselves. Each student agrees to prepare a brief presentation on one topic. Here is what they have come up with when they return the following week.

MONEY AND HAPPINESS

The first student to speak is Joy. She's been shopping around for courses in different departments, including psychology, philosophy, religion, and literature, trying to figure out what will make for a satisfying course of studies, and what she might make use of in later life. The way of thinking Professor Doe is introducing her to is interesting, she thinks, but the course has yet to help answer some of the popular criticisms of market society that she's being reading for other courses. She wishes Professor Doe would make contact with some of those issues.

"I took an intriguing course on psychology and philosophy in which it was suggested," Joy begins, "that advertising and competition for status encourage people to think that if they have more money and more possessions, they will be happier. But money does not in fact buy happiness. The desire for money just puts people on a sort of 'hedonic treadmill,' always believing that with a little more, they'll be happy. What they usually find, though, is that when they have obtained that little bit more, there is yet something else that they are without. Now, it's that something else that they think would do the trick. A good illustration is a study by a social psychologist who asked people in both a poor country, India, and a rich country, the United States, what it would take to make them really happy. A forty-year-old skilled worker earning thirty dollars a month in India replied: 'I hope in the future I will not get any disease. Now I am coughing. I also hope I can purchase a bicycle. I hope my children will study well and that I can provide them with an education. I also would sometime like to own a fan and maybe a radio.'

"A twenty-eight-year-old lawyer in the United States replied: 'I would like to provide my family with an income to allow them to live well—to have the proper recreation, to go camping, to have music and dancing lessons for the children, and to have family trips. I wish we could belong to a country club and do more entertaining.'[2]

"It's easy to see that once the Indian worker and others around him get the bicycle, they'll begin to dream of having motorcycles, and after that of having cars, and after that maybe sport-utility vehicles, and there will be no real end. It is this ratcheting of aspirations that explains why, once a basic minimum of material needs is satisfied, further increases in income show no real tendency to increase happiness in surveys that ask people how happy they are. In a given country at a given time, to be sure, people with higher incomes tend to report that they are somewhat happier, on average, than do people with lower incomes. But as everyone's income goes up, an income once high enough to make people relatively happy

2. From a study by Cantril, 1965, cited in Easterlin, 1996, chapter 10.

produces no more self-assessed happiness than did a low income in the past. A striking example is that as real per capita income rose fivefold in Japan between 1958 and 1987, there was no improvement in self-reported happiness. Likewise, there is no trend in average self-reported happiness in the United States between the early post–World War II period and 1991, a period in which real per capita income more than doubled.[3]

"A political scientist who studies these issues from a psychological perspective, Robert Lane, agrees with economist Tibor Scitovsky that most of the sources of real satisfaction in life have no price and do not pass through the market. Lane cites studies that suggest that self-reported happiness is more closely linked with happiness in marriage, number of friends, and satisfaction with aspects of one's job other than pay than it is with income. However, Lane argues, many people are misled by market culture into placing a higher premium on seeking more income and goods than is consistent with their own well-being. This leads them to concentrate on making money at the expense of doing fulfilling work and investing in emotionally satisfying relationships, with the result of declining real happiness. Lane supports the last point by referring to declining survey reports of happiness with marriage, job, and overall situation in the United States from 1946 to 1994. He also suggests that a rise in clinical depression in industrial countries is linked to these trends."[4]

"Perhaps putting too much of a premium on wealth and goods is foolish," says Professor Doe, "but how is any of this the fault of the economy? Doesn't the market simply supply the goods that people demand?"

"That's just it," Joy replies. "Economists seem to think of people's wants as a given. You assume that you have a bunch of people who have certain existing wants. You then claim that you are going to evaluate possible mechanisms that will help those people satisfy those wants. After looking at the alternatives, you conclude that the market is great because it fills the place of such a mechanism with great efficiency and freedom. The problem with this approach is that the economy is not only a satisfier, it is also a *creator* of wants. Let me quote from Frank Knight, who my philosophy professor tells me was an influential economist active in the 1920s and '30s. I brought a book of Knight's with me, in which he says,

3. These results are summarized in the chapter by Easterlin, 1996. For another discussion, see Lane, 2000.

4. See Lane, 2000, and the more condensed discussion in Lane, 1998.

'the economic order does far more than select and compare wants for exchangeable goods and services; its activity extends to the formation and radical transformation, if not to the outright creation, of the wants themselves; they as well as the means of their gratification are largely products of the system.'[5] Well, the kind of economy we have may be preventing us from being happy by creating new wants as quickly as it can satisfy them, and by turning our attentions away from the equally or more important things that it cannot provide."

"This is all very interesting," says Doe, "though I'm not sure it's all exactly as you contend. After all, people in poor countries, at least, do have very legitimate needs that go unmet, and even in very rich countries there are some at the bottom who are wanting for certain basics. Market economies have by and large proved better able to meet more people's needs than any other kind of economy that has yet existed. And the idea that the man in India who is hoping for a bicycle will soon want an SUV may be a bit exaggerated. I'd wager that if he gets as far as a motorcycle in his lifetime, he'll count himself lucky."

"Perhaps," replies Joy, "but let's look at the industrial economies, and at the bulk of the people there, who are not poor. This is where I have my main problem, because it is there that more money and more goods are most likely to have lost their ability to contribute to happiness. Think of it from a biological point of view. People are endowed by nature with the drive to procure the things that they need for their survival. Without this drive, the human race would never have survived. But modern technology makes it possible for us to obtain more than we really need, creating a revolutionary new situation. Our biological cravings for sugar, salt, and fat, which are difficult to obtain in nature, were no problem to us until we found the means to supply ourselves with these things in enormous quantities. Now people must struggle to control their intake of foods that are harmful if taken in excess of needs. Similarly, our bodies need a certain amount of exercise, which we naturally obtained when we foraged and when we engaged in agriculture and other labor-demanding activities. But in today's world where a great many jobs require little exercise, people experience ill health unless they regularly exercise. What this suggests to me is that adjustments to possibilities of abundance may be required

5. Knight, 1935, p. 46. The essay from which the quotation is taken originally appeared in the *Quarterly Journal of Economics* in 1923.

still more generally. But our economic mechanism works relentlessly against our making the needed adjustments. It keeps telling us that we need more things.

"To make money, companies must sell products, and to sell products, they must convince people that the products will satisfy needs. While people are amusing themselves with television, magazines, and other media, they are exposed both to explicit advertisements and to more subtle messages about what 'successful' or 'cool' people consume. One estimate is that 'by the time the typical American reaches college, he or she will have spent three to four hours a week watching TV ads, about 100,000 of them in all.'[6] These advertisements and messages take advantage of human nature, appealing to sexual drives and to the related desires for status that are built into us by evolution. Once the use of a new product becomes widespread, this in itself creates expectations and pressures that make others feel the need for it. If everyone else is using mouthwash and deodorant, I'm afraid that I'll attract unwanted attention unless I do the same. Likewise, I may once have been content to communicate with my friends and relatives by letter or phone, but now they're enjoying the convenience of e-mail, leaving me out of the loop until I spring for a personal computer and accompanying software. And so on."

"Those are certainly interesting points," says Professor Doe. "Perhaps advertising *is* sometimes harmful, but I'm not sure it would be beneficial to limit it. After all, the right to advertise is part of free speech, and besides, advertising and the industries it makes possible are large sectors of our economy, without which millions of people might be without a source of livelihood. I'm not sure what, if anything, can be done about this. But let's first hear from the others before thinking about how these problems might be addressed."

"Agreed," says Joy, "but just one more thing. Before I finish, I want to suggest to you that advertising as such may be merely the tip of the iceberg. It reflects the drive to produce more that is built into our economic system, a system that needs growth and profits in the same way that a person needs air to breath. The possibility that a good life might be measured in other ways — for instance in terms of satisfying relationships with other people, or of finding ways to help others who are in need, or of cultivating a spiritual sensibility, or of broadening one's cultural horizons —

6. Goodstein, 1999, p. 208.

those possibilities are shoved aside 365 days of the year because they have no spokesmen in the market economy. Our very success in creating prosperity has pushed aside the things we used to have more time for when we were resigned to more modest standards of living, unlikely to leave our places of birth, and forced by circumstances to rely upon one another in more immediate and intimate ways."

THE STRESSFUL SOCIETY

Next up is Chase, an anthropology major who is taking his first course in economics. In today's conversation, he takes on the issue of stress and overwork. "My issue is closely related to Joy's," he begins. "But I want to focus on the work demands and stress that we take on in our efforts to meet those insatiable needs for things, things, and more things."

"In my anthropology classes, I've learned that people in industrialized societies work longer hours than do people in foraging and horticultural societies. Apparently, people took up, and then intensified, agricultural production when there were no longer enough edible plants and animals to be obtained by gathering and hunting. Agriculture made it possible to support far larger populations, but the increased productivity was of no benefit to the average individual, who in fact had to work far longer hours to wrest a living from the soil. Once dense populations had to feed themselves on small resource bases, there was no going back to the earlier way of life, and many new problems set in, including large-scale warfare, epidemics, and the exploitation of peasants and slaves by small elites.

"Well, my immediate concern is not about why life failed to improve for the first agriculturalists," says Chase, "but why we haven't regained the leisure of earlier times even after all the technological progress that's taken place in recent generations. Today's developed countries support vastly larger populations at a far higher standard of living with far less physically onerous work. We've made advances in health care, we've outlawed slavery and serfdom, we have governments that are accountable to our people, and we in the developed countries have even managed to avoid wars with other advanced countries for over half a century. But instead of relaxing and enjoying the fruits of this progress, we're running around faster than ever, and many of us feel intense stress day in and day out.

"The amount of work that we do shows a declining trend between the days of the nineteenth-century mills, notorious for their twelve- and fourteen-hour workdays, and the middle of the twentieth century. Yet the time we devote to work probably *hasn't* yet fallen below the work hours of our medieval ancestors, or those of many horticulturalists, pastoralists, and hunter-gatherers. And work hours may even have begun to increase again in recent years. A controversial book by economist Juliet Schor, for instance, argues that the average American worker performs about 1,950 hours of paid labor a year, down from 3,650 hours in 1850, but still more than is estimated for a typical male peasant in thirteenth-century England (1,620 hours). And Schor argues that work hours display a rising, not a falling, trend between the 1960s and the early 1990s. In addition to that, she reports that since 1945, the proportion of married women participating in the market labor force has risen from around 20 percent to almost 60 percent. Average American wages have been stagnant in recent decades, so modest gains in living standards for typical families have depended on having more than one wage-earner in the labor force. Among other things, this means that a married worker who is working more hours is much less likely to have another adult at home to take care of the house and children. Women who enter the labor market may cut back on their work at home somewhat as men expand their help with household chores, but total hours worked between the market and the home are up for both sexes."[7]

"You said that Schor's book is controversial," notes Professor Doe.

"Yes," replies Chase. "John Robinson and Geoffrey Godbey, for instance, conclude from reviewing a series of 'time diary' studies that leisure has actually increased since the 1960s. But the difference between theirs and Schor's findings is not enough to cast doubt on the conclusion that work hours in the United States have in any case not declined much, if at all, in recent decades. More educated workers work especially long hours, according to Robinson and Godbey. And Americans have failed to increase their vacation time as have Europeans: Schor contrasts the four- or five-week vacations guaranteed by law in Austria, Belgium, Finland, France, Greece, Iceland, the Netherlands, and Switzerland, and the five- to eight-week vacations commonly agreed to by employers in France, Germany, and Sweden, to the much shorter vacations, and absence of such legal guarantees, in the United States. And Robinson and Godbey

7. Schor, 1992.

report survey results that show that the proportion of Americans who say they 'always feel rushed' rose from 22 percent in 1971 to 35 percent in 1992, while the percentage who 'almost never have time on their hands that they don't know what to do with' rose from 48 percent to 61 percent during that same period. Again, the higher the education, the greater the perception of stress: the proportion reporting moderate to great stress rises from 46 percent, among high school dropouts, to 65 percent for college graduates and 67 percent for those with some education beyond college. By attending college, it looks like *we're* signing up for lives of high anxiety," he says, glancing around at the others.

"Just one more thing," Chase adds, preparing to conclude. "So far, I've been focusing on the balance between work and leisure time. But I don't want to leave you with the impression that I assume that the goal of society should necessarily be to minimize work time. Many social scientists and philosophers argue that work can be the most fulfilling part of one's life, a source of challenges, of a sense of identity, of self-respect, of a sense of belonging. Almost all agree that few prefer to be unemployed, even if receiving an adequate stipend from the government, over being employed in a reasonably satisfying job. So, in a more perfect world, we might want to see people being given more choices about their work hours and more flexibility to adjust them as needed to take care of family responsibilities and such, but we don't necessarily want to see average work time contracting dramatically from present levels. The issue, then, may be not so much how much time we spend at work, but rather whether or not our work is satisfying, or contributes as much as it might to our development as individuals. And some critics argue both that the market doesn't respond to workers' desires for satisfying work, and that market culture fails to cultivate the concern with workplace satisfaction that would be in workers' best long-term interests.[8] Satisfying work might be work that gives more decision-making autonomy to the worker, that provides more variety of tasks and responsibilities, that gives more opportunities for teamwork.

"There's been experimentation with things like 'quality circles' and 'job enlargement,' which have some of these features, and there is evidence that adopting these ideas can increase worker satisfaction without sacrificing productivity. But it's not clear that the changes have gone far

8. See Lane, 2000, and sources cited there.

enough yet, since overall job satisfaction, at least in the United States, still shows a downward trend.[9] Could it be that, at the same time that our society breeds an appetite for consumer goods, it inculcates the attitude that work is a necessary evil, that you should expect to dislike your job, and that it is the necessary price to pay for all the goodies you can have when you go home with your paycheck? In other words, is the dichotomy that we draw in economics between work and leisure — where work is assumed to bring disutility while leisure is the time for utility from consumption — is that dichotomy itself part of what prevents us from demanding and designing more satisfying jobs?"

ECONOMY AND FAMILY

Next up is Mary, a soft-spoken sophomore who has been gravitating toward sociology courses. "I have only a little bit to add to what Joy and Chase have said. I want to raise some issues about families and the economy.

"Our textbook talks about the household as a unit that makes consumption and labor market choices," Mary continues, "but it doesn't discuss ways in which the economy affects the composition and stability of that unit. It seems that this ought to be a concern of economics, but is it? My grandparents grew up in large families that their dads were somehow able to support, with moms at home all day to manage the household, and marriages that stayed together. But now look at *my* family. My dad left my mom when I was seven and remarried; this kind of thing is pretty common among my friends. Mom was already working and of course had to keep doing that, and until I was old enough to start getting

9. Freeman and Rogers, 1999, rate firms based on their use of "advanced human-resource practices" and then see how these correlate with workers' reported happiness with their jobs. They find (p. 99) that 78 percent of workers in firms in the top 10 percent for advanced practices report that they look forward to going to work, versus 44 percent for workers in firms in the bottom 10 percent. Of workers in the latter firms, 46 percent say they wish they didn't have to go to work, compared with 15 percent in the former group. In the high-advanced-practice firms, 83 percent of workers rate labor-management relations excellent or good, versus only 35 percent in the low-advanced-practice firms. Freeman and Rogers find most firms clustered closer to the low than the high end of their scale. Lane, 1998, shows a downward trend in reported job satisfaction in the United States.

out on my own with friends, I seem to have spent the better part of my time being babysat by the TV and amusing myself with video games. I've looked up the statistics, which show that about half of all marriages begun in the United States in the 1980s were expected to end in divorce, and that divorce rates rose beginning in the 1960s throughout the developed world, including Japan. The number of children growing up without both parents has also risen because more are born to mothers who are unmarried. The proportion of births to unwed mothers was under 10 percent before 1960, but rose to over 30 percent in the United States and Britain in the early 1990s, and over 50 percent in Sweden. Some say there's an epidemic of neglect of children, both in poor homes and rich, and even in homes with two parents.[10]

"Families that don't stay together and parents who are too involved in their work to spend time with their children seem to be products of the way our economy works, not just social trends independent of the economy. Isn't this something that concerns economists? I wonder whether the social norms involved here aren't a function of economic forces. I mean, many sociologists believe that it was urbanization and the movement of work and consumption from home to market that weakened the extended family. So, might these same forces also be breaking the bonds of the nuclear family today? Is the movement of women away from full-time domestic work part of the larger trend toward specialized, large-scale workplaces? Was the economic 'emancipation' of women a facilitator of the rising rate of divorce?

"Related to all this, it seems to me, are some questions about our values and beliefs. Society relies on families to teach children the basic values of honesty, fairness, mutual obligation, and the idea that gratifying one's senses isn't the only purpose in life. These days, it looks like these things are going by the wayside along with the family . . . that popular culture, driven by the profit motive, is becoming the real purveyor of standards. The political scientist Robert Putnam argues that television may be a major cause of the decline in people's interactions with one another, and that the closer-knit world of clubs and community organizations that existed a generation ago has given way to a world of low trust in which people do what was once unheard of: go bowling alone![11] Could the

10. See, for instance, Hewlett, 1991.
11. See Putnam, 1995a and 1995b.

cooler kinds of gadgets and forms of entertainment that we have now really be worth the price we're paying in terms of declining trust, family, and community?"

POLITICAL PARTICIPATION
AND INEQUALITY

Polly and Justin have decided to bring up their issues together. They've discovered that they have something in common: both have parents who are active in various social causes, and both are thinking of majoring in political science. "When my parents were my age," Justin begins, "people used to talk a lot about what they called 'social justice.' They still teach us this stuff in school, but the message we seem to get from the media is that those are old-fashioned notions, now that we've figured out that it takes lots of competition and economic insecurity to keep a nation on its toes and able to compete."

"Another thing they teach you about in school is democracy," Polly says. "But it's the same story. Just a lot of rhetoric. The reality is that the individual carries almost no weight in the political arena, and that the money to buy campaign advertising is what really does all the talking. Now, isn't that the economy trampling on our supposedly sacred political rights? Doesn't this belong in the scope of a course in economics? But I don't see where it will be touched upon at all. Income distribution, on the other hand, at least gets *some* coverage in our textbook."

"Right," says Justin. "In fact, one of the things that I like most about our course is that it touches on the question of who pays taxes, how people with higher incomes are asked to pay more, and the role of the government in various welfare programs. I can see that a lot of the action in the social justice area lies in the field of economics, and I'd like to take some more economics courses for that reason. But I worry that the types of measures that economists are used to considering, when it comes to redressing injustice, are not much better than band-aids, partial fixes that don't deal with the deeper, underlying problems. I mean, we're told in school that inherited status died with the great revolutions of the eighteenth century, but it seems that people born today have far from equal chances. I've found estimates suggesting that the top 1 percent of households in the United States own 35 percent of all household wealth, and the top 5 percent together own 56 percent, leaving less than half of total wealth to be shared by 95 percent of all households.[12] That estimate is for 1983, and it's generally agreed that both wealth and income distribution have become significantly *less* equal since then. Some estimates say that you'd have to add the combined net assets of the bottom 40 percent of all households to equal the wealth held by the single individual at the top of the whole heap. And while the incomes of the top 5 percent of American households ranked by income grew by 26.3 percent during 1989–98, the incomes of the bottom 20 percent of households grew a negligible 0.7 percent in the same period.

"Even more distressing to me than this inequality is the fact that the children of people at the bottom of the income distribution are much less likely than are those at the top to earn high incomes as adults. An economist named Gary Solon finds that the correlation between the adult earnings of American fathers and those of their sons, a generation later, is as high as 0.4 or 0.5. This means that if a man's father was in the bottom fifth of the labor force based on earnings in 1967, the son had about a 45 percent chance of also being in the bottom fifth, and about an eight in ten chance of being somewhere in the bottom half, of the earnings distribution in 1985.[13] And it's not only a matter of *relative* well-being: there is real *poverty* out there, even in rich countries. People at the bottom who are forced to choose between adequate food or a well-heated place to live in the winter or medical care. Homeless shelters filled up, even with working families; people depending on soup kitchens for a meal; children being bitten by rats as they sleep. And a significant statistical correlation between income and life expectancy, at least part of which seems to be due to differences in access to health care and information. Is it impossible to design an economic system that gives people more equal chances, one in which further technological progress needn't mean the further widening of inequalities?"

"That relates to my concern, too," says Polly. "I mean, Justin mentioned that the large inequalities of wealth that we see translate into differences of economic prospects for the next generation, contradicting the ideal of equality of opportunity. And what I sense is that economic inequality also spills over into the political system, turning equal par-

12. Wolff, 1994.
13. See Solon, 1992. Solon's paper also refers to others that obtained similar results.

ticipation there into a myth. For instance, in the United States in the mid-1990s, about a million dollars was spent campaigning for each seat in the House of Representatives in a single election. Almost nine million was spent on each Senate seat, and over 450 million dollars were spent in the race for president.[14] Ordinary citizens don't have the necessary funds, so running for the highest offices means raising money from businesses, labor unions, and wealthy individuals. With this money, the politician is marketed to the public like a hair spray or a laundry detergent, using slick television advertising that is expensive to produce and to air. Getting the money means an implicit promise to keep the interests of the donors in mind. It's much worse than that, too, because politicians want to be re-elected, and they know that to do this they'll need to raise money again. So they keep their doors open to potential contributors, and their official acts and decisions are inevitably swayed by their fund-raising needs.

"Money and politics have always been intertwined, but lately things seem to get more and more out of hand. Advertising gets more expensive, people are busier and harder to reach, campaigns require larger outlays for travel and other expenses. So politics begins to look like another industry, another marketplace. And from what I hear, the American style of electioneering is spreading to Europe and elsewhere, with campaign financing scandals becoming an everyday staple in country after country."

THE ENVIRONMENT

Only one student hasn't spoken yet. "I've waited patiently for my turn," begins Glen, an environmental studies major. "But after hearing the others out, I think the issues that I've been waiting to raise are still the most important ones. They are about the environment and the sustainability of the economy.

"At a first pass, of course, you can raise questions about the environment that pretty much parallel the kinds of issues raised by Joy, Chase, and the others. These are the 'trade-off' and 'quality of life' type questions. Joy and Chase ask whether our abundance of gadgets and conveniences is worth the sacrifice of other sources of happiness and meaning. Justin and Polly ask whether the consumption of the economically well

14. Based on Federal Election Commission reports cited by Common Cause, a citizen's action group, in a report titled "Overall Campaign Finance Statistics, November 15, 1999" posted at www.commoncause.org, January 2000.

off justifies forgoing a more concerted quest for social justice and democracy. There's a trade-off question for an environmentalist, too, which is whether these gadgets are worth the destruction of natural bounty that is in danger of being preserved only in a few national parks and nature sanctuaries, and eventually perhaps not even there. The environmentalist's trade-off question asks how many species of animal are worth sacrificing for faster computer operating systems, more highways, more housing developments, and more theme parks. Environmentalists point to the degradation of woodlands by acid rain, to the increasing incidences of various cancers, and to the accelerating growth of urban sprawl around American cities and the loss of open green space that results from it.

"From a different point of view, however, my issues differ from those of Joy and the others, because trade-offs are in my case only the tip of the iceberg. The question of the environment differs in kind from the others because, unlike social justice or the 'quality of life' issues, unless we address the environmental issue successfully today, future generations may not even have the opportunity to worry about social justice and meaning."

"A nice beginning," says Professor Doe, "but surely this is one area that our textbook can't be faulted for ignoring."

"Well," says Glen. "it's true that your course has touched on the environmental issue. You've explained to us that a company whose factories pollute the air and water as they turn out products to sell to consumers imposes costs upon many individuals that don't automatically affect its bottom line. The company has to recoup from its customers the costs associated with its employees' time and with the inputs that it uses in order to remain in business; but the market mechanism doesn't force the company to cover the environmental damages that it causes. You economists call this an 'externality.' You point out that one way of addressing the problem is to have the government charge the polluter a tax or penalty for each ton of pollution released, so that the costs the company imposes on society are borne by that company as direct monetary costs, giving it an incentive to reduce them where possible."

"That's exactly right," says Professor Doe. "That's a lesson you've mastered well and can pass on to others. And if you are interested, you can delve into the topic further and learn about alternative ways of discouraging pollution, about the costs and benefits of different kinds of tax schemes, and much more."

"This may be a start," says Glen, "but with all due respect, this sort of thing doesn't begin to go far enough to reassure me. The notion that pollution is an 'externality' implies that it is merely an unfortunate by-product, something we can adequately treat by some kind of after-thought. That might have been OK in the world of a century ago, when the sum of human economic activity was still small relative to the waste-absorbing capacities of the planet. But we human beings are no longer ecologically insignificant. The effects of our activities can now tip the balance between a habitable and an uninhabitable planet, so those ac-tivities must be planned for from the foundation up in the realization that they are part and parcel of the earth's biosphere. We can't any longer go on without harmonizing our activities with the overall needs of that natu-ral system.

"Here are just a few facts to consider, facts that might help convince all of you that our problems are too serious to be treated as 'externalities.' Let's start with ozone. It's a naturally occurring compound consisting of three oxygen atoms. At ground level, ozone is a health hazard, a dan-gerous constituent of industrial smog. But it is a normal part of the upper atmosphere, the stratosphere, where it plays a critical role in protecting us from ultraviolet rays from the sun that can cause skin cancer and damage to vegetation. In the mid-1980s, it was discovered that the ozone layer above Antarctica was at only about half of its normal level. The scientists who made the initial measurements are said to have been so startled that they disbelieved their own readings and sent for new equip-ment. But when the new equipment arrived, it confirmed the original measurements. There was a relatively rapid international response in the form of an agreement first to reduce by half and then to largely eliminate the production of chemicals called CFCs (chlorofluorocarbons), which are used in refrigeration systems, air conditioners, aerosols, and else-where, and which are believed to be responsible for much of the ozone depletion. However, that response is in some respects too late, because CFCs are very persistent and stay in the upper atmosphere for decades before breaking up. The ozone level has continued to decline, and thin-ning has been detected over the Arctic and other parts of the globe. Optimists believe that the new limitations will lead to a recovery of the ozone layer by the year 2050, but there are pessimists who expect it to take much longer.

"More alarming still is global climate change. There is considerable evidence that burning fossil fuels and putting other greenhouse gases into the air, while at the same time rapidly reducing the earth's forest cover by logging and clearing forests, causes the atmosphere to trap additional heat, raising temperatures around the world. At current rates, the amount of carbon dioxide in the atmosphere will double by the end of this century, resulting in an estimated 1.5 to 4.5 degree Celsius rise in temperatures. If the higher estimates are correct, global sea level may rise by about seventy centimeters. Far larger increases in sea level, on the order of fifteen to twenty feet, would occur were the West Antarctic ice sheet to break up, a contingency still considered unlikely by many but by no means all scientists. Many coastal cities and residential areas might have to be abandoned, and agriculture in the vulnerable poor countries of the Third World could be hard hit.[15] Global warming may also be associated with increasingly turbulent weather patterns, including increased incidence of severe storms like the ones that swept through Europe in December 1999. Some steps have been taken to cut back on CO_2 emissions, with big conferences in Kyoto and elsewhere, but so far the response is sluggish, because governments are hesitant to risk damage to short-run economic growth. And what hope is there of cutting down on the pollution associated with automobiles and industry if countries like India and China, which have combined populations eight times that of the United States, continue racing toward American levels of industrialization and automobile use?

"Finally, there is the state of the world's ecosystems. In getting it into their heads that nature is something to be tamed and used as they like, human beings forgot that they themselves are part of nature, dependent for their very survival not only on their ability to cultivate and harvest certain quantities of foodstuffs, but also on diverse species, including countless types of plants, insects, and microorganisms, that help to recycle nutrients and atmospheric elements and perform other services critical to our own survival and the survival of the plants and animals that we directly consume.

"Take trees for example. Some people think that when we run out of them, we'll find substitutes for the lumber, paper, and fuel that we get from trees today. That may be the case from the standpoint of these materials, but anyone who talks blithely about substitution is forgetting that those same trees play less visible but more important roles in absorb-

---

15. This discussion follows Tietenberg, 2000, pp. 401–4.

ing carbon dioxide from and adding oxygen to the atmosphere, in providing habitats for wildlife, and in preventing erosion and stabilizing watersheds. An estimated 35 percent of the world's land surface is covered by forest today, but the World Resources Institute reported in 1992 that forty-two million acres of tropical forests, an area comparable in size to the state of Washington, are cut down each year.[16] Very little of this logging is done on a sustainable basis. Deforestation is an important cause of an ongoing wave of species extinctions, which include, for instance, 'nearly half the exclusively freshwater fishes of peninsular Asia, half of the fourteen birds of the Philippine island of Cebu, and more than ninety plant species growing on a single mountain ridge in Ecuador,' according to biologist E. O. Wilson. Wilson points out that 'the ongoing loss of biodiversity is the greatest since the end of the Mesozoic Era sixty-five million years ago.'[17] In other words, the current effect of humans is comparable to that of the meteor impact that caused the extinction of the dinosaurs and other species, possibly the greatest environmental disaster since the evolution of multicellular life.

"Trees are only one example of a resource that we're harvesting at unsustainable rates. The Worldwatch Institute says that at the end of the twentieth century, the world was pumping 160 billion tons of water a year for irrigation, drinking, and other uses.[18] This is more than the planet's aquifers can provide without running dry. Yet the demand for water will continue to grow steadily with population growth and rising living standards.

"Talk about efficient trading of rights to pollute, in the face of the kind of crisis we're bringing on, makes me think that most economists, and the politicians, still don't get it. In looking into this, though, I did find a few writers on the economy and the environment who see that a more radical approach is called for. As early as the 1960s, Kenneth Boulding suggested looking at the earth as a spaceship, a largely closed physical system that can continue to support life only if relevant chemical and thermal balances are maintained within tight limits.[19] Nicholas Georgescu-Roegen pointed out the relevance of entropy laws to economics, noting that the

16. Ibid., p. 255.

17. Wilson, 1998, pp. 292, 294.

18. Brown et al., 1999.

19. See "The Economics of the Coming Spaceship Earth," reprinted in Markandya and Richardson, 1992.

one-way flow from resources to wastes is a fundamental constraint on the 'circular flow' of the market usually focused upon by economists. More recently, Herman Daly has argued that economics as a discipline needs to be rebuilt on ecological foundations.[20] Economists have always recognized that resources are scarce in comparison with human wants, Daly says, but they've tended to treat them as mere things to be allocated toward one human end or another, without recognizing that the human economy can't exist apart from a viable ecosystem. Daly argues that economics is founded on the assumption that the earth is an 'empty' planet from which human beings can extract as much biological and mineral matter as they like, and into which they can dump as many toxic outputs and by-products as they care to, without significant impact. That was roughly true a thousand years ago, and still mostly true a hundred years ago, but the size of the human economy — and population — has now grown to the point at which a 'full earth' metaphor is what's called for. The economy, in other words, must begin to be understood as a subsystem of a natural ecology that can sustain human life only within the limits of various elemental and energy balances.

"Resistance to such ways of thinking by the proponents of economic growth is keen, however. Daly recounts how, while working at the World Bank, he and a group of fellow 'environmental resisters' within that institution were unable to convince bank officials to include in a report titled *Development and the Environment* either a diagram that shows the input and output flows of the economy as part of a larger system called the environment, or a half-page insert mentioning the controversial view that consumption in the rich countries may need to be curtailed if there is to be a rise of living standards in the poor countries and an equitable division of the world's finite resources.[21] 'That's not the right way to look at it,' he was told again and again. He argues that we are beyond the point at which modest adjustments of lifestyle will do. What is needed is to substitute, for the old concept of economic *growth*, a new notion of sustainable *development* where the focus is on increasing the *quality of life* without increasing resource use, and on radically reducing the volumes of toxic wastes that are dumped back into the environment. To reach these goals,

20. See, for instance, Daly, 1996. Daly comments extensively on Georgescu-Roegen's fairly technical work (Georgescu-Roegen, 1971).

21. Daly, 1996, pp. 5–10.

the growth of material 'throughput' (the movement of material from processing to utilization to disposal as waste) must be ended in the developed countries, population growth must be stopped, and rich countries must help poor ones to achieve satisfactory living standards on a sustainable basis.

"But how can we be optimistic that the policymakers will get the message in time, given that companies that rarely think past a one- to five-year planning horizon have the ear of the government, for the sorts of reasons that Polly talked about, and that many politicians still ridicule environmental warnings as if they were just so much ranting by anti-growth cranks. More to the point for our purposes today, are economists doing enough by simply talking about efficient pollution abatement without seriously considering the need to limit growth?"

DR. DOE'S RESPONSE

"That was a masterly presentation," says an impressed Dr. Doe. "You've laid out a lot of issues in a compelling fashion. You'll never find me underestimating my students again, if I ever have before. And I'm glad that you felt it worthwhile to address all of this to me, rather than just writing me, and economics, off. The fact of the matter is that my training is in economics, and that discipline is no more prepared than are others with ready answers to the kinds of questions that you raise. And yet, the first point that several of you have made seems unassailable: the economy *is* inextricably bound up with virtually every dimension of life. So we economists would be remiss if we didn't join others in helping to puzzle these things out. And I hope that, though I don't have all the answers, I can at least show you that economics can contribute a great deal to this task by virtue of the tools it gives us for understanding human behavior. If enough students take up these methods and continue to be motivated by these sorts of issues, we might have more of the answers by the time that some of your generation sit where I'm sitting and have your own students come to you as you've come to me today.

"I want to begin by pointing out that economics is the study of the economy, that is, of how people provide themselves with their needs and wants through production and exchange. But it is also a methodology for studying human behavior through the lens of goal-directed decision making in the face of constraints. As a result, economists may be able to help answer your questions at two different levels: first, in terms of our substantive understanding of how economies function, and second, in terms of our understanding of human behavior more generally, as decision making subject to constraints.

"Substantively, economics speaks to your issues in a great many ways. For instance, insofar as some of the issues that you raise imply criticism of markets as an institution, economics contributes its understanding of how markets accomplish the tasks of coordination and incentive provision. If we want to consider replacing markets with some alternative mechanism, we'd best know what that other mechanism's features are. The field of comparative economic systems looks at the characteristics and performance of nonmarket economies, and it finds the institutions of such economies even more problematic than are those of market systems. By studying in detail the way in which markets address coordination and incentive problems, microeconomics too can give you a better sense of the problem one faces in trying to design a better system. For instance, you may want to limit certain kinds of advertising in order to reduce the exposure of children to some messages. Contrary to the way it's sometimes caricatured, economics doesn't tell you *not* to do that, simply because it would interfere with the free market. Instead, economics can help you to analyze the potential costs of doing it, for instance whether there are kinds of useful information that consumers might have to do without, whether there would be a reduction in quality competition among companies, what the effect would be on revenue for the operation of certain broadcast and print media, and so on. You yourself then must determine how much benefit you attribute to reduced advertising, and weigh it against these costs. If you are interested in the benefits that others derive from reduced advertising, you can also turn to economic analysis for help in inferring the magnitude of those benefits from people's decisions. In general, the more fully you are informed about the costs and benefits of a policy decision, the better the decisions you are likely to make, and economics provides considerable guidance in the measurement of costs and benefits.

"For another example, let's take inequality, the issue that Justin presented to us. It would be quite erroneous to characterize economists in general as being advocates of economic growth or wealth creation without regard to distribution and poverty. Immense amounts of research are done to measure inequality and poverty, and more important to determine what factors, including government programs and policies, affect the incidence of poverty and the degree of inequality of income and wealth distribution. One doesn't find in economics, any more than in society as a whole, any single consensus about how much poverty alleviation is worth pursuing. Some economists feel that poverty or large inequalities are necessary costs of having an efficiently functioning economy, but that is only one viewpoint. In fact, there is much evidence that too much inequality may not only offend many people's moral sensibilities but may also be harmful to economic growth and efficiency.[22] Furthermore, the tools of economic analysis can be put to good use to study how poverty can be combated at least cost, and also perhaps with the least erosion of popular support for the measures needed.

"We know from experience that the market system can function quite well despite considerable amounts of government intervention aimed at altering distributive outcomes. Welfare states with extensive protections for working people coexist with economic liberalization and increasing competitiveness in virtually all of the rich industrial economies today. Studies suggest that the distribution of income after taxes and transfers is far more equal in those countries than that before it. Through progressive taxation and government expenditure, the poorest 20 percent of the population gain almost 6 percent in their share of all household income, and the next poorest 20 percent gain something similar.[23] Although there has been a decisive slowing in the growth of the welfare state in Western Europe and North America, there is no sign that the public wants such programs to be eliminated. Moreover, it is possible that more creative ways can be found to offer the same or better benefits more efficiently, with less cost to the taxpayer or to incentives for productivity. In the last analysis, the kind of income and wealth distribution that we have can be significantly shaped by the public. Economic analysis is also useful for understanding the nature of social choice, that is, how the interests of

22. A survey of the large literature on the determinants of economic growth that arose in the 1990s notes that the effects of inequality on growth has been one of the topics most actively studied. The author finds that there is an unusual degree of concurrence among relevant studies that inequality tends to be harmful for growth. See Temple, 1999, p. 146, and the surveys of the inequality and growth studies that are cited there.

23. Milanovic, 1999.

different groups within a population get aggregated into the decisions of nations and communities through voting and other mechanisms.

"For a third example, let's take Glen's issue, the environment. Yes, it's a biggie today all right. But there's no truth in the caricature that economics as a discipline teaches that growth is good at any cost. Remember, it was an economist, Malthus, who first warned that population will tend to grow beyond the earth's capacity to produce food, leading to war, disease, and starvation. There has been lively debate within economics ever since his time about the pros and cons of population growth. The majority of economists today believe that high population growth is inimical to economic development in poor countries, and economists are doing important research on the determinants of population growth, for example demonstrating that female education has a strong negative effect on child bearing. We now understand a lot more about the tendency for birth rates to decline following a decline in death rates, and we have greater confidence that the rate of world population growth will slow and that population will ultimately stabilize, although at a level that may indeed be dangerously high.

"Probably as important as the absolute number at which population stabilizes is the manner in which people use the resources around them. Here, economics is also making contributions. The field of environmental economics has grown enormously in the past twenty years, and at the undergraduate level you can choose from a good number of thick and substantive textbooks covering a wide range of topics and viewpoints.[24] We not only have models of how to efficiently reduce pollution, to which you referred, Glen, but we also study, for example, how communities can engage in collective measures to protect a common resource, such as a water source or a fishery. We're studying ways people in developing countries organize themselves to protect woodlands and endangered species, so that these goals won't just be concerns of the rich that are unaffordable to the poor. And economists are helping to define new measures of well-being that will not count more output as good without accounting for its costs. For instance, there's a proposal to substitute for gross domestic product a measure called 'Net National Welfare,' which adds to GDP the value of services like childcare that are provided outside the market, while subtracting from it the social costs of externalities, the cost of

---

24. Examples include Goodstein, 1999, and Tietenberg, 2000.

pollution abatement and cleanup, and a measure of the depreciation of both physical and natural capital.[25]

"Certainly, the solutions of the world's environmental problems are not all clear yet, and economists might do more to increase the attention given to environmental concerns in their teaching. That would be desirable if the environmental pessimists are right that industrial civilization as we've known it is headed for disaster unless changes far more radical than anything currently contemplated are adopted in the near future. Unfortunately, I'm no expert on these things, so I can't assess the relative merits of optimistic or pessimistic outlooks. But no matter how dramatic are the changes needed, it's likely that economic analysis will prove critical in designing and monitoring them. Our ability to analyze the incentives that underlie the choices of individuals, firms, and communities, for instance, is likely to be an indispensable tool for crafting appropriate policies. Even radicals like Daly fully endorse the idea that markets are appropriate mechanisms for allocating scarce resources, and that incentive-based mechanisms should play an important part in solving problems of environmental decline. So, far from having to be tossed out, the insights of economic analysis will be of even more value in a more ecologically conscious world. It's been said, in fact, that economics is the material ecology of human society, while ecology is the economics of nature. The two fields are very closely related and intertwined. So I would urge you, Glen, not to write off economics. In fact, if you really want to help the environment, studying as much economics as you can would be a very good idea.

"Now I could give many more examples of the substantive relevance of economic analysis, but let me give just one more, concerning the types of jobs that are available in the economy, which is one of the issues that Chase raised. Someone who hasn't studied any economics might assert that people have no control over their working lives, that they have to accept whatever is offered to them by business owners. Economic analysis tells us that that view is too simplistic. First, workers are free to be self-

25. See Goodstein, 1999, pp. 82–84. A group called Redefining Progress proposes as an alternative a "Genuine Progress Indicator" (GPI). In addition to the adjustments included in Net National Welfare, the GPI adds the value of the service provided by consumer durables and infrastructures like highways, and subtracts (a) expenditures to combat declines in welfare from social "bads" like crime and auto accidents, and (b) estimates of the social costs of divorce, lost leisure, and similar factors.

employed or to get together to organize their own companies. Second, there are two sides to a labor market, the workers' side and the employers' side. In a competitive labor market, employers have to attract workers by competing against other employers with job offers that incorporate bundles of attributes, including not only pay and work hours but also task variety, autonomy, and so on. If there is perfect competition in the labor market, the kind of jobs that will be offered and accepted will reflect both the objective trade-offs that exist among the attributes (for instance, how much if any output must be sacrificed to give a worker a more varied job) and the preferences of workers over attributes (how much if any pay the worker is prepared to give up to have a more varied job). The idea that employers care only about profits and that they pay no attention to job satisfaction makes absolutely no sense in a competitive labor market framework.

"But we cannot leave the analysis hanging there. Chase's concern can't be thrown out just by reciting some abstract theory. Perhaps workers do *not* in practice get enough input on how work is organized. Our analytical framework can help us to sort out why that might be, because the perfectly competitive model is only a starting point, a bench mark against which the real world can be judged. The problem could be that the labor market doesn't work perfectly because employers have what we call monopsony power.[26] Or there may exist a buyer's market for labor, where employers get to call the shots more than employees, because there is endemic unemployment (which may be due to any of several factors that are analyzed extensively in macroeconomics).[27] Perhaps workers' decisions on which jobs to take and to stay with fail to communicate to employers their real preferences over job attributes, as suggested by some labor economists.[28] Perhaps a lack of symmetry between the nature of

26. Monopsony is said to exist when the buyer of an input such as labor can influence the price (or wage) paid by varying the number of units (or workers) hired. The analysis of monopsony is presented in standard microeconomics texts.

27. For example, in "efficiency wage" models, firms hire fewer workers at higher wages so that workers can be induced to work harder lest they lose their jobs and become unemployed. As more firms raise their wages and reduce the number of workers hired, unemployment rises in the economy as a whole. The efficiency wage model is now discussed in most intermediate macroeconomics textbooks. The "buyers market" idea is developed especially by Bowles and Gintis, 1990.

28. See, for instance, Freeman, 1976.

labor and the nature of capital prevents most workers from organizing their own firms.[29] All these possibilities and more can be investigated systematically to understand the causes of low workplace satisfaction, where it exists, and accordingly also the best possible remedies, be they a voice for workers on firms' boards of directors, more participation at the shop floor level, introduction of job enlargement, or other measures.

"Enough examples, I hope. I want to leave time to say some things now about the more methodological side of economics' contribution. Economics, that is, provides an approach to studying human decision making, an approach that is being emulated today by more and more social scientists. Our approach is undoubtedly partial, leaving out some aspects of psychology and social dynamics. But we work on important pieces of the overall puzzle, and our cooperation with other disciplines is often quite fruitful. If you'd really like to see fundamental changes in society, I would encourage you to get as strong an understanding as you can get of how it is that people actually behave in practice. I think economics can contribute a lot there.

"What is the economic approach to explaining social behavior? To begin with, economics builds models of social processes that have individuals as their basic building blocks. Everything is explained in terms of individuals pursuing goals in the face of various constraints. Of course, the constraints include the behaviors of other individuals, so social systems are complex. But the basic idea is that the 'society' or 'system' is composed of individuals making choices. Problems can't be blamed on society and left at *its* doorstep because whatever society does wrong, it does as the consequence of the actions of many individuals. Sometimes, it is true, a social outcome can be detrimental to almost everyone involved; for instance, a community may destroy some resource on which all of its members depend because each individual, acting without having coordinated her actions with the others, pursues self-interest in a way that ends up hurting everyone (the famous 'tragedy of the commons').[30] If we want to know why negative social outcomes occur, and to find ways to prevent

29. Alternative explanations of why workers usually take employment in firms not controlled by workers are reviewed by Dow and Putterman, 1999, in a book with other useful contributions on workers' roles in enterprise governance.

30. The seminal contribution is Hardin, 1968. More up-to-date discussions based on subsequent writings in economics will be found in environmental economics textbooks, such as Goodstein, 1999, and Tietenberg, 2000.

them, we have to understand the nature of the individual incentives that lead to those outcomes, and then appropriately alter the incentives.

"Sometimes economics is criticized for assuming as its basic elements rational, self-interested individuals with fixed tastes. The critics say we need to allow for a large amount of *irrationality* in human behavior, as well as for more complex interests, such as altruism and jealousy. Some critics say, too, that we miss a lot by viewing society as only the sum of its individual members. And it is pointed out that tastes may be shaped in important ways by social environments, including forces like advertising.

"There may be a point to some of this criticism, but often the critics underestimate the sophistication and flexibility of economic analysis. Group-level phenomena are indeed more complex than individual choices, but we can obtain a lot of insight into group and individual behaviors by using game theory and other approaches to examine group dynamics, allowing for feedbacks both from individual to group outcomes and from group processes to individuals.[31] As far as self-interest goes, economics already makes considerable allowance for altruism, for instance as part of the explanation of bequests and of parental investment in children's education. The study of how choice is affected when the well-being of one individual influences that of another has been a growth area of economics in recent years. So has the study of how tastes or preferences are influenced by past choices and exposures — for instance, the study of addiction.[32] And some economists even relax the assumption of perfect rationality, looking, for instance, at how the perceived value of objects changes depending on whether one is buying or selling them — a phenomenon that should be ruled out if people are strictly rational.[33]

"What, then, do the methods of studying decision making that economists employ contribute to considering the sorts of issues that, say, Joy

31. For an intriguing and relatively nontechnical discussion of individual and group behavioral interactions, see Schelling, 1978. For an introduction to game theory, see Dutta, 1999, or Gintis, 2000. A widely used advanced text is Fudenberg and Tirole, 1991.

32. There are several books by economists that consider altruism quite broadly, including Collard, 1978, and Margolis, 1984. On both family altruism and addiction, see Becker, 1996. Family altruism is also discussed by Bergstrom, cited in Chapter 1.

33. Work that tests or drops the assumption of rationality is discussed by Kahneman, 1994, and Rabin, 1998.

and Chase and Mary raised? First of all, economics offers a framework and a vocabulary for talking about individual and group welfare. It is indeed the case, as Joy said, that the usual assumption in economics is that the market satisfies preexisting wants. Many economists judge markets to be efficient because they are thought to satisfy wants effectively. However, the vocabulary and framework of the theoretical area that deals with such questions — what we call welfare economics — can also be used for treating the issues raised by the fact that tastes can be manipulated by advertising and popular culture. The problems do become complex and esoteric, but both economists and philosophers have found the framework useful.

"At bottom, many of the questions that you've raised are questions about human nature. Are human beings basically selfish and acquisitive, or do they have the potential to cooperate, and needs demanding fulfillment in more dimensions than the material only? Economics looks for evidence on these matters from actual behaviors and choices. Such an approach may have some blind spots, because present culture and institutions may not provide enough opportunities to observe behaviors and preference patterns that could potentially exist, but simply don't exist under prevailing circumstances. Nevertheless, the approach of inferring dispositions from behaviors has a lot to recommend it, in comparison with simple introspection or assertion. Furthermore, the evidence that we find is very complex, hardly supporting the caricatured view of a strictly self-interested humankind, but also making clear that self-interest and material wants are very much part of the human makeup.

"The relatively recent field of experimental economics is a good and growing source of evidence about human nature. In one type of experiment, volunteers are given a certain amount of money, say ten dollars, and are permitted to choose between keeping it for themselves and putting it in a group fund where it grows in value. The money in the group fund is then divided equally, without regard to who contributed and who did not. This is an example of the so-called prisoners' dilemma: each individual will be better off if everyone contributes their money to the group fund and earns, say, twenty dollars. However, each individual is better off still if he or she keeps the money while the *others* contribute to the group fund. If all individuals follow this self-interested logic and keep their money, they earn only ten dollars.

"Now, the prediction of a model of perfect self-interest and rationality is that if the game is played only once and there is no possibility of making binding agreements, the participants will always choose to keep their money and each will earn the inefficient amount, ten dollars. In actuality, though, a little over half the money provided is typically put in the group fund, suggesting that some individuals try to cooperate for mutual gain. If the game is played repeatedly and there is no special way to communicate plans, make deals, or punish a noncooperative player, the contributions to the group fund tend to decline from round to round.[34] But the declining trend is not seen in certain circumstances, for instance when the experimenters make sure that the more cooperative types of subjects are grouped with one another, or when the subjects can have some face-to-face communication, or when one subject can punish another by reducing that subject's earnings at some cost to himself. This kind of research, some of which is still at an early stage, holds out the promise of revealing the mix of selfish and group-minded, altruistic, reciprocal, and other behaviors characteristic of typical individuals. It can show how this mix of behaviors differs from person to person, and demonstrate how the interactions of individuals of different types leads to different kinds of outcomes in different groups.[35] Thus, it may play a part in the discovery of ways people can cooperate more effectively on social objectives, including the collective protection of an environmental resource mentioned earlier, a problem that has a strong prisoners'-dilemma-type component.[36]

WHAT FUTURE, THE MARKET ECONOMY?

When Professor Doe has finished speaking, Chase picks up the conversation on the students' side. "What you've just said is certainly interesting," he says, "and I, for one, am now even more likely than I was to spend more time learning what economics has to teach, as a way of getting further insight into the types of issues that we've been discussing. But

34. The early research in this area is discussed in Davis and Holt, 1993, chapter 6.

35. An example is Fehr and Gächter, 2000.

36. In brief, most individuals might prefer that the environment be protected by having people desist from actions that benefit them at its expense; yet a strictly selfish individual might be best off by "free riding" on the public-spirited acts of others, to which she herself does not contribute. The problem is to induce people — whether by threat of penalty or some other method — not to treat themselves as justifiable exceptions to the rule.

you've mainly told us in very general terms how a knowledge of economics can be useful to making headway on those issues. You haven't said
much about your own opinions."

"I was curious about that too," says Mary. "I mean, you're an economist and you already know about all of these tools. Can't you tell us what
you yourself think about the problems of stress, family breakdown, justice, and so on? Don't you have some opinion of your own?"

"Well, no, I don't have fully formed opinions about all of these issues.
And where I do have opinions, I've hesitated to express them to you
because you came to me in my role of economics professor, and what I
happen to think as an individual is not necessarily related to that role. I
emphasized the sorts of things that economics as a discipline has some
agreement on, rather than opinions that differ from one person to the
next, much of which has little to do with my professional training."

"I'd still like to hear what you think, though," says Mary.

"Fair enough," says Doe. "But let me just think for a moment about
how I should proceed." He leans back and rubs his forehead in concentration, then after a few seconds begins to speak again.

"OK. Let me start with those issues that Joy, Chase, and Mary raised.
Glen's right that each generation might get its own chance to deal with
these matters if its day in the sun arrives (we hope without too many
ultraviolet rays). So a viable physical environment is indeed critical. But
we each have only one go at life, and it would be a damning indictment of
the way we manage things if our way of life is as fatally flawed as Joy and
the others seem to suggest.

"Now, much of the indictment seems to me to come down to this: that
the market economy is very efficient at making and distributing things,
but that its operation also has a strong and pernicious influence on what it
is that people come to want. Our type of economy is said to pump up
people's felt needs for material things and to teach them to devalue their
human relationships, their personal development, their free time, their
interior lives, and perhaps anything on which a price can't be placed. This
causes people to end up leading less satisfying lives than they might have,
despite having more goods."

"Exactly," says Mary. "So, what's your answer, Professor?"

"Well, to begin with, I think we ought to rid our minds of any grand
notions of conspiracy. What is going on is definitely *not* that nasty advertising companies and CEOs and multimillionaires get together to hatch

plots against the rest of us. The set of institutions that we find ourselves with was designed by no one with no particular end in mind. It's the result of tens of millions of individual human beings reacting as nature and nurture bid them to react to the opportunities that they face. I'm not saying, by this, that our contemporary form of economy is the only 'natural' one. But I think it *is* clear that our economy is at least one historical product of human nature, and not the artificial concoction of a few individuals or of some outside force. I also conclude, from what I see, that acquisitiveness is not an artificial concoction of capitalism, but is rather a part of human nature that capitalism builds upon and caters to, conceivably strengthening it in the process, as you worry. More important, though, I would remind you that acquisitiveness is not the only side of human nature. The idealism that appeals to you and your friends, and the sense that you share with many other people, the sense that pursuing material ends only will not satisfy, is very real. All this shows that the human is indeed a very complex animal."

"OK," nods Justin. "Or should I say: touché!"

"Now, one way to rephrase the questions that you are asking is: Is it possible for us to enjoy the fruits of a market economy, their spur to productivity and invention and their low-cost and nondictatorial coordination of resource allocation, without suffering some attendant loss of sight as to what might most enrich our lives? A possible response to that question is to challenge its implicit premise, the premise that it is the market that sidetracks us from what we would otherwise be doing. It may well be only the atypical individual, an unusually philosophically or aesthetically inclined person, or one who gets exceptional utility from sociability, who feels a conflicting tug against the culture of the market. On the whole, people may basically be getting what they want, and your real complaint may come down to the idea that people just don't want the things *that you think they should want.*

"If economists have a bias in this respect, it is to be skeptical of the idea that someone knows better than the decision maker herself what it is that makes that person best off. The idea that there may be some way of judging what is good for people other than by looking at what they themselves choose is often labeled 'paternalistic' in economists' writings. To be sure, their stance against paternalism can be questioned. We don't assume that a small child or a drug addict will make the best choices about any resources that happen to be put at their disposal, and there are compelling cases for some objective standards of well-being, like nutritional status. But whatever one thinks of the anti-paternalist stance, it is worth stopping to make sure that the virtue that the market economy possesses with respect to granting a great deal of freedom to individuals is not overlooked or underappreciated. Remember, while markets are criticized with respect to some dimensions of nonmaterial well-being or quality of life, like those mentioned by you, it is rare to see them upbraided for failing to let people make their own decisions. To some, the freedom that accompanies a market economy is sufficient reason for defending it against all challenges.

"But now, let me grant for the sake of argument that there *is* something to the complaint that the commercialism of our economy is a corrosive force tending to eat away at our sense of proportion, at our family ties, at our 'higher values.' It doesn't follow that the market is so dominant an aspect of our existence that it is in danger of winning any time soon, of destroying every other facet of society. There seems still to be 'space' left in the overall social picture, space in which people can pursue interests apart from those driven by commerce, space in which people can bake their own bread or pursue other hobbies that 'don't make sense' from a dollars-and-sense standpoint, space for institutions like churches and schools and voluntary organizations that nurture values somewhat distinct from those promoted by the market.

"One of the things that strikes me about the past hundred years is that the market economy has shown an extraordinary capacity to accommodate changes in social and political values. Take the concept of the equality of individuals. It's been a driving force behind social changes that are still working themselves out after a dozen generations. The rhetoric of equality—which was ready at hand in some strains of Judeo-Christian thought, among other sources—may have been used in the eighteenth century mainly by propertied white males aiming to improve their positions vis-à-vis hereditary nobles and monarchs. Yet the concept seems to have had an impetus that's carried through to the movements for universal education and suffrage, for equality between the sexes, and for racial justice.

"Consider, too, the fact that capitalism was not born in a setting of political democracy. In fact, a century or two ago, most educated and politically 'enlightened' people did not think that democracy could coexist with private property and economic freedom. At the American constitutional convention of 1787 in Philadelphia, for example, James Madison argued that one of the two legislative branches of the U.S. government should be elected only by holders of property, since the 'great majority of the people' who 'will not only be without landed, but any other sort of property' would have no interest in protecting property rights.[37] Likewise, nineteenth-century thinkers, including Karl Marx, believed that unless capitalists prevented the emergence of real democracy, democracy would do away with capitalism.[38] Yet the extension of the vote to ordinary people did not in the end undermine the market economy, which on the contrary has reached new heights, perhaps in part because it was strengthened by popularly demanded programs to stabilize it and to provide certain economic assurances to citizens.

"Now a cynic could claim that this is all sham democracy that is promoted by the movers and shakers of the world as a superficial palliative, something to smooth out the social ripples that might otherwise make rough seas for market economies. But a different interpretation is that we live in a pluralistic society in which a number of distinct but compatible ideals coexist, and in which people are not willing to stake their well-being on any one institution (the market, for example). Rather, people look to a set of complementary institutions (markets, bills of rights, political democracy, schools, religion, and so on) to answer to diverse needs. In this vein, I see a widely shared value of political democracy, and I think the fact that it is as yet imperfectly achieved does not mean that there will not be further progress in that direction. Let's not forget where we have come from in just a few generations."

"Very interesting," interrupts Joy, "but I'm not as concerned about democracy as I am about well-being. My worry is that the commercialization of life is putting the lid on our quality of life, and that this relentless commercialization is an unstoppable by-product, a kind of cultural pollution, pouring out endlessly from our economy."

Justin steps in. "What I think the professor is saying, Joy, is that not everybody is a robot of advertising jingles. Some people get pretty brainwashed, I suppose, but most people are able to keep some perspective. If I have kids five or ten years from now, I'm not just going to program them to be good consumers. They'll be exposed to other things, and they

37. Quoted in Wood, 1969.
38. See Przeworski, 1985.

can become well-rounded people in spite of the commercial messages they see."

"I got something else from what the professor said earlier," says Chase. "That part about the welfare state and worker protections and so on made me begin to realize that placing some limits on markets won't necessarily destroy them. In some cases, it might actually make them do more for us. Markets show a lot of vitality. So perhaps we could limit more kinds of advertising (not just that on cigarettes), exercise more control over the messages to which kids are exposed, and so on without these changes clashing with the basic market mechanism. The market would still deliver its efficiencies in resource allocation and innovation, getting people the goods they want. In fact, there's been a fair amount of legislative action in the United States in recent years that has required some educational and public service content in children's television, or makes it harder to broadcast programs that are just concealed advertising, or easier for parents to prevent kids watching certain kinds of things. And I've read that TV advertising aimed at children is completely banned in Sweden. So far, there's no sign that that's wrecked the Swedish economy, which sustains one of the highest incomes in the world."

"Hmmm. And campaign finance reforms *might* do similar things to right some of the flaws in our democracy," Polly muses.

"Perhaps yes," says Doe, returning to the conversation. "Without taking a position there, what I think may also be worth saying is that not everything has to depend on legislation or government action. We've seen important changes in social values and norms that have taken place mainly within the sphere of popular culture and perceptions, through changes in attitudes. In some of these cases, legislation or the courts or other institutions play an important facilitating or validating role, but in others law and government are barely involved at all. That's been the case with respect to the movement for equality of the sexes, which has had a few legal successes but has mainly gained ground in the court of public opinion. Another example is the environmental movement. The idea that uncontrolled industrial growth poses a threat to human survival was advanced mainly by a radical fringe thirty years ago, but that way of thinking is now so commonplace that corporations and politicians trip over each other trying to cultivate 'green' images. Glen may be right that the environmental threat is still not being addressed adequately, but the shift in public awareness here has been a dramatic one, and it wasn't brought about by government. I'd say it's more the other way around, that is, that government and industry have responded to a shift in public opinion."

"Well, I wonder how that idea might apply to the issue of advertising and tastes," asks Joy. "Could it really be that we don't have to impose legal constraints on advertising? Can we hope that there will be in the offing some sort of cultural shift against materialism that forces advertisers to appeal to a more humane outlook if they want to win over customers? That seems doubtful to me. How will this shift get started so long as people continue to grow up being exposed to the commercialism of the media at every turn?"

"My concern, too," says Glen. "Sure, it's hopeful that attitudes have begun to change on environmental issues. But this could be too little, too late. We need action now."

AFTERMATH TO AN AFTERNOON

The conversation could have gone on a lot longer, but it was fast approaching four o'clock, and several of the students had activities or classes to attend. Professor Doe himself wanted to attend a seminar on economic theory being given by one of his colleagues in the department seminar room. It was agreed that the meeting would be followed up by another one where some of the students would discuss the idea of working on independent study projects related to their interests. Most of the students left seeming pleased that they were heard out and that they received some new views from their professor. Doe found three of them still talking in the hallway when he emerged from the seminar ninety minutes later!

Not all are happy with how this afternoon has gone, though. When Doe reports the encounter to his wife that evening, she reminds him that he needs to stay more focused on his own research. He'll never be given tenure, she says, if he makes himself so accessible to his undergraduates.

"But," protested Doe, "if I'd turned them away, they might have lost interest in economics and concluded that we economists care about nothing but our theories and economic indicators. By helping them to see the connections between economics and the issues that concerned them, I may have encouraged one or more of them to become further engaged with economics, with who knows what results. In the end, I believe that there are young idealists out there who may really be able to help make a better place of this world, and I think they need all the understanding they can get in order to make a go of it. If I didn't believe economics was part of the solution, I wouldn't have gone into teaching it."

CONCLUSION

Economics mainly studies one sphere of social life, that in which people satisfy their material needs and wants through the production and distribution of goods and services. However, it employs a general method of analysis, looking at social outcomes as consequences of decisions made by individuals in the face of constraints. Both because the economy itself is inextricably bound up with every aspect of life, and because the methodology of economics makes it relevant to a very wide range of social issues, the discipline of economics is a participant in society's broadest discussions about values, social goals, and the obstacles to their fulfillment.

From their broad studies of the economy, most economists conclude that competitive markets are highly efficient mechanisms for fostering innovation, motivating enterprise and effort, and causing resources to be allocated where they can most effectively meet human needs. And in economically developed countries, most people agree with the view that the market economy has delivered desired material goods. But some people wonder whether this comes at a high price. They cite, among other things, the apparent weakening of social ties, declining self-reported happiness, rising levels of stress, mixed indicators of job satisfaction, more fragile marriages, and larger inequalities of wealth and political influence, all of which appear to have accompanied past decades of economic change in advanced economies. Some worry, too, that further industrial growth could spell ecological catastrophe, and that the economic and political mechanisms of industrial societies are not sufficiently responsive to the alarm bells that have already begun to ring.

Are there really conflicts between an efficient market economy and a high quality of life in terms of overall well-being, rights, and their equitable distribution? Does the pursuit of more prosperity today endanger the possibility of a good life for future generations? How might the substantive knowledge and the methodological strengths of economics be brought to bear on such problems? These are some of the big questions that one might wish to see addressed but that receive little attention in most textbooks. Economists do have useful things to say about these questions, and a place needs to be reserved at the table when such issues are discussed so the insights that the substantive knowledge and methodology of economics offers are part of the conversation.

Of course, the issues raised are so broad that no brief discussion can list even the most important arguments, facts, and viewpoints. We did no more in this chapter than scratch the surface of a few of the questions listed in the imaginary conversation of Professor Darin Doe and six articulate students. Along the way, references were made to a variety of books and articles to which you can turn to pursue some of these issues in greater depth. If your appetite has been whetted and you have been freed of the notion that "economics" and "human concerns" are two mutually exclusive domains, then your journey has just begun.

REFERENCES

Becker, Gary, 1996, *Accounting for Tastes*. Cambridge: Harvard University Press.

Boulding, Kenneth, 1992 [1966], "The Economics of the Coming Spaceship Earth," pp. 27–35 in Anil Markandya and Julie Richardson, eds., *Environmental Economics: A Reader*. New York: St. Martin's, 1992.

Bowles, Samuel, and Herbert Gintis, 1990, "Contested Exchange: New Microfoundations of the Political Economy of Capitalism," *Politics and Society* 18:165–222.

Bowles, Samuel, and Herbert Gintis, 1991, "The Economy Produces People: An Introduction to Post-Liberal Democracy," pp. 221–45 in Michael Zweig, ed., *Religion and Economic Justice*. Philadelphia: Temple University Press.

Brown, Lester R., et al., 1999, *State of the World, 1999: A Worldwatch Institute Report on Progress Toward a Sustainable Society*. New York: Norton.

Cantril, Hadley, 1965, *The Pattern of Human Concerns*. New Brunswick, N.J.: Rutgers University Press.

Collard, David, 1978, *Altruism and Economy: A Study in Non-Selfish Economics*. New York: Oxford University Press.

Daly, Herman, 1996, *Beyond Growth: The Economics of Sustainable Development*. Boston: Beacon.

Davis, Douglas, and Charles Holt, 1993, *Experimental Economics*. Princeton: Princeton University Press.

Dow, Gregory, and Louis Putterman, 1999, "Why Capital (Usually) Hires Labor: An Assessment of Proposed Explanations," pp. 17–57 in Margaret Blair and Mark Roe, eds., *Employees and Corporate Governance*. Washington, D.C.: Brookings Institution Press.

Dutta, Prajit, 1999, *Strategies and Games: Theory and Practice*. Cambridge: MIT Press.

Easterlin, Richard, 1996, *Growth Triumphant: The Twenty-first Century in Historical Perspective*. Ann Arbor: University of Michigan Press.

Fehr, Ernst, and Simon Gächter, 2000, "Cooperation and Punishment," *American Economic Review.*

Freeman, Richard, 1976, "Individual Mobility and Union Voice in the Labor Market," *American Economic Review (Papers and Proceedings)* 66:361–68.

Freeman, Richard, and Joel Rogers, 1999, *What Workers Want.* Ithaca, N.Y.: Cornell University Press.

Fudenberg, Drew, and Jean Tirole, 1991, *Game Theory.* Cambridge: MIT Press.

Fukuyama, Francis, 1999, *The Great Disruption: Human Nature and the Reconstitution of Social Order.* New York: Free Press.

Georgescu-Roegen, Nicholas, 1971, *The Entropy Law and the Economic Process.* Cambridge: Harvard University Press.

Gintis, Herbert, 2000, *Game Theory Evolving: A Problem-Centered Introduction to Modeling Strategic Interaction.* Princeton: Princeton University Press.

Goodstein, Eban, 1999, *Economics and the Environment,* 2d ed. Upper Saddle River, N.J.: Prentice Hall.

Hardin, Garrett, 1968, "The Tragedy of the Commons," *Science* 162:1243–48; reprinted in Anil Markandya and Julie Richardson, 1992, *Environmental Economics: A Reader* (New York: St. Martin's).

Hewlett, Sylvia, 1991, *When the Bough Breaks: The Cost of Neglecting Our Children.* New York: Basic.

Hirshleifer, Jack, 1987, "On the Emotions as Guarantors of Threats and Promises," in John Dupre, ed., *The Latest on the Best: Essays on Evolution and Optimality.* Cambridge: MIT Press.

Kahneman, Daniel, 1994, "New Challenges to the Rationality Assumption," *Journal of Institutional and Theoretical Economics* 150:18–36.

Knight, Frank, 1935, *The Ethics of Competition and Other Essays.* New York: Harper.

Lane, Robert, 1998, "The Joyless Market Economy," pp. 461–88 in Avner Ben-Ner and Louis Putterman, eds., *Economics, Values, and Organization.* New York: Cambridge University Press.

Lane, Robert, 2000, *The Loss of Happiness in Market Democracies.* New Haven: Yale University Press.

Margolis, Howard, 1984, *Selfishness, Altruism, and Rationality: A Theory of Social Choice.* Chicago: University of Chicago Press.

Markandya, Anil, and Julie Richardson, 1992, *Environmental Economics: A Reader.* New York: St. Martin's.

Milanovic, Branko, 1999, "Do More Unequal Countries Redistribute More? Does the Median Voter Hypothesis Hold?" unpublished paper, World Bank.

Mill, John Stuart, 1929 [1848], *Principles of Political Economy with Some of Their Applications to Social Philosophy,* ed. Sir W. J. Ashley. London: Longmans, Green.

Przeworski, Adam, 1985, *Capitalism and Social Democracy.* Cambridge: Cambridge University Press.

Putnam, Robert, 1995a, "Bowling Alone: America's Declining Social Capital," *Journal of Democracy* 6:65–78.

Putnam, Robert, 1995b, "Tuning In, Tuning Out: The Strange Disappearance of Social Capital in America," *PS: Political Science & Politics* 28 (4):1–20.

Rabin, Matthew, 1998, "Psychology and Economics," *Journal of Economic Literature* 36:11–46.

Robinson, John, and Geoffrey Godbey, 1997, *Time for Life: The Surprising Ways Americans Use Their Time*. University Park: Pennsylvania State University Press.

Schelling, Thomas, 1978, *Micromotives and Macrobehavior*. New York: Norton.

Schor, Juliet, 1992, *The Overworked American: The Unexpected Decline of Leisure*. New York: Basic.

Solon, Gary, 1992, "Intergenerational Income Mobility in the Unites States," *American Economic Review* 82:393–408.

Temple, Jonathan, 1999, "The New Growth Evidence," *Journal of Economic Literature* 37:112–56.

Tietenberg, Tom, 2000, *Environmental and Natural Resource Economics*, 5th ed. Reading, Mass.: Addison-Wesley.

Wilson, Edward O., 1998, *Consilience: The Unity of Knowledge*. New York: Knopf.

Wolff, Edward, 1994, "International Wealth Inequality in the 1980s," paper presented at the American Economic Association Meetings, Boston.

Wood, Gordon, 1969, *The Creation of the American Republic, 1776–1787*. Chapel Hill: University of North Carolina Press.

SUGGESTIONS FOR FURTHER READING

Aaron, Henry, 1994, "Public Policy, Values, and Consciousness," *Journal of Economic Perspectives* 8:3–21.

Axelrod, Robert, and William Hamilton, 1981, "The Evolution of Cooperation," *Science* 211:1390–96.

Ben-Ner, Avner, and Louis Putterman, eds., 1998, *Economics, Values, and Organization*. New York: Cambridge University Press.

Boulding, Kenneth, 1978, *Ecodynamics: A New Theory of Societal Evolution*. Beverly Hills, Calif.: Sage.

Boulding, Kenneth, 1985, *Human Betterment*. Beverly Hills, Calif.: Sage.

Bowles, Samuel, 1998, "Endogenous Preferences: The Cultural Consequences of Markets and Other Economic Institutions," *Journal of Economic Literature* 36:75–111.

Bowles, Samuel, and Herbert Gintis, 1986, *Democracy and Capitalism: Property, Community, and the Contradictions of Modern Social Thought*. New York: Basic.

Frank, Robert, 1988, *Passions Within Reason: The Strategic Role of the Emotions*. New York: Norton.

Frank, Robert, 1999, *Luxury Fever: Why Money Fails to Satisfy in an Era of Excess*. New York: Free Press.

Galbraith, John Kenneth, 1996, *The Good Society: The Humane Agenda*. Boston: Houghton Mifflin.

Galbraith, John Kenneth, 1998, *The Affluent Society*, 40th anniversary ed. Boston: Houghton Mifflin.

Hayek, Friedrich A. von, 1949, *The Road to Serfdom*. Chicago: University of Chicago Press.

Heilbroner, Robert, 1996, *An Inquiry into the Human Prospect, Updated and Reconsidered for the Nineteen Nineties*. New York: Norton.

Mansbridge, Jane, ed., 1990, *Beyond Self-Interest*. Chicago: University of Chicago Press.

Mishel, Lawrence, Jared Bernstein, and John Schmitt, 1999, *The State of Working America, 1998–1999*. Ithaca, N.Y.: Cornell University Press.

Nussbaum, Martha, and Amartya Sen, eds., 1993, *The Quality of Life*. Oxford: Clarendon.

Rothbard, Murray, 1973, *For a New Liberty*. New York: Macmillan.

Schelling, Thomas, 1980, *Strategy of Conflict*. Cambridge: Harvard University Press.

Schor, Juliet, 1998, *The Overspent American: Upscaling, Downshifting, and the New Consumer*. New York: Basic.

Scitovsky, Tibor, 1992, *The Joyless Economy: The Psychology of Human Satisfaction*, rev. ed. New York: Oxford University Press.

INDEX

abstract formalism, and economic theory, 81

"adverse selection," and insurance, 118, 119

advertising: and market economy, 235, 250, 263, 264; and political campaigns, 243; and social psychology, 81

Africa: and colonial expansion, 33–34; economic development of, 149; foreign debt crisis in, 157, 160; and large-scale migration, 32

Africa, sub-Saharan: economic development of, 158–60; and historical framework for growth, 171; hunter-gatherers in, 21; life expectancy and adult literacy in, 164, 176

aggregate balance, and neoclassical school, 83

agriculture: in developing economies, 161; development of, 7, 13–22, 136; and economic modernity, 144–45; and economic theory, 173–74; as manual labor, 26; and price-setting by government monopolies, 160; by private farmers, in socialist economies, 124n; and Ricardo's law of rates of return, 65; and specialization, 29–30

AIDS epidemic, 139

altruism: and economic analysis, 256; parental, 13

American Economic Association, 90

American Economic Review, 91

American Revolution, 37

animals, domestication of, 15

Argentina, 157

Aristotle, 56, 226

Arrow, Kenneth, 85

Asia: economic development of, 149–50; and European colonization, 34–35; GDP in (1966–96), 159. *See also* China; East Asia; India

asset ownership, and globalization, 46

atmospheric pollutants, as externalities, 106, 244–45

Austrian school of economic theory, 80

Aztec empire, in Mexico, 23, 26

band form of organization, in prehistory, 9–10, 15

bank credit, and corporation financing, 121

"barbarians," and host cultures, 19–20

Barr, Nicholas, 118

barter, and primitive trade, 11

"basic income grant," 214

behavioral predispositions, and human evolution, 12

Bentham, Jeremy, 69, 71, 189, 192

bequest taxes, 208

Bergson, Abram, 203n

Bernstein, Jared, 209

biology, and economics, 64, 75, 86–87, 234

Blaug, Mark, 72

Bohm-Bawerk, Eugen von, 188, 192